DESIGNING IN *Ivory and White*

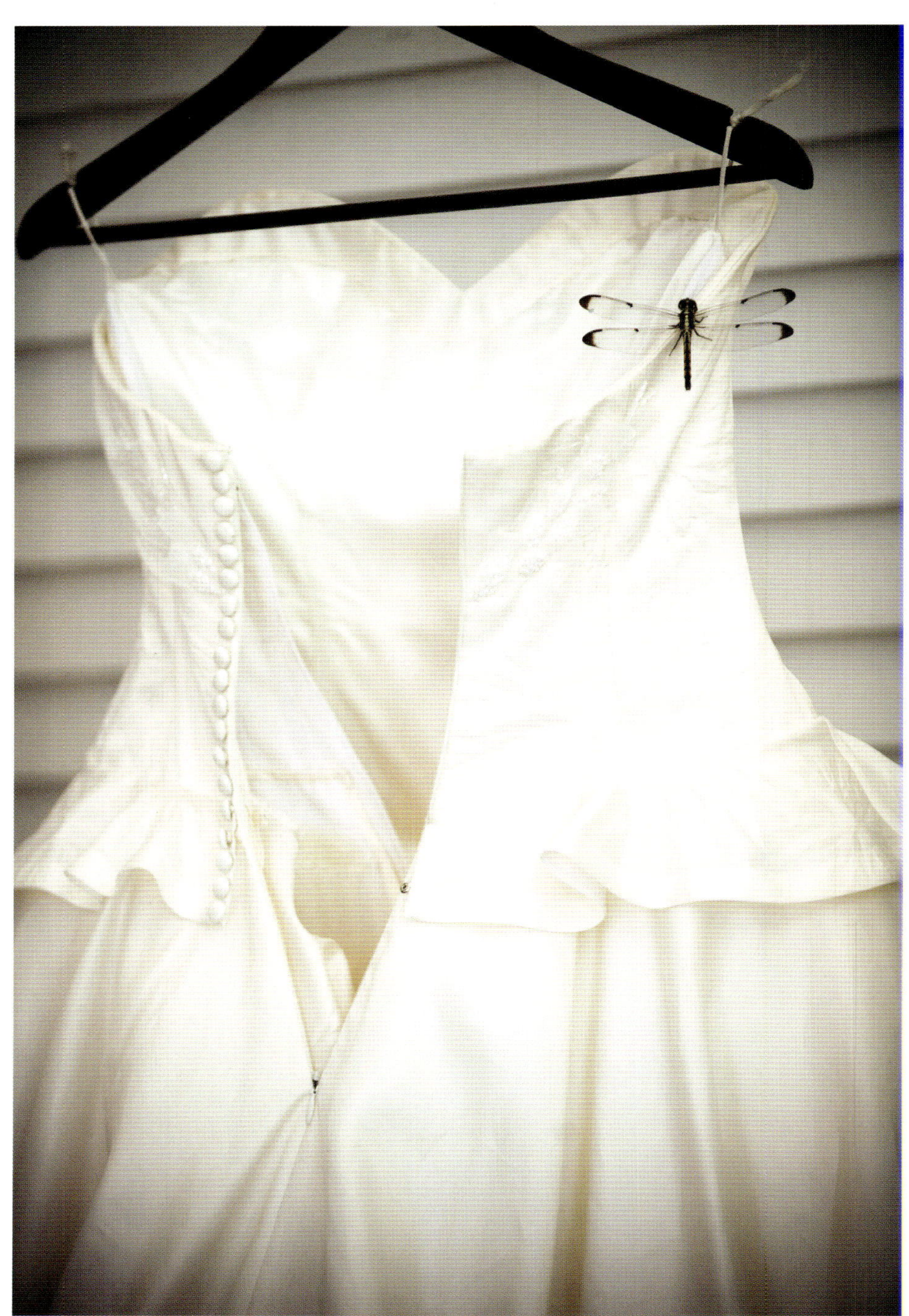

DESIGNING IN

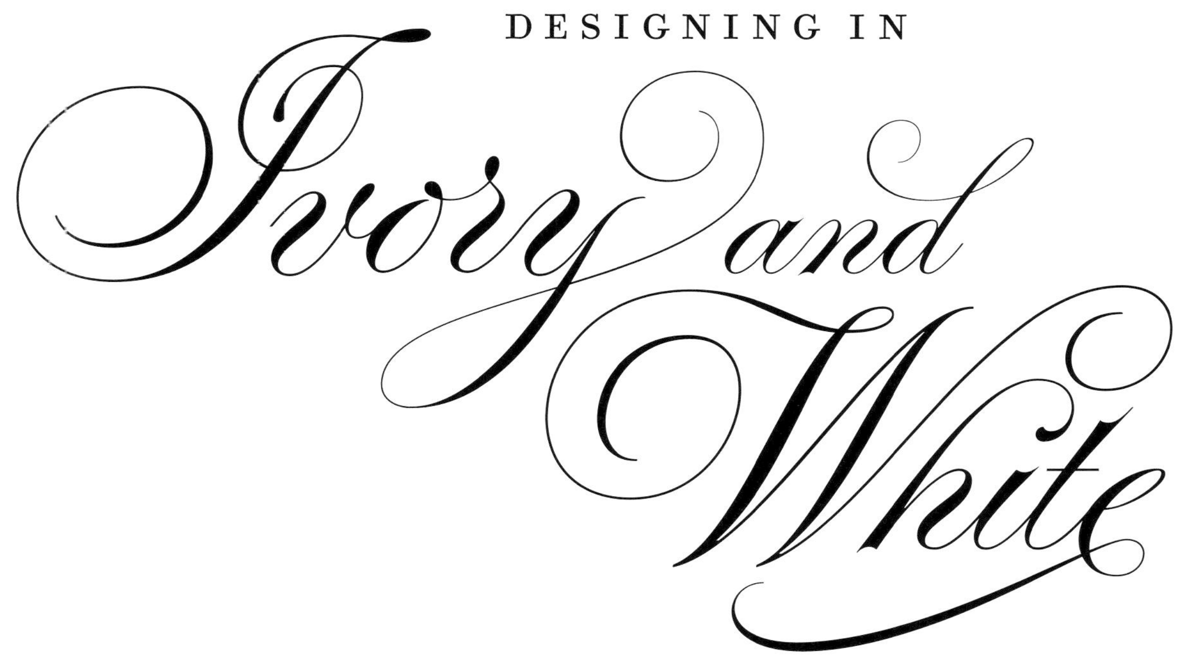

Designing in Ivory and White

Gowns from the Inside Out

SUZANNE PERRON

PHOTOGRAPHS BY JASON COHEN AND BRIAN BAIAMONTE

LOUISIANA STATE UNIVERSITY PRESS BATON ROUGE

Published by Louisiana State University Press

Manufactured in China
First printing

DESIGNER: Michelle A. Neustrom
TYPEFACES: Whitman, text; Filosofia and Parfumerie Script Pro, display
PRINTER AND BINDER: Regent Publishing Services

Note: Photographers are identified by initials in the captions. Credits for photographs without captions are as follows:

Brian Baiamonte: page viii
Jason Cohen: frontispiece, pages vi, xiv, 40, 48, 132

LIBRARY OF CONGRESS CATALOGING-IN-PUBLICATION DATA

Perron, Suzanne, 1968–
Designing in ivory and white : Suzanne Perron gowns from the inside out / Suzanne Perron ; photographs by Jason Cohen and Brian Baiamonte.
p. cm.
ISBN 978-0-8071-4370-4 (cloth : alk. paper) — ISBN 978-0-8071-4371-1 (pdf) — ISBN 978-0-8071-4372-8 (epub) — ISBN 978-0-8071-4373-5 (mobi)
1. Perron, Suzanne, 1968– —Themes, motives. 2. White. I. Cohen, Jason, 1983– II. Baiamonte, Brian, 1972– III. Title.
TT505.P375A5 2012
646.476—dc23

2011029994

The paper in this book meets the guidelines for permanence and durability of the Committee on Production Guidelines for Book Longevity of the Council on Library Resources. ♾

For Ruth Hackett East and Caroline East Perron,
in appreciation of their never-ending support and inspiration

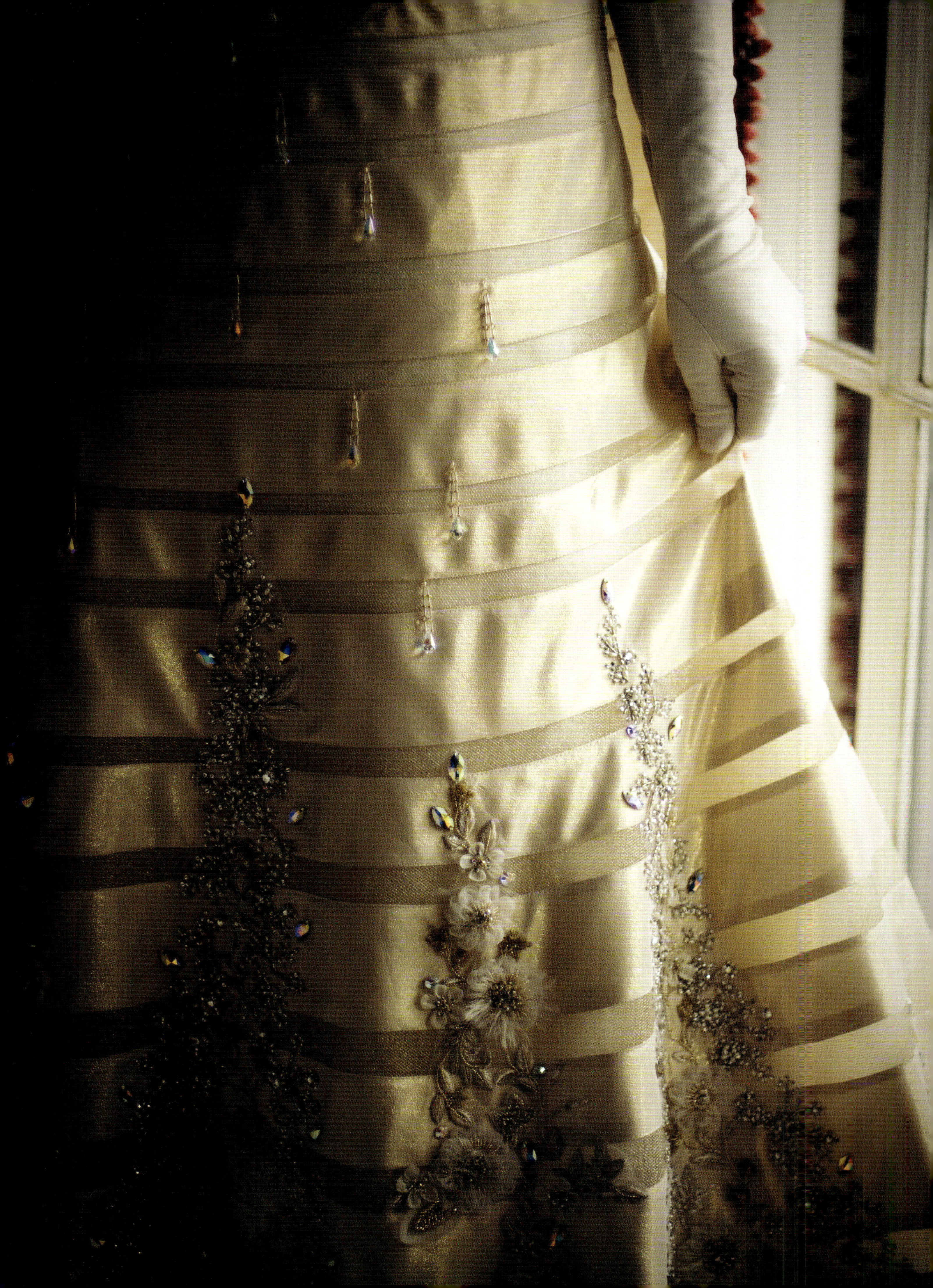

Contents

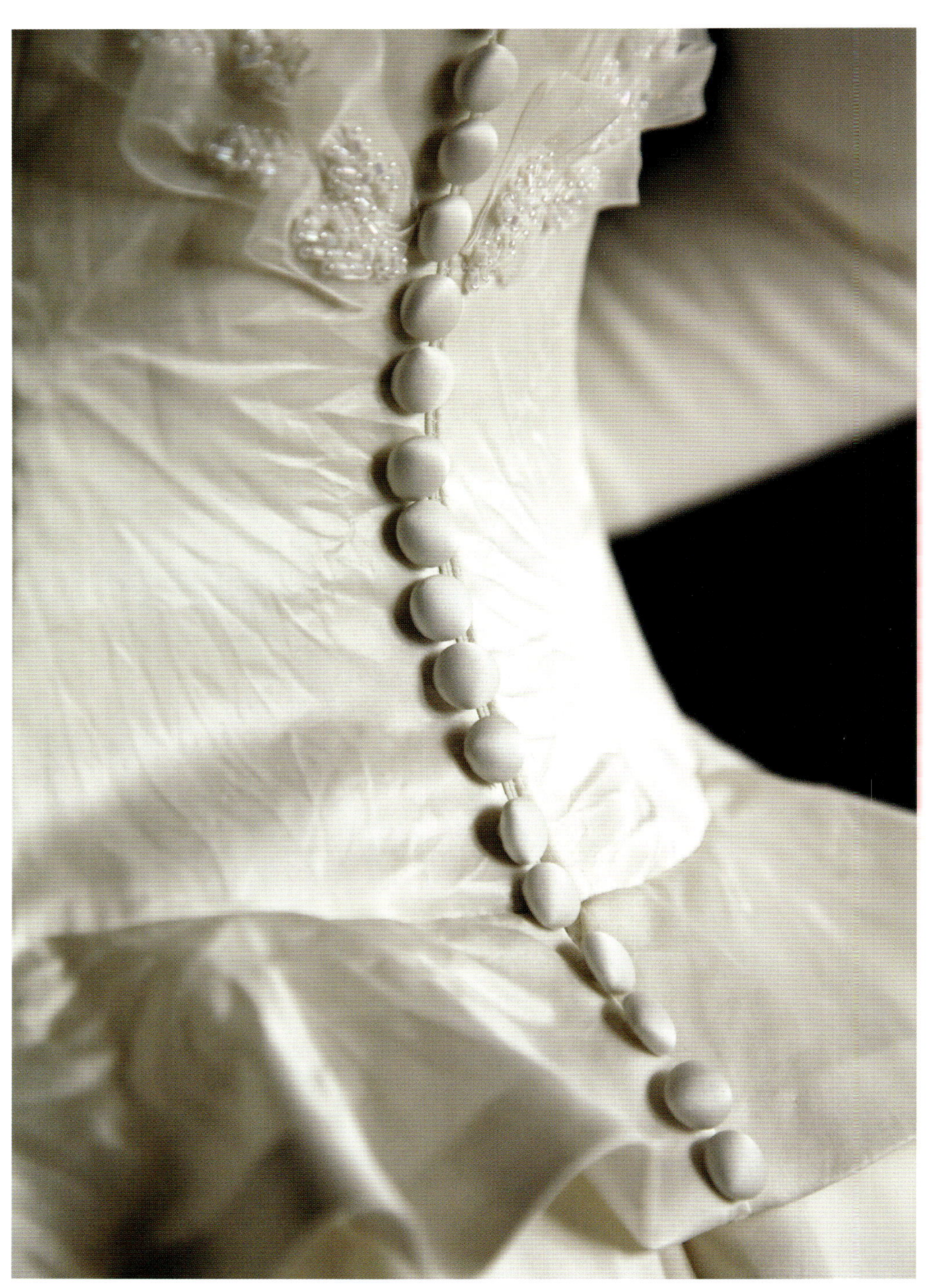

Foreword

The world comes in standard sizes these days. Small, medium, large. Six, eight, ten. Petite, tall, misses.

We pull a garment off the rack at the local mall or at our favorite boutique, slip into it in the dressing room, and admire a reasonable approximation of fit—though the waist may gape slightly and the legs may drag the floor. When we're lucky, it works enough, especially with a little tailoring. If the dress skims our curves and the pants fall appropriately, we head to the checkout counter.

The majority of us shop this way, whether our tastes and budgets run to Dillards or Dolce & Gabbana, whether we're looking for work clothes, play clothes, or a dress for a special event. Modern lives require the efficiency that comes from mass production. Everything moves in a hurry.

But, in our fast-paced world, is there still a place for couture—the art of intricately designed, custom-fitted, hand-finished clothing?

Boiled down to its most basic elements, couture is custom. It's a one-of-a-kind, a perfect fit designed by an artist for an individual. If you're reading this in your home, take a quick glance around the room and stop to think how many things around you were designed to your specific preferences, wants, and desires. How many were created to fit just you? In our off-the-shelf culture, such intimacies are rare pleasures indeed.

Couture—often lamented as the endangered species of the fashion industry—survives, hanging on to its antique ways—the sketches, the draping, the muslin, the hand-sewing, the multiple fittings—even as the world zips by it with the speed of an online shopping click.

Asked in a 2007 *New York Times* interview why couture was still relevant to his business—which includes ready-to-wear and accessories—designer Alber Elbaz of Lanvin replied, "I think it's important to still support couture because we're supporting a technique, a dream."

"It's a big question you are asking," he continued. "Do you keep the past by going forward, or do you have to maintain it in order to exist?"

Suzanne Perron is a gifted designer, helping to establish a vibrant, albeit small, fashion industry in Louisiana. She's doing it in the most traditional of ways. And that seems so fitting for New Orleans, a city that in the early part of the twenty-first century is both leading the country in young entrepreneurship and previously untried school reform and yet still rooted within our venerable cultural traditions of Carnival and cotillions.

To be technical, Perron does not, by definition, do haute couture. Only those designers working in Paris under the auspices of the Chambre Syndicale de la Haute Couture garner that label—just as sparkling wines produced in the Champagne region of France are the only bottles properly called champagne. It's more accurate to say that Perron works in the couture tradition, crafting gowns, each as individual as the woman who will wear it, one at a time.

Couture is more than just a custom fit. Like a commissioned painting or sculpture, a client's desires add to a designer's vision in crafting a final product. In such calculus, two designers, each working with the same client, would produce two different dresses, just as two chefs working with the same ingredients create two different meals. There's no recipe to follow. The artistry comes out in the details.

To fully appreciate a couture piece, you need to inspect it up close, to marvel at the miracles of handwork, the finished seaming, the beading and fabric manipulation. Unfortunately, most couture gowns are worn for the grand entrance, not the close inspection. A bridal gown and a debutante dress stand apart in fashion—both mythical robes, designed to be worn only once. No other garment is held to such significance.

Such once-in-a-lifetime dresses are a modern invention. Until the mid-nineteenth century, brides went to the altar in their best dress, sometimes custom designed, often in a color. It would be worn for the wedding and then throughout the next year. Elaborate gowns of white or ivory lace only became popular after Queen Victoria wore white for her wedding to Prince Albert in 1840. She was the first princess bride. Then and now, couture remains a lab for innovation and trend-setting, a place where designers can experiment and clients can find the dress that's a perfect fit.

SUSAN LANGENHENNIG
Fashion Editor, *New Orleans Times-Picayune*

Preface

Some little girls dream of their wedding dress. I dreamed of everyone else's. That childhood fantasy of designing dresses marked the beginning of a remarkable adventure through the fashion industry. The journey from Louisiana to New York and eventually back to my home state was seasoned with an extraordinary range of experiences and the invaluable influence of others. From the adrenaline of Fashion Week to the exhaustion of ninety-hour work weeks, from celebrity clients to New Orleans Mardi Gras royalty, from a high-rise building on Seventh Avenue to a shop on Magazine Street, the journey has been one of an almost fabled existence. There were, of course, the challenges that kept me grounded and firmly planted in reality. Persevering through demanding work loads and the almost unrealistic expectations of the New York City fashion industry proved arduous but with much reward. The onslaught of Hurricane Katrina and my plans to open a couture gown business collided with much devastation. My idea of home and my business plan appeared to have been destroyed. But the tenacity I gained from years of working in the New York fashion world prepared me to rescue my shattered dream. Just months after Hurricane Katrina, I made New Orleans my home and shortly thereafter opened my business. My endeavors in New Orleans provide continually unfolding chapters as each client and gown offer a unique opportunity for growth and development.

My personal journey as a designer began early in life. Many of my childhood projects foreshadowed the deep love and affinity for fashion I would carry into adulthood. In my first chapter, I have related the hopes, tears, laughter, and triumphs of that journey thus far, hoping that knowledge of my background will provide insight into my work and into fashion design generally.

Next I describe the steps of the couture design process—from sketch to muslin to finished garment—to give a greater understanding of a gown's construction. Much of the beauty of a couture gown is the result of invisible details and painstaking techniques requiring untold hours of work. The perfectly sculpted foundation and carefully engineered crinoline are not in view, and yet they dramatically impact the look of the finished product. The final shape and silhouette of the gown are the result of skillful patternmaking and artful draping.

The client experience is also integral to understanding the couture process. I have chronicled in these pages the four phases each client experiences: her consultation, her gown sketch, her muslin development, and her final fitting. Working closely together at every stage makes the couture experience unique for both designer and client.

The book culminates in sixteen gown stories highlighting the individual client's particular needs and her unique dress details. I explain how each dress design was executed and brought to completion through specific techniques ranging from beading layout to draping. Full portraits and fine-detail photographs showcase each gown.

With that, I invite you to turn these pages and enjoy learning all about Suzanne Perron gowns from the inside out.

DESIGNING IN *Ivory and White*

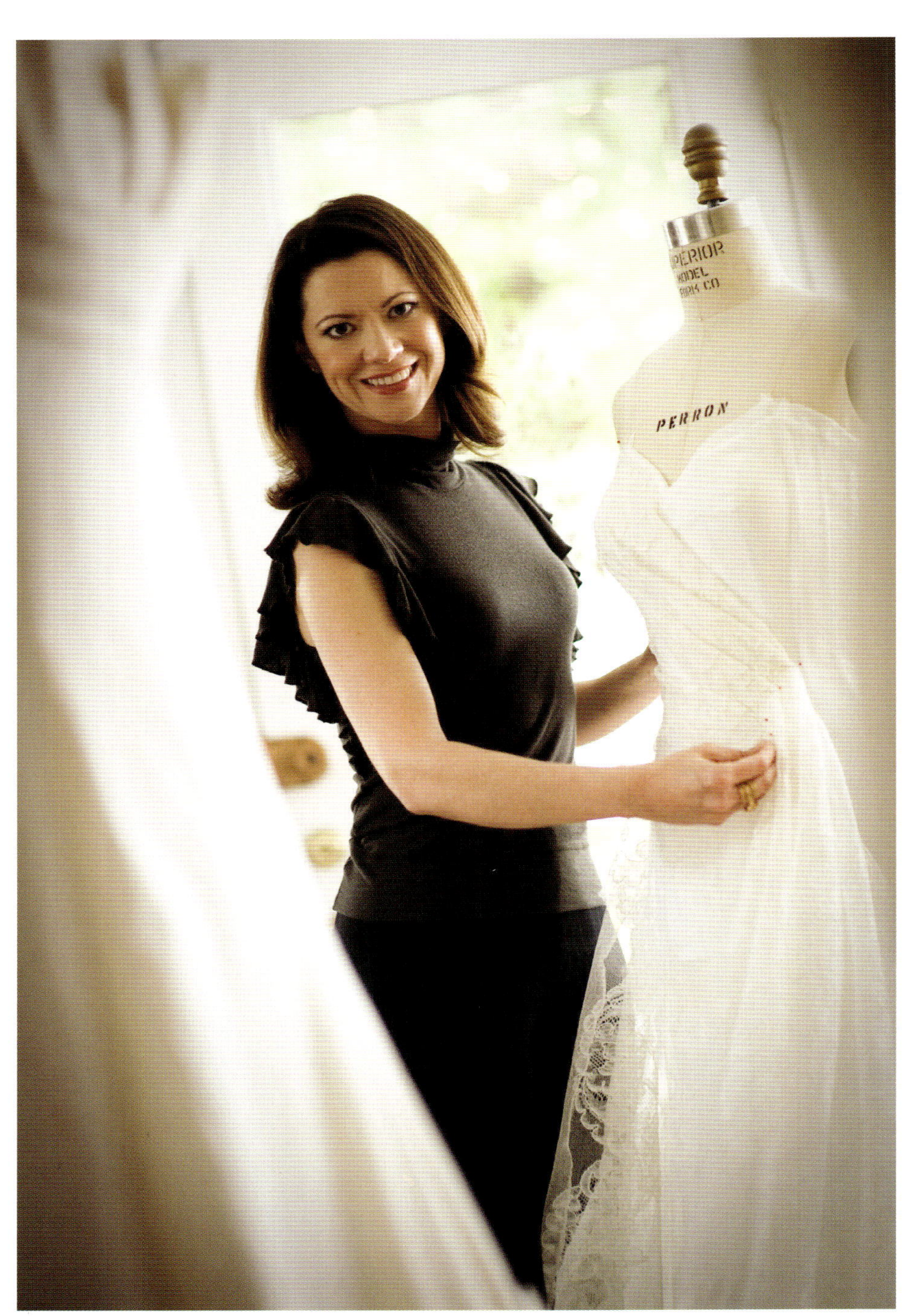
PERRON

INTRODUCTION

The Designer

A CHILDHOOD OF INSPIRATION

When I fell in love with fashion as a child, I was intrigued by the work of the great artists who had not only gifted vision but the technical ability to make that vision reality. I was mesmerized by the work of those designers who used fabric as their artistic medium by shaping and manipulating it into exquisite creations. I was enthralled by the remarkable examples of fine sewing and almost incomprehensible technique, and by the concept of the designer as true craftsman, dressmaker, pattern cutter—not the celebrity designer or the famous personality pervasive in fashion today.

Dover Paper Dolls, illustrated by Tom Tierney, exposed me to the fashion greats when I was too young to realize who they were. I collected the paper doll books and pored through them time and time again. The work of Charles Frederick Worth, Paul Poiret, and Madame Grés leapt from the pages in collections of gowns from *Godey's Ladies Book* and *Harper's Bazaar* from over a century ago. The exceptional work of gifted costume designers Edith Head and Adrian excited me about making and designing clothes and costumes. The paper doll forms dressed in Schiaparelli, Balenciaga, Chanel, or Dior were the most luxurious of toys to me. My imagination would soar with the gowns I would one day create.

During my childhood we lived in many places: Baton Rouge, New Jersey, Delaware, Tennessee, and West Monroe. No matter where we lived, we would spend extended holidays and summers in New Orleans with my grandparents. I would cherish visiting the Presbytere or the Cabildo in Jackson Square with my grandmother. Within these historic buildings would be various exhibits of gowns from the extensive costume collection of the Louisiana State Museum. My heart would race with the sight of magnificently designed gowns ranging from historic pieces to elaborate Mardi Gras queens' gowns. I fondly remember fabric shopping in New Orleans with my grandmother. We would visit the third floor of Krauss to browse the fabric department. I was always on the lookout for the perfect goods for my next project. We would also shop at Halpern's and later Promenade. Metairie Fabrics, which was within walking distance of my grandparents' Oakridge Park home, was one of my regular stops. As a little girl, I was mesmerized by the shimmering trims and fabrics waiting to be transformed into the wears of Mardi Gras royalty.

When I entered my teen years, my interest in fashion became more current and grew beyond historic paper dolls with the birth of a CNN program called *Style with Elsa Klensch*. Beginning in 1980, Elsa Klensch covered fashion shows from New York, Milan, and Paris. I rarely missed an episode of the Saturday morning program. By the end of the 1980s, VH1 was airing the Canadian series *Fashion File* with Tim Blanks. The immense talents of John Galliano, Karl Lagerfeld, Jean Paul Gaultier, Valentino, Gianni Versace, and Alexander McQueen were on display before my eyes. I was introduced to the work of New York designers, including Oscar de la Renta, Geoffrey Beene, and Carolina Herrera. Although I dreamed of working among such talent, I never thought it would become reality.

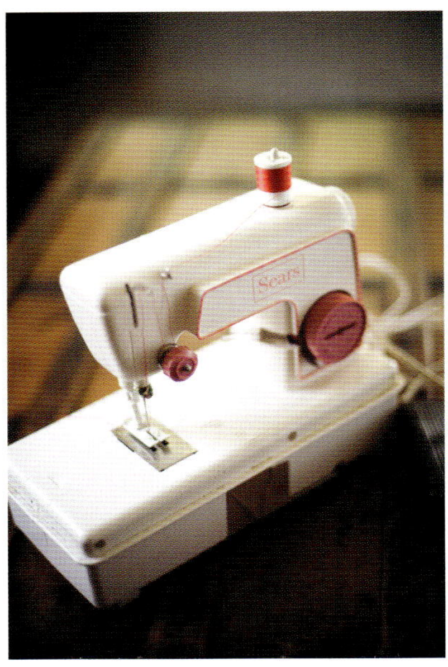

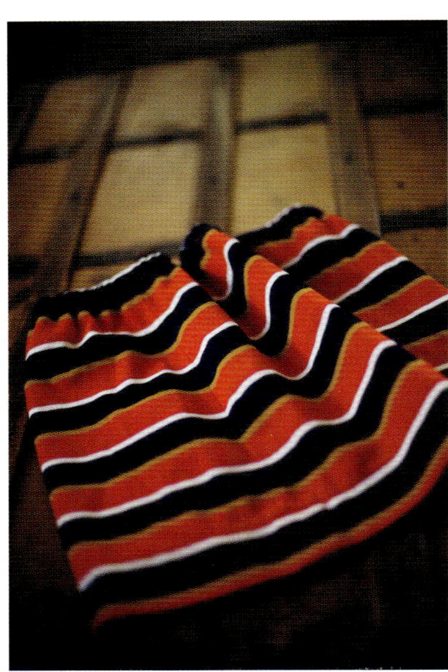

My first sewing machine from Sears (JC)

My first sewing project, an elastic-waist skirt of double-knit polyester (JC)

A CHILDHOOD OF PURSUING A PASSION

Before the age of five, I became intrigued with sewing. I was always preoccupied with some sort of creative endeavor. When my mom could no longer satisfy me with hand sewing projects, she decided I needed a machine of my own. At five, I was too young and too small to use her machine, although (I have been told) I had been pestering her to do so for some time. With Christmas and my November birthday too far away for this very determined child, the Easter Bunny had the privilege of delivering a precious gift. It was this Sears child's sewing machine left for me by the Easter Bunny that was the beginning of my vivid memories of sewing. I remember thinking I must be very important, being only five with a toy "for girls 8 to 12." I can still recall the recommended ages printed on the box. I remember the pink case housing the pale pink plastic machine with bright pink detailing. The word "Sears" was embossed on the front in hot pink. The machine had a top thread and a bobbin thread, which was unusual in a child's machine.

I was not interested in sewing clothes for dolls. I wanted to sew clothes for me. My first project on my new sewing machine was an elastic-waist skirt. My mom had made a peasant dress out of blue, red, yellow, and orange striped, double-knit polyester. (Okay, it was 1973!) The scrap left behind was a long, narrow piece of the stripe. The scrap would have gone around me perfectly had I wanted vertical stripes. But no . . . I envisioned horizontal stripes! I had a very specific vision of what my skirt should look like. I somehow decided that if I cut the scrap into four pieces and seamed them together, I could get the fullness I wanted and have horizontal stripes. My mom showed me how to pin the fabric to make the stripes match. I still have a hard time believing I had the hand dexterity at five to pull it off, but she insists that I did it myself. I am amazed every time I look at that skirt.

The polyester striped garment was the beginning of my kindergarten skirt wardrobe. I soon advanced to patch pockets and gathered ruffles. The child's sewing machine satisfied me for about two years. By the time I was in second grade, I was sewing on my mom's Singer sewing machine. This was the 1962 Singer my mom took with her to college. The "green machine," as it was known, is a gem: the perfect tension, an adapted buttonhole attachment from my grandmother's machine, an easy-to-control stitch-length lever and reverse control. In its day it was considered portable, though it is quite heavy with its all-metal parts. That machine is now my prized possession. It traveled with me to LSU and the Fashion Institute of Technology, and is still with me today as I work in my New Orleans studio. I even used that machine to make buttonholes in jackets for one of Carolina Herrera's runway shows. Anytime I need precise sewing, I go for the green machine! Those of you who sew would appreciate the stitch-control lever that allows for hand-free back stitching. The lever allows for the most infinitesimal adjustments when extreme accuracy is necessary. I do not make bound buttonholes without it. When I moved to New Orleans from New York, the movers shattered the top of the machine. Of all the stress related to the delayed post-Katrina move, the damaged green machine was what brought me to tears. I gathered all of the pieces I could find and glued them back together. With a few tweaks, it still works beautifully.

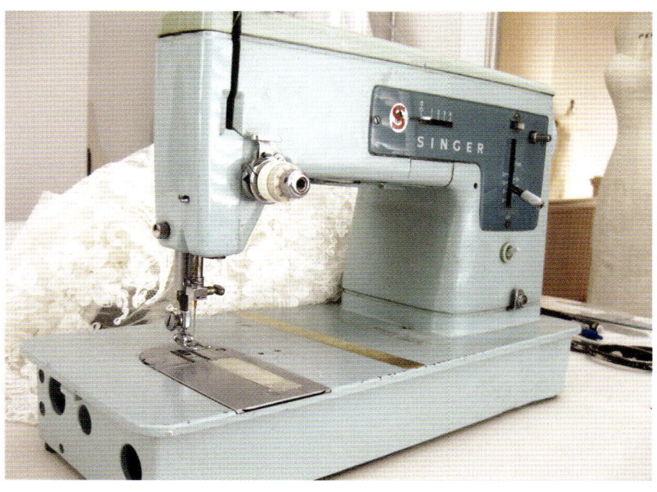

The "green machine," my most-valued sewing machine (SP)

I was a very imaginative child and would get inspiration from anything around me. The pre-glamour Cinderella was one of my early Halloween costumes, when I was about seven years old. My sister's stuffed mouse with a pink tummy was my inspiration. I wanted to be Cinderella before the ball and carry a broom and my sister's stuffed mouse for props. I was obviously more interested in completing the look than having a free hand for my candy bag. I made a skirt with brown fabric. It was a simple elastic-waist skirt with a raw hem cut into jagged triangles. Was this the forerunner of the "distressed" look? I sewed patches of colorful fabric with big whipstitches of contrasting thread. I called them Frankenstein stitches. The T-shaped dolman top was jagged and patched to match. I tied a square of fabric that matched my patches as a kerchief on my head. Only my memory remains of this costume. The garment and our photos of it have yet to surface post-Katrina.

I was so fascinated with clothes and sewing that I would bring fashion into my school art projects. I remember playing with Play-Doh in the back of my second-grade classroom. I shaped the dough into a girl and a boy. I fashioned outfits for them out of the dough, complete with buttons, collars, and skirt and pants. They even had Play-Doh hairstyles. When I finished, I wanted to take them completely apart because they did not live up to my expectations. The teacher intervened. She was so impressed with my creations that she wanted to keep them intact until parent night. I was upset. I would have preferred to take them apart than to have anyone see work that I thought was substandard!

Another art project with fashion influence was a construction-paper cutout for a PTA cultural arts contest. I was a ten-year-old student at the time. I had unusual hand dexterity at a young age, and I also had a long attention span if creatively engaged. I would cut and paste at my art table for hours. I came up with a concept of a paper doll chain encircling a globe to fit with the theme "What the World Needs Now." I remembered my grandmother teaching me how to cut out paper doll chains. I wanted the pairs of children in the chain to be dressed in native costume. Every detail was cut out of construction paper. I weaved narrow strips of colored paper to make the plaid of the Scottish kilts. I cut curved bands of construction paper to define the flare of the Spanish costumes. I re-created style lines of embroidery with layers of intricately shaped construction paper. Even hair, headdresses, eyes, and mouths were crafted in construction paper. I am so

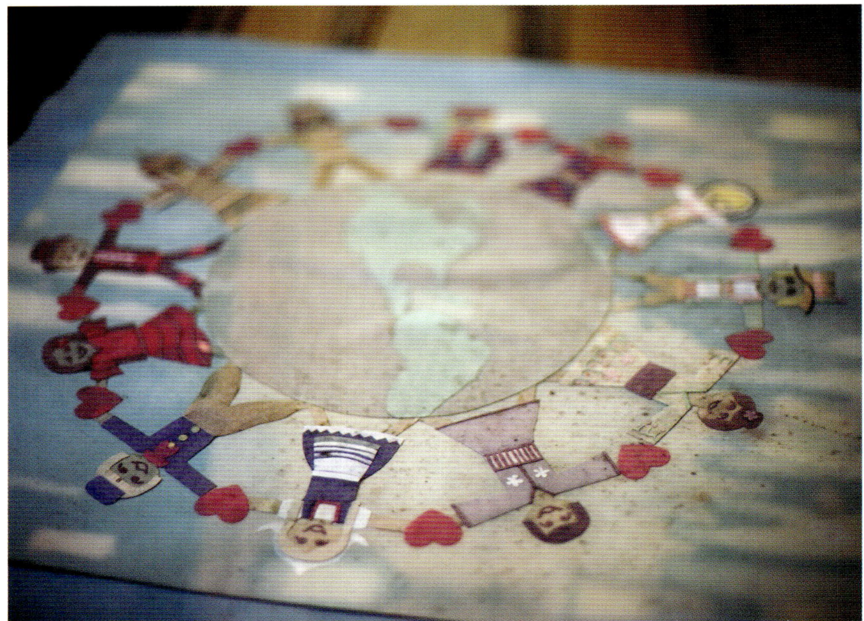

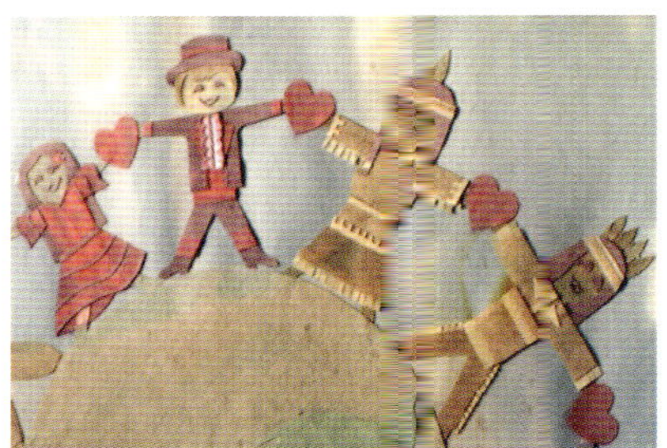

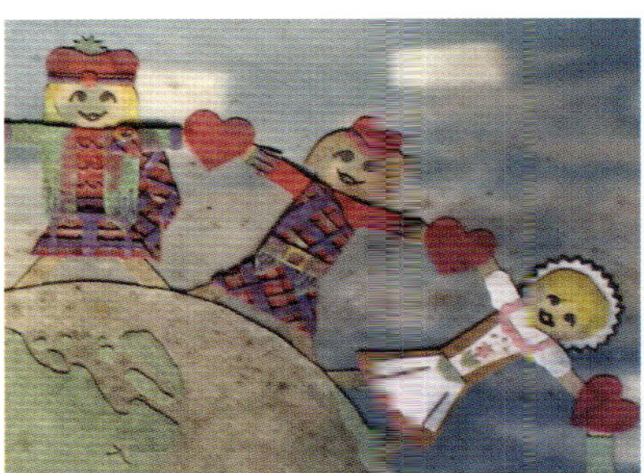

Fashion-inspired art project from elementary school (JC)

Details including headdresses and garment trim cut from construction paper (JC)

Plaid detail created with cut construction paper (JC)

fortunate to have this sample of my childhood artwork. When searching for keepsakes at my parents' house after Hurricane Katrina, this was the one item I was determined to find. With relief I discovered it had survived the submersion quite well. The oceans of the construction paper globe now have a water effect not original to the piece.

When deciding on my next project, I would lean toward undertakings that allowed me to learn and practice new sewing techniques and applications. I would challenge myself with each activity. One of my more ambitious childhood projects was a green-velvet knicker pants suit. I was twelve. The suit consisted of a bolero, knickers, and ruffled, collared shirt. I trimmed the edge of the bolero and the sleeves with gold piping. This was a challenge as I changed the pattern to accommodate the piping. Without any patternmaking training, I simply used my best judgment and changed the jacket and sleeve hems to facings. I practiced on scraps with the zipper foot and taught myself how to sew in the premade metallic gold piping. The velvet knickers even had plackets and cuffs at the knee. Making a fly front in velvet was quite an accomplishment. I loved looking at pictures of historic costumes and was fascinated by the intricacy of dress in the Elizabethan era. I wanted to finish my velvet suit with a white shirt and lace ruff collar inspired by a photo of Queen Elizabeth I. I achieved this by making a white cotton, jewel-neck long-sleeve shirt from a commercial pattern. I ran a gathering stitch about one third into a wide piece of lace. I gathered the lace to the measurement of the finished neckline. I attached the lace around the neckline, creating a two-tier lace ruff. The shorter ruffle stood up around my neck, and the longer ruffle fanned out around the neckline. The idea in my head became reality.

When I was in junior high school, the prairie dress was in fashion. I envisioned the dress I wanted and set out to create it. First I scoured the local fabric stores. I found a floral printed, gray cotton fabric and a white eyelet lace. I envisioned a prairie dress with very full puffed sleeves. I was working with a commercial pattern. I thought if I had more fabric to gather, the sleeves would have more fullness. Before I ever studied patternmaking, I was making patterns. I cut and spread out the pattern on the fabric. I had no idea I was using the very basic "slash and spread" patternmaking technique I would later learn in school. I further personalized my prairie dress by drafting my own ruffle for the hem of the skirt. I loved how the skirt would move and swish as I walked. I was intrigued with fabric movement.

Halloween presented great opportunities to design. In sixth grade, I had an idea of a Jetson-like red space costume. The color scheme was dictated by a red bishop-sleeved shirt that I already owned. I wanted a skirt to go with the shirt. Not just any skirt, but one that stood out like a saucer. I first thought of a hula hoop to make the skirt saucer shaped, like a hoop skirt from antebellum dress. Wanting more flexibility, I opted for upholstery cord. I covered thick upholstery welt cording with silver lamé and stitched it around the hem of the red satin skirt. The skirt stood out like a saucer. I created cardboard shoulder pieces trimmed with silver lamé–covered cord. I literally put the cardboard through the sewing machine to attach the cord. A cardboard cumberbund with red ribbon laces completed the look. The outfit was such a hit that a friend borrowed it for a costume function at her school a few months later.

I got my first taste of once-in-a-lifetime gowns with my sister's prom dress. When I was in junior high school, my older sister was invited to the high school prom. We went dress shopping together. She was old enough to drive, so it was just the two of us. After visiting every store in town, we had not really seen anything we liked. The only dress that piqued our interest was far above our price range. I offered to make her gown if our mom bought the fabric. On our way home, we stopped at the fabric store. I found fabric, I estimated yardage, and presented a proposal. Mom was impressed with my design and follow-through for the blue-green organza gown with ruffled shoulders, puffed sleeves, and scalloped hem. I designed the dress to be convertible. It was two pieces: a tea-length dress with a scalloped hem and separate underskirt with a ruffle to the floor. I rummaged through our stock of commercial patterns. I found something similar to my design and then drafted what was missing. I made patterns for the ruffles, scalloped hem, facings, and an underskirt. I reshaped the sleeve to have a ruffle extending below the casing. The detail I put in this project was tedious. The garment was made by layering silk organza over satin. The two layers were framed together in the same manner I often work with layers today. All of the ruffles were made of organza and finished with a narrow rolled hem on the serger. I hand twisted strips of hemmed organza into rosettes. The back closed with fabric-covered buttons and hand-crocheted thread loops.

When my sister came home from the prom, she hung the dress up in the laundry room. The next day I noticed a hole and diagonal pull in the front of the skirt. I immediately set out to remedy the situation. I collected fabric scraps and shaped them into additional rosettes and petals. I appliquéd the spray of flowers and petals over the damage. A few months later, when this gown became my first entry in a 4-H sewing competition, the main comment on the score sheet was "beautiful floral appliqué on skirt front."

An unlikely outlet that prepared me for my fashion career was Louisiana 4-H. My best friend from high school was very active in 4-H. When she saw how well I could sew, she suggested I get involved and enter the clothing competitions. Our high school did not have a 4-H club, so we competed through the Ouachita Parish at-large club. The parish agent came to see my work and immediately helped me join the organization and encouraged me to participate. The biggest competition of the year was coming up, the State 4-H Short Course. I had the perfect garment, my sister's prom dress, to enter in the special occasion category. When competing in 4-H, you model your own garment. I was a little smaller than my sister, so I stitched a tuck in the waist and wore a higher heel.

I was competing against entrants from each of the sixty-four parishes, and I was one of the youngest and newest competitors. The clothing competition is quite involved. Garments are submitted in advance of the competition for judging of construction. They are evaluated from the inside and outside. The judging panel looks at every element of construction: even seam allowances, proper stitch length, pressing, appropriate interfacing, and quality hand stitching to name a few. During the competition, garments are modeled and evaluated for fit, design, and style. Once the judging is complete, a fashion show is staged. The fashion show concludes with the announcement of the blue ribbon group or top ten of each category.

At the final state 4-H awards ceremony, which incorporates all areas of competition and involves hundreds of competitors, the winners are announced. The clothing winners are announced with much drama, almost like Miss America finalists. With the top blue ribbon winners already announced, the longer you go without hearing your name and parish, the higher you placed. What excitement as the names in my category continued to be announced. As we counted, we realized I was at least third, then second . . . and the WINNER! I was floored. I called my mom from the pay phone in the lobby of the LSU Assembly Center to share the great news. For me it was like winning an Academy Award. I went on to participate in 4-H activities throughout high school. I learned so much from the judges' construction critique sheets. I was a regular participant in the state 4-H Sew with Cotton contest. I also entered garments in the local and state fair, earning prize money to put toward future fabric purchases.

Many activities outside of sewing and drawing were instrumental in preparing me for the pursuit of fashion design. Dancing with the Twin City Ballet Company in Monroe, Louisiana, helped shape my appreciation for beauty and movement. Rigorous training, high expectations, and working on deadlines prepared me for a successful college and professional career. Competition, rejection, respect for authority, and acceptance of constructive criticism specifically prepared me for the rigors of a fashion industry career. Evening gown and bridal design was a natural extension of my love of the stage, performance, and beauty developed from years of classical ballet training and performing. Boned bodices and the tulle skirts of ballet costumes are of similar construction to the components that make up bridal and evening gowns. Helping and learning from my mom—who designed ballet costumes for Twin City Ballet—enhanced my construction knowledge when working with structured bodices or hundreds of yards of tulle. I developed a greater understanding of fit having worn so many boned-bodice ballet costumes in performances. The grace, elegance, and femininity of ballet carry through in my work today.

Another venue for showing off my work was the Louisiana Junior Miss scholarship program. I was first drawn to the program because of the emphasis on talent and academic achievement. I had an outstanding academic record and jumped at the chance to put my years of ballet training to practice on stage. I recognized the opportunity to earn valuable scholarship awards that would help defray the cost of my college education. Participating also gave me a venue to design and wear my own gown, talent costume, and interview dress. The floor-length white evening gown I designed was the second white gown I had made for myself. The first was a tiered taffeta and lace gown made for the freshman choir concert. Rows of taffeta and lace alternated from the waist to the floor. The Junior Miss gown was made of organza and satin. Organza ruffling created a portrait neckline. Lace appliqués blended into a dimensional ruffled hem. Lace appliqué is one of the most common adornment techniques used in my current bridal work. For talent, I made a peasant-inspired ballet costume for my Little Red Riding Hood divertissements from *Sleeping Beauty*. The bodice was embellished with hand-sculpted fabric flowers and cording. Today I often add design interest and dimension to gowns with similar fabric-sculpting techniques. The interview dress was of white-on-white cotton jacquard and was styled with horizontal stitched pleats in the bodice and vertical inverted box pleats in the skirt. Fabric pleating is a signature design element commonly incorporated into my current work. My Junior Miss experience was a success: I placed as first runner-up and won the overall scholastic award.

FAMILY LEGACY

You may wonder how I not only became intrigued with fashion but also developed sewing and fashion design skills at such a young age. Sewing and fashion design are all in the family. My mother and grandmother were both talented designers and seamstresses. The tradition of needlework goes back even further.

My grandmother Ruth Hackett East, known as Gran to me, was first exposed to sewing when she was five years old. She and her older sisters were on their own when school recessed at noon. Gran's sisters were usually off on their skates and bikes while my grandmother spent her time with her dolls. My great-grandmother enjoyed dressing her four daughters alike, so she hired a seamstress to come in twice a year to make their dresses. My grandmother and the seamstress had a deal: Gran would not bother her, and the seamstress would set aside the smaller scraps in a special place in the scrap drawer. The minute the seamstress left, my grandmother was into the scraps and planning new outfits for her dolls. Having watched the seamstress cut from patterns, hand baste, and machine stitch, my grandmother knew just what to do. She remembers listening for the seamstress's footsteps going down the stairs so she could hurry to the machine and get to work.

When Gran entered all-day school, she took her pastime with her. Instead of passing notes to classmates, she passed paper dolls. Under the guise of taking notes, she would design outfits for the dolls. When she almost got sent to the

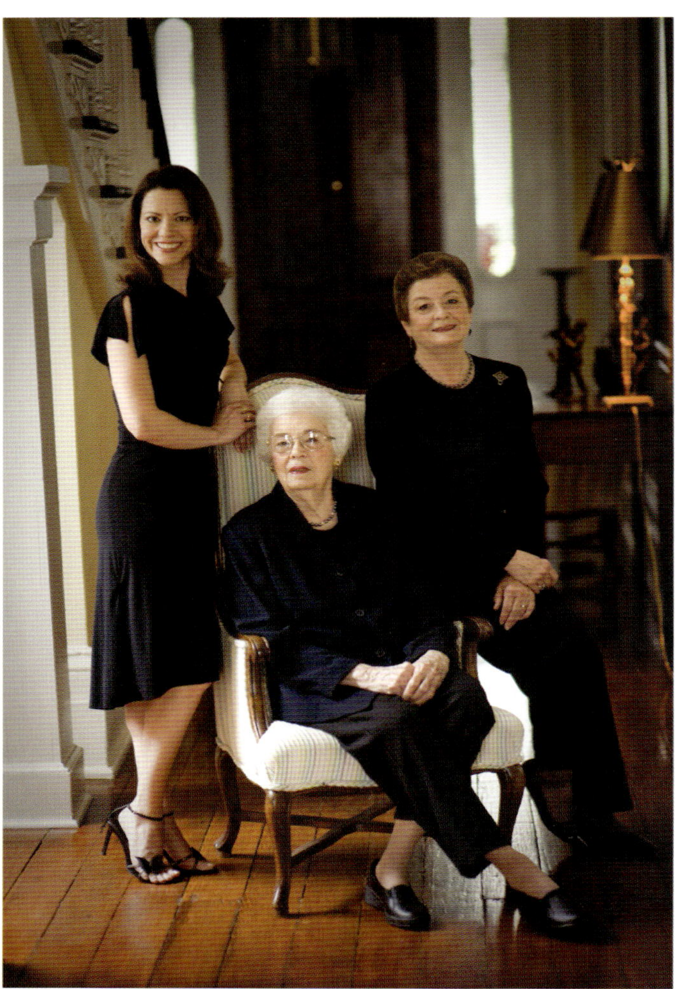

Three generations of designers. I am pictured with Ruth Hackett East and Caroline East Perron (JC)

principal's office, she gave that up. Sewing was added to her school's curriculum when she was in seventh grade. She remembers two of the three machines being treadle machines. The emphasis in that class was on making baby squares and embroidered dresser scarves.

In her spare time at home, Gran created evening gown designs in watercolor and pen and ink. Her mother would pass by at 11 p.m. and snap off the light without comment. Homework and extracurricular activities limited her sewing time, but fortunately a newly widowed seamstress had been recommended to her soft-hearted mother, who gave Gran the go-ahead to have evening dresses made according to her designs. The summer before her junior year, she had the bright idea of making dirndl skirts, which were just coming into vogue, with large matching squares that could double as either a head scarf or bandana top. Much to my great-grandmother's dismay, Gran received quite a few orders.

With college looming, Gran was in a quandary. She had been registered at Vassar College, her mother's alma mater, when she was six months old, but dress design was not included in the curriculum. Gran's mother solved the dilemma by writing a letter to the famous designer Edith Head via a mutual friend. Edith Head in return wrote a letter to my grandmother stating that a liberal arts college foundation followed by technical training at a design school such as Parsons was the recommended path.

With history, art history, drawing, and painting leading her course of study, my grandmother was on her way. She and her freshman-year roommate made dirndl skirts and matching bandanas to raise money for Vassar's seventy-fifth anniversary. Then along came Pearl Harbor and World War II. My grandmother graduated from Vassar in 1943. Studying at fashion school during the war was out of the question. The next time she had a chance to think about dress design, she was in Laramie, Wyoming, with a military husband and a three-month-old daughter, my mother. My grandmother saw an ad in a magazine for a fashion correspondence course through a school in Chicago. The course was in patternmaking and design. My grandmother finally had her chance to study fashion. It took her almost two years to finish the course. Her final exam entry was a fashion business concept. She designed a children's shop complete with an architectural plan. Included in her final exam evaluation was the comment, "the most professional entry I have ever received."

Seven years later, my grandmother and a business partner opened a children's clothing enterprise in New Orleans called "Jibby." Jibby owed its great success as much to well-fitting garments as to attractive designs and appropriate fabrics. By this time Gran had eight years of patternmaking experience. With the help of a government guide to patternmaking and sizing, she came up with patterns that could fit multiple sizes. Along the way, she introduced shoulder and waist length tucks along with conventional hem tucks to add years of wearability. My grandmother was known for how well her children's clothes fit. At one point, the mother of Gran's business partner, who was active in the New Orleans fashion scene, commented to my grandmother, "You are a civil engineer, just like your father."

Evidence of an interest in fashion as a longstanding family trait turned up on my grandmother's cousin's wall. Framed, under glass, is a chatelaine belt from which hang seven or eight sewing notions including tiny scissors, an emory board, and a thimble. To be so carefully preserved suggests its historical value; perhaps it was handed down from previous generations.

My mother, Caroline East Perron, was likewise interested in sewing at a young age. She, like my grandmother, began making clothes for her dolls at age five. Although she made numerous such fashions, the most memorable was a wedding dress she made for an 18-inch poseable doll when she was sixteen. I remember the sleeveless dress of ivory satin. A bateau neckline framed the face. The skirt was gathered vertically creating a scalloped finish similar to a balloon shade for a window. A miniature crocheted lace added detail to the neckline and the scalloped hem. A ruffled tier extended beyond the scallops to create a full-length gown with train.

In junior high and high school, my mom was sewing clothes for herself. She made dresses for church and school. Pleated skirts were a staple in her custom wardrobe. Engineered stripes, patterns, and prints gave the skirts design interest.

When my mother went to the University of Southwestern Louisiana, she majored in home economics. At the time there was no apparel design degree. Mom tailored her curriculum as much as possible to fashion by taking every class related to clothing and design. Whether it was interior design, dress design, or tailoring, Mom made sure to work the classes into her schedule.

All through my early childhood, my mother sewed for us. She made matching outfits for my older sister and me. Mom incorporated all of my grandmother's ingenious children's clothes techniques of growth tucks and adjustable seam allowances. I was able to wear the same dress for about five years. About the time I grew out of my dress and all of the growth tucks, I could fit into my sister's. No wonder I wanted to make my own clothes! My earliest involvement with sewing was standing behind the sewing machine while Mom was sewing our clothes. I would remove the pins as the fabric passed under the presser foot and behind the machine.

Although never formally trained as a fashion designer, my mother had quite a natural talent. She sketched beautifully and had an instinctive eye for color and proportion. Her talent, sewing knowledge, and sketching ability led her into costume design. For twenty years she was the wardrobe director for Twin City Ballet in Monroe. She would also oversee the design and construction of costumes for entire productions, including *The Nutcracker*, *Coppelia*, and newly commissioned works for the company. At a recent anniversary performance of the ballet company, costumes designed by my mom were still in use. I was especially impressed by her use of color and hand dying of silk. The body-flattering shape and construction of her corsetlike ballet bodices influenced my love for constructing evening and bridal gowns. Mom refined her costume skills by attending workshops with other costume designers at regional ballet festivals. What my mother accomplished during her costume design career is astounding. Many of the techniques I incorporate in constructing bridal gowns are techniques I picked up from her. I am grateful for the legacy passed down through the family and for the opportunity to learn from previous generations.

MY COLLEGE EXPERIENCE

I initially planned to go to New York City straight from West Monroe High School. I had my sights set on Pratt Institute. I had learned about Pratt through its national high school talent search. Although I did not win, I was awarded a partial scholarship by placing in the finals. Even with that partial scholarship offer, Pratt was a cost-prohibitive choice for me and my family. I had shipped the three garments I made for the Junior Miss competition to Pratt as part of my portfolio evaluation. When my mom called to inquire about the garments being returned, the Pratt staff mentioned how impressed they were with my construction ability and even wondered if I had actually made the garments myself. My mom assured them I had, and was then informed that I may not have placed higher in the finals because my designs were "too southern." My mom's response was "Why do you think she wants to go to design school in New York?"

With New York City temporarily off the plate, LSU won out with an offer of an academic honors scholarship. Additional scholarships including 4-H and Junior Miss further defrayed my college expenses. In the end, attending LSU was the best college choice I could have made. Maturing into a young adult while experiencing all that a traditional four-year college had to offer was priceless. I earned a place on the revered LSU Golden Girl dance line, pledged Kappa Kappa Gamma sorority, and became involved in several campus organizations, including Student Government, Mortar Board, and Leadership LSU. LSU provided a strong fashion and academic base without the student loan debt that would have accrued at the private institutions I had investigated. Preparing for the transition to New York without that debt burden was yet another benefit of choosing LSU. On-campus living and the sorority house life prepared me for the close living quarters that are a way of life in New York City.

LSU may be far removed from any world fashion capital, but the education I received in the fashion design department gave me a great base on which to build. Apparel classes in patternmaking, draping, and construction provided an ideal foundation for the intensive training I would receive in New York. Textile science gave me an understanding of fabric construction and content continually applicable when designing. Classes in the art department, including charcoal drawing and watercolor painting, helped me develop useful skill sets for fashion illustration.

The class that most prepared me for working with the layers and structure of bridal wear was tailoring. They may seem unrelated, but the same principles of layering apply to both. Yvonne Marquette Leak taught us the basics of tailoring: framing, pad stitching, staying, easing, and more. We worked with a little boy's size-four jacket. We made half of the jacket with every detail executed longhand, in the tradition of old-fashioned hand tailoring. Working on a smaller scale gave us great hands-on experience and an understanding of tailoring and shaping in short period of time. Having only made half, we could peek inside and refresh our memory when working on later projects. The understanding of how layers of fabric can be permanently shaped with stitching, interfacing, and steam is applicable to numerous design and construction applications. The concept taught in tailoring of how circumferences must change within a cylindric or cone shape also applies to the design of layered skirts and crinolines.

An educational base beyond the arts added to the value of the LSU experience. The campuswide core curriculum requirements encouraged achievement in multiple disciplines outside of a declared major. Opportunities to build leadership skills in the broader campus community and interdisciplinary study prepared me for the fashion industry through exposure to both competition and teamwork. Holding leadership positions within organizations helped me learn to effectively delegate responsibility to others as well as develop good study habits, manage time, and establish priorities. Attending LSU and being an active part of the community laid the groundwork for a future back in Louisiana. Forging lifelong friendships and relationships set the stage for opening a business in Louisiana. The support of my alma mater has been a crucial part of my business success.

THE FASHION INSTITUTE OF TECHNOLOGY

In the fall of 1992, I found myself in a New York City taxi with two yellow suitcases asking the driver to take me to the corner of 27th Street and 7th Avenue. My destination was the campus of the Fashion Institute of Technology. I had embarked on a journey that would far exceed my expectations. My room was secure in an on-campus dorm, and I was enrolled in a one-year accelerated program in fashion design. I had earned one of fifty available spots filled through a selective admissions process.

The Fashion Institute of Technology is a public institution under the umbrella of the State University of New York system. Located just blocks from the center of the fashion industry, FIT has offered a world-renowned fashion curriculum since 1944. The school's close ties to the industry and its strategic location allowed me to be immersed in the fast-paced world of fashion. The design programs at FIT are committed to nurturing creativity while preparing the student for the real demands of the fashion world. This unique educational experience fostered my successful entry into the challenging industry of fashion.

The first semester began with a series of orientations intended to acclimate us both to the immediate campus of FIT and the bigger New York City campus around us. I was surrounded by students of every nationality, background, and style imaginable. Many of my peers had tattoos, nose rings, body piercings, and wildly colored hair. This conservative southern belle that had barely pulled the sorority bow out of her hair felt like a fish out of water. I was initially very intimidated by New York and the FIT environment. It did not take long for me to see, however, that I had an instinctive talent for the technical disciplines of draping and patternmaking. I realized that I had the skill level to compete. Illustration was not as natural a gift. I really had to work when it came to illustration assignments. My ability to quickly complete assigned muslin sew-ups and other construction projects afforded me the time to devote to illustration. I rendered fabric and garment details competently. It was faces, hands, and feet that gave me the most trouble. Through the tutelage of gifted industry professionals, I was able to build on my underdeveloped illustration skills while realizing my technical abilities were truly unique. Draping, patternmaking, and construction were always easy for me.

A twelve-hour intensive draping class was the core of the first semester. Our professor, Eva Bernard Nambath, taught with unbridled enthusiasm and passion. She taught the textbook basics while keeping us motivated about design with glimpses of how to apply these basics to more creative, artful manipulation. She was a motivator who prepared us for the industry by expecting a lot in both the content and quality of our work. She expected attentive students with a strong work ethic.

The exposure to fashion design legends during my studies at FIT was epic. The first of the great designers I met was Valentino. An exhibit of his work was being staged at the Seventh Regiment Armory on the Upper East Side of Manhattan to commemorate his thirty years of work in the industry. A representative of Valentino's staff called the fashion design office and offered twenty-five tickets to design students to attend a tour of the exhibit personally led by Valentino. Professor Nambath happened to be in the office when the call came. She quickly spread word to our class, and the twenty-five of us scooped up the tickets. We all enjoyed a personal tour of the exhibit "Valentino: Thirty Years of Magic." The legendary designer was very generous with his time and eager to share his comments. He patiently answered numerous questions in his heavy Italian accent. He took the time to sign the beautiful hardcover books companion to the exhibit that were available for purchase in the gift shop. It was an expensive purchase for a student, but well worth working into the budget.

The year I was at FIT was also the year French-born American designer Pauline Trigère celebrated her fiftieth anniversary in fashion. Trigère did not sketch her designs. She was an innovator of shape as she would cut and drape from bolts of cloth directly on the mannequin, model, or client. In one student presentation I attended, she wielded scissors and a bolt of fabric around a student volunteer until there was a lovely cape perfectly draping from the volunteer's shoulders. With a fiftieth-anniversary milestone unique among American designers, an elaborate benefit fashion show and dinner were staged on campus. Hundreds of the most influential figures in the fashion world joined socialites and theater personalities for the gala event. Many were Trigère's personal friends and longstanding clients. These same socialites and contemporaries modeled garments spanning the breadth of her career. I had a very personal perspective of this event, having been chosen by the faculty to be one of the few students allowed to work backstage.

An elaborate retrospective celebrating Gianni Versace was staged at the FIT museum while I was a student. I frequently walked through the exhibit and would spend hours in awe of the masterfully made decadent creations of sparkle and glamour. The retrospective was titled "Versace: Signatures." As a tie-in to the exhibit, Versace himself was a guest lecturer during our final-semester lecture series. I can picture him sitting on a stool before us in the auditorium, holding a microphone and answering questions as images of his work were projected behind him. He generously gave the companion book to the exhibit to participating students and even took the time to sign a few. I was not one of those lucky ones getting the autograph, but I did receive a copy of the book.

Another prominent and revered designer to speak at FIT was Geoffrey Beene. I was particularly interested in meeting him because of our parallel roots. Beene was a native of north Louisiana. He studied medicine at Tulane University before dropping out to move to New York City to pursue fashion. He studied at the Traphagen School of Fashion in New York. Hearing his personal accounts of the fashion industry while seeing images of his collection projected on the stage was tremendous. After the presentation, I had the opportunity to introduce myself to him. He was unimpressed that I too was from Louisiana, though it was still a privilege to meet such a critically acclaimed designer. He was an innovator who blurred the lines between sportswear and eveningwear and was a master with geometric shapes and soft tailoring.

During my final semester at FIT, I selected a design studio with an eveningwear specialization. The first half of the semester, we learned couture and evening techniques. We studied foundation development, hand fluting and fabric techniques, as well as hand beading and embroidery. The second half of the semester was dedicated to designing and making a garment for the student runway show. Each specialization class worked with an industry critic. Our critic was Carolina Herrera. We met with Mrs. Herrera and her design director several times throughout the semester. When Mrs. Herrera came for our final critique, she commented on my work. She pointed to my garment and told my professor that if I was graduating, they were interviewing for a design assistant. It sounded like a fairy tale or a great piece of fiction—but it was real. I could barely comprehend what was happening. The next day I was headed up 7th Avenue from the FIT campus, portfolio in hand, with my feet barely hitting the pavement. I was overwhelmed thinking this kid from Louisiana, who sewed for 4-H, had an interview scheduled with Carolina Herrera! My student career could not have ended on a better note. I received the Bill Blass Award recognizing the one-year program's outstanding graduate during commencement exercises at Radio City Music Hall.

MY 7TH AVENUE INDUSTRY CAREER

An industry career spanning thirteen years far exceeded my expectations. Each designer I worked with provided a unique experience. I was exposed to a range of design processes with each designer possessing different strengths and different methods of collection development. With each position I further expanded my craft and built on my existing skill set. I was exposed to various style sensibilities, price points, and target customer bases. Career opportunities with Carolina Herrera, Anna Sui, Chado Ralph Rucci, Christina Perrin, and Vera Wang combined for a fairytale-like industry career. I was exposed to a legacy of talent and am committed to continuing in the tradition that preceded me.

My career with Carolina Herrera began with an interview, portfolio review, and a hands-on tryout. I draped a gown from a sketch and made a paper pattern.

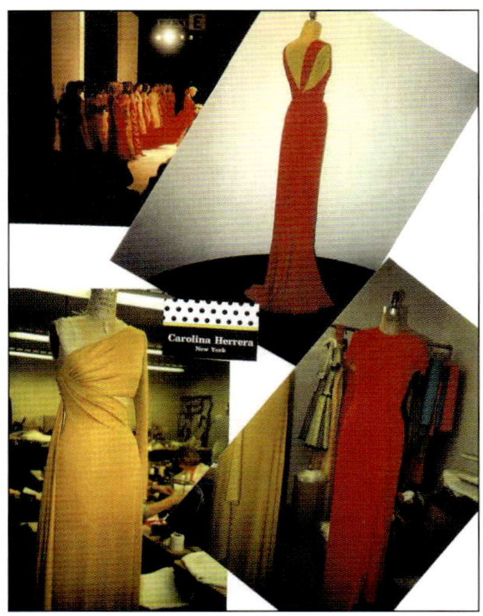

Scrapbook collage of some of my work for Carolina Herrera (SP)

A sample gown was cut and sewn from my pattern. With my work being up to standard, I was offered a position as a design assistant. The red layered chiffon and 4-ply silk crepe gown that was my tryout project became part of the Resort collection. It is not unusual for design companies to have prospective employees work under a trial period. This process gives the employer personal knowledge of a candidate's skill level while giving the candidate the opportunity to see how he or she works within the organization.

Although my job title was design assistant, my responsibilities were draping, patternmaking, and sample room supervision for the couture collections. My role was to interpret a sketch in three-dimensional form by draping fabric on a mannequin. I would follow through by transferring my draping to a paper pattern and directing the cutting and sewing of the garment.

There was much to learn from my immediate boss, who had interned under Pauline Trigère. Not only was he a talented illustrator, but he was a wealth of knowledge with a critical eye for garment construction and shape. He was gifted in shaping garments, particularly suits, with steam. I learned many steaming and shaping techniques from him. I also learned many tailoring and sculpting techniques from one of the sewers who had worked with legendary American designer Norman Norell. When someone asked her a question, she would hold a lesson and teach us all by sharing her treasure of information. I was able to witness the utmost of couture techniques put into practice. Raw edges of seams were bound. Linings were set in by hand. Hems were invisibly secured by hand. Labor-intensive French seams were the norm. The most delicate of hand-rolled baby hems would finish chiffon edges.

Mrs. Herrera is a designer with impeccable style and taste. She was very involved with collection development in the initial stages and again with garment fittings. We would do the majority of the garment development in the workroom and then show her our progress in a model fitting. It was amazing to watch Mrs. Herrera make the slightest adjustments to length, pocket placement, and detail shape. Her attention to detail, style, and proportion would bring the garment to a different level. When I was with Carolina Herrera, she was mostly known for impeccably made suits, dresses, and gowns for elegant and fashionable clients. Today she creates collections with more of a youthful fashion edge.

Assisting Mrs. Herrera gave me the first opportunity to work with celebrity and notable clients. I fit garments on the Duchess of York, Princess Margaret, and numerous socialites. Here were also some of my early brushes with fashion royalty. John Galliano visited the design room one evening. On another evening Polly Mellen, then the creative director at *Elle*, passed through the design room. Mrs. Herrera told Mellen that I had "good hands," the greatest compliment a designer skilled in draping could receive.

Preparing for the Carolina Herrera traditional Monday-morning time slot in fashion week was always exhilarating. I helped with many of the model fittings. Mrs. Herrera booked the most beautiful models. Her choice of model embodied old-style glamour. Mrs. Herrera's gowns were stunning on the models' statuesque womanly curves that are almost absent from today's runway. In preparation for one fashion show, I draped a gown on a mannequin for display in the hallway of the showroom. Mrs. Herrera saw my draped gown and liked it so much that she wanted it in the show. By the next morning, a wearable version was ready for the runway. The "green machine" also made its runway debut with Carolina Herrera. The machine had traveled with me all the way to New York. We were in need of buttonholes in garments for the Monday morning show. Using our traditional out-of-house resources was not an option over a weekend, so the company gave me cab fare to bring my machine to the office. My grandmother's attachment on the green machine made professional-quality keyhole buttonholes with beautifully rounded edges The Carolina Herrera shows were the first of countless Bryant Park Fashion Week experiences for me.

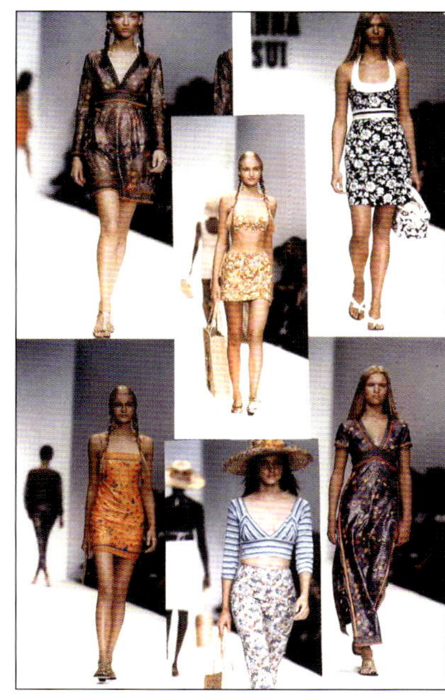

Scrapbook collage of photos from the Anna Sui runway (SP)

With three years of Carolina Herrera experience behind me, I was ready for a pay increase. I was hired at Herrera as an entry-level design assistant but found my responsibilities to be almost exclusively draping and patternmaking. Entry-level design assistants are paid far less than drapers and first patternmakers. When inquiries of a pay increase with Herrera went unanswered, I sent out a few résumés. I almost immediately found opportunities for substantial pay increases with reputable and desirable fashion houses. I interviewed with Anna Sui and was offered a temporary position four days a week. I took the risk and accepted. Within a short period of time, my status changed to full-time draper and patternmaker. Although the word *designer* was not in my title, I had a tremendous impact on the design of the garments for the collection. I was responsible for all of the design between sketch and finished garment. I was an integral part of the design team and played an active roll in developing runway collections and conducting model fittings. I would remain in the position of draper/first patternmaker throughout my New York career.

The vintage-inspired atmosphere of Anna Sui was quite a departure from the conservative couture atelier of Carolina Herrera. The whimsical prints of Anna Sui in vibrant colors and patterns sharply contrasted with the sophisticated textiles of Carolina Herrera. As a twenty-something, I welcomed the change. Construction techniques were completely different too. Instead of expensive, labor-intensive hand techniques, garments were finished with more affordable machine-enhanced production techniques better suited to her clients. I was a typical young professional Anna Sui client, making the experience that much more enjoyable. I especially appreciated the perk of a clothing allowance in stock merchandise.

One of the most valuable experiences at Anna Sui was working with seasoned patternmaker and Parsons instructor Anna Lou Plott. She was so generous with her wealth of knowledge, and was an experienced sounding board for problem solving. I once told her I wanted to enroll in her pants class at Parsons. She told me not to bother with the class; she would bring me her notes. Not only did she bring the notes for the pants class, but she shared a career's worth of notes. The information ranged from flat patterning a bodysuit to drafting an entire suit jacket based on a bust measurement. I am so grateful for her generosity. I cherish the opportunity to continue passing on and sharing such valuable knowledge.

What I found most unique about Anna Sui was her process for collection development. In her office she had erected a bulletin board that covered an entire wall. The board was divided into four sections, one for each of the four groupings of the show. In design school and in the industry, you may see a story board for a collection. Anna had an entire wall. Early on in the development process, a few fabric swatches would be placed on the wall. Then inspiration photos would be added. Maybe a vintage garment or two, followed by embroidery swatches, then a few pieces of trim. As the wall filled up and garment sketches appeared, a dynamic yet cohesive story would evolve. Anna's inspiration walls were works of art in themselves. There was such beauty in her story development that seamlessly translated onto the runway.

The challenge of coming out with a new and fresh product from the vintage-garment inspiration was one at which Anna routinely excelled. With barely a thread of the vintage inspiration remaining, the new incarnation would be uniquely Anna and perfectly current. Her historic inspirations mixed with eclectic styling merged in a way that set trends and inspired other designers. The sample room would cut hundreds of samples for Anna to style with for the show. Mixing and layering furthered her artistic vision.

Although Anna Sui's runway shows were celebrity-studded events, the focal point was the beautifully designed garments presented in an entertaining, theatric setting. The fashion shows had the vibe of a rock concert. James Iha of the Smashing Pumpkins even graced the catwalk. With Anna's good friend and renowned fashion photographer Steven Meisel often in attendance, Anna would attract the top models of the day to her runway. During my tenure in the mid-1990s, models included Amber Valletta, Shalom Harlow, Naomi Campbell, and Gisele Bundchen. Preparing for the shows involved working long hours at a frenzied pace. I would participate in the model fittings and follow up with all necessary corrections. With fittings occurring only a few days in advance of the show, there was a lot to accomplish before the fixed deadline of the show. The only option was to get everything done, and done well. Once, when Naomi Campbell missed her fitting, Anna suggested I go with her in a cab to Naomi's apartment. The quick road trip was averted when Naomi rescheduled for the next morning.

While I loved the trend-setting, energy-infused dynamic with Anna Sui, I missed being immersed in the impeccable couture techniques and fabrics that I was introduced to at Carolina Herrera. Through a chance crossing of paths on 7th Avenue with a former co-worker, I was referred to Ralph Rucci. Ralph Rucci is an American couture designer who also studied fashion design at the Fashion Institute of Technology. He was heavily inspired by Balenciaga and worked with Halston and a Balenciaga-trained patternmaker before launching his own collection. Ralph's collection, Chado, is almost as meticulous as the 33-step Japanese tea ceremony it is named after. Ralph's work embodies the same attention to detail, precision, and integrity as the ancient tea ceremony.

I met Ralph early on in his development of Chado. He pulled together a talented group of industry professionals not only passionate about his vision of exceptional craftsmanship but also gifted with the unique skills necessary to advance that vision. We worked freelance on evenings and weekends. I was part of his committed team of freelancers for six years. We developed silhouettes in which seams combine function and artistry. Nontraditional armholes were often unique blends of raglan, dolman, kimono, and gussets. His signature articulations in seaming required absolute perfection in patternmaking. Nothing short of the perfect fit was acceptable.

Ralph wisely focused his valuable creative talent and energy on the made-to-measure couture tradition rather than the exhausting, never-ending treadmill of setting the next trend. His work is reminiscent of the great masters of art, architecture, and fashion he emulated. Sculptural silhouettes, impeccable craftsmanship, and to-die-for fabrics set Chado apart as a true couturier. Being exposed to his mastery shaped my approach to form and structure.

Wanting to get back to couture full time, I began seeking new design opportunities. In an ever-changing industry, it is not unusual to regularly peruse the job listings. I was drawn to a job posting by an up-and-coming designer named Christina Perrin. The classified ad in *Women's Wear Daily*, our industry's trade publication, listed a job for a draper/first patternmaker with leather experience. In college I had participated in a student-exchange program that allowed me to study the leather and suede industry in Argentina. I had learned construction and patternmaking techniques specific to leather, suede, and fur. I occasionally applied my leather knowledge with Anna Sui and was excited by the possibility of enhancing my expertise. The new employment opportunity came to fruition. I was working not only with leather and suede, but also with python, alligator, and ostrich.

My responsibilities quickly grew beyond leather and suede. I was developing garments from daywear to swimwear to gowns. I was soon the lone draper/patternmaker working with an assistant. For the first time, I was on my own. There was no one with more experience to ask questions or bounce ideas off. I had to figure it out all on my own and rely on my own years of experience. I flourished in this position, as it really pushed me to perform. It was almost overwhelming at times to know that every garment going down the runway was my responsibility.

Christina Perrin became a regular during New York Fashion Week and was known for celebrity dressing during the late 1990s. She would design elaborate gowns with fabrics from some of the most prestigious fabric houses in the world. We would work with beading and embroidery from Lesage, France's oldest embroiderer. Beading for one gown alone could be in the six figures. Patterns that I developed for gowns and beading layouts were sent to the Lesage workrooms in Paris. We would create with Jakob Schlaepfer's innovative textiles and laser-cut fabrics. Schlaepfer's fabrics can cost hundreds of dollars per yard and are known for layers and dimension. We even created garments with Whiting & Davis metal mesh, more commonly used for accessories.

When the tragic event of 9/11 unfolded, I was at the office of Christina Perrin. We had a fashion show scheduled for five p.m. that day. We had worked through the previous night finishing model alterations. The entire staff was bleary eyed that morning and preparing to go home when we heard news of a plane hitting the World Trade Center. New York City changed before our eyes, and from that we will never be the same.

Prior to that fateful September I had been looking for new opportunities. I had been with Christina Perrin for three years and was ready for a change. Her focus was increasingly on the celebrity and social aspect of fashion design. Building an image had greater import than building great garments. I wanted to utilize my skills to their fullest in an environment in which the garments are the focal point. Not long after 9/11, an ad in *Women's Wear Daily* caught my eye. There was an opening for a draper/first patternmaker with designer experience. The position was with Vera Wang! So few people had been hiring during the post-9/11 environment, and I was thrilled to see such a fantastic opportunity. Further piquing my interest, I knew that Vera was coming into prominence far beyond the realm of bridal. I was excited by the idea of designing bridal while keeping my hands in the more fashion-forward ready-to-wear and runway industry.

I faxed my résumé to Vera Wang during my lunch break. By the time I got home from work that day, I had a message from Vera Wang's human resources director. I followed up first thing in the morning to schedule an interview. I interviewed with a portfolio of magazine tear sheets of my work with other designers and samples of all the couture seam finishes I had mastered during the course of my career. Although sewing would not be part of the job, the evidence of my sewing skills particularly impressed the creative director. As supervising sewers and cutters is an integral part of the design process, my sewing skills have continually contributed to my success as a draper and patternmaker in the industry. My interview led immediately to a three-day tryout period, after which I was offered a position. Less than a week had passed between seeing the ad and securing a job with Vera Wang.

Of all the amazing career opportunities in New York, working with Vera Wang was unparalleled. I was able to unequivocally advance my draping expertise and truly contribute creatively to the collections of one of the most highly regarded designers in the industry. I worked well with Vera. She respected my talent along with the aesthetic and skill set I brought to the table. My ability to interpret what she wanted allowed for a seamless relationship to develop whereby we pushed each other creatively.

Vera's design process was unique to her and shaped by her years of experience in fashion editorial. Vera was not one to sew or illustrate, yet she had a clear, defined vision for her collections. Her ideas and very stylized flat sketches would come to life through the design director's illustrations. We would further interpret her vision through draping and patternmaking. Vera worked with us much like an editor or stylist. She would see our draping on the model and further style and develop the silhouette. She realized her designs through working directly with our muslins and first sew-ups on the model. Vera's discerning eye for proportion, fit, and fabrication yielded esoteric modernity. We would work together in preparation for fashion shows with model fittings and styling.

Even though more of my time was dedicated to ready-to-wear fashion shows, bridal is where my skills advanced the most. I had no intention of pursuing bridal but quickly fell in love with the challenge of applying structural and engineering principles while achieving a soft, ethereal finished product. My skirt shapes evolved as I perfected crinoline shapes to support them. I applied geometry to calculate lengths of subsequent crinoline ruffles as the cone shape expanded. Continually improving construction techniques for bodice foundations was satisfying. Developing techniques to minimize bulk while maintaining structure required a combination of my sewing and construction expertise. I gained experience with framing layers of fabric to reduce seam puckering, camouflage seam allowances, and shade translucent bridal goods. Attention to flattering seam placement, sculpted supportive inner structures, and meticulous hem finishings were carried through many Vera Wang bridal collections. Experience I gained in working with delicate tulle, organza, and lace translates to the confidence I have in gown making today.

My work with Vera received much public exposure. Our runway shows garnered a lot of press. Our work from runway collections would grace the pages of numerous publications, including *Vogue, Women's Wear Daily,* and *Harper's Bazaar.* The gowns were popular choices with celebrities. More particularly, our bridal gowns were constantly featured in a range of bridal magazines. Garments that I draped have been on the covers of many magazines, including *Vogue, Martha Stewart Weddings,* and *Brides.*

Our work was most in the public eye when worn by celebrities. One of the most notable was Jennifer Lopez. For her private wedding to Marc Anthony, she wore a bridal gown sample I had developed for a runway show. On a Thursday afternoon, I came in from lunch to find the tiered-lace bridal sample hanging next to my worktable. The note attached said to alter the gown according to the pins by four o'clock as requested by celebrity stylist Andrea Lieberman. Although we were not told whom the gown was for, I knew immediately it was for Jennifer Lopez. I knew Lieberman was her stylist, and I could also tell by the needed alterations. We did a quick alterations job and had the gown out of the door in two hours. I assumed Jennifer Lopez would be wearing it as a presenter for the Tony Awards that weekend. The gown had an array of ivories and festive ruffling. It would have been as appropriate as an awards dress as a bridal gown. On Sunday morning, I awoke to hear on the news that Jennifer Lopez had married Marc Anthony. It was one of our working Sundays. About three hours into the workday, it all clicked. Jennifer Lopez got married in our gown! Although no official photos were released, we were able to confirm with Lieberman that she was indeed married in the gown we altered.

When Holly Hunter was nominated for numerous awards for her performance in *Thirteen,* I worked with Vera on three of her awards dresses. For the Golden Globe ceremony, she wore a gold lamé bias gown that I had draped. She wore another project of mine for the Screen Actors Guild presentation. For the Academy Awards, she wore a lavender tulle ethereal gown with an open back and sweeping train. I traveled to Los Angeles with Vera and our design director, Robert Barnowski, for the final fittings. It was one of many experiences with Vera Wang that seemed unreal for a former Louisiana 4-H sewing champ. We stayed at the Regent Beverly Wilshire, dined in the piano bar, and used my hotel suite as the site of our fittings. We fit Holly in the marble bathroom because of the lighting and the almost completely mirrored walls. Holly even stood on the ledge of the tub to get the best full-length back view of her gown. On the day of the awards, I went to Holly's hotel room, helped dress her, and walked her to her limo. Later in the evening, I rode in the limo with Vera to the InStyle after party and walked through the paparazzi line with her. I was not on the guest list but Vera wanted me there, so she grabbed my arm and walked me through check-in as if we were in deep conversation.

The first notable bride I dressed with Vera Wang was Nadja Swarovski of the Austrian crystal family. Nadja is responsible for bringing Swarovski to the forefront of fashion and design by forging relationships with some of the most talented artists in the industry. Just weeks before her May 2002 Innsbruck wedding, she was not happy with her European-designer couture wedding gown. She went to the Vera Wang flagship store and selected a pleated, satin-faced organza gown. To best fit her and to make the necessary adjustments to accommodate the 15,000 crystals that would bubble from underneath the train and peek beyond the bustier, I was asked to make a custom gown for her. When we had the first muslin fitting on Nadja at our design office, there was too much length in the torso. I was working from the measurements from the bridal salon. Although they were accurate, they did not include a measurement for torso length. Chett, the president of Vera Wang, mentioned that I could travel with the dress to Austria for additional fittings if necessary. A week later we all met again. The gown fit to perfection. Chett commented, "I guess Suzanne does not need to go to Austria." So much for the rewards of a job well done! The impeccable finished product was featured in a multipage spread in *Town & Country Weddings*.

Several celebrity fittings brought me to unique venues. When dressing Mariska Hargitay for her victorious appearance at the 2005 Golden Globes we went to the New Jersey soundstage of *Law and Order: Special Victims Unit*. I fit the gown of pink crepe back satin between takes. Mariska captured the essence of old Hollywood glamour with her sinuous shape and striking appearance. When fitting Katie Couric for the Kennedy Center Honors in 2004, I made two trips to her Uptown apartment. Her home was welcoming and warm with a daughter practicing piano and book bags stacked at the door. We fit the taupe sequin-trimmed cotton taffeta ball gown with all the accessories. She even opened her closet and asked my advice as to what purse to carry.

Fitting Anna Wintour in the Vogue fashion closet was the epitome of a fashion moment. I fit her in Vera Wang for numerous occasions, ranging from fashion week to a British royal wedding. She would come in with the signature dark sunglasses, occasionally lifting them to get a better view. There was often a frenzy of activity before her arrival, particularly if the room was not immaculate. The frenzy would change to utter calm with her entrance—as if everything had always been perfect. During one fitting, André Leon Talley's booming voice could be heard in the hall. He soon joined us in the fitting for an even more unreal experience. All I kept thinking was "How did I get here? . . . With Anna Wintour and André Leon Talley . . . in the Vogue closet!" Although Anna Wintour was quick with comments and sharp in opinion, working with her was always pleasant.

THE ROAD HOME

With a dream job at Vera Wang and an amazing experience in general in New York, I found the initial homeward tug surprising. I could not imagine a better professional career or a more encouraging circle of friends. This circle of accomplished friends had, like me, followed a passion through to a career—not just in fashion, but also in piano, classical ballet, opera, theater, and more.

The pull to move home only intensified. I wanted to be near family. I wanted to be back in Louisiana. Over the years, I had grown weary of missing family events big and small: weddings, anniversaries, family dinners at the yacht club. I missed weekends in Pass Christian, Mississippi, with extended family. New York's lifestyle, though exhilarating, had grown exhausting over the course of thirteen years. My personal life was dictated by my professional life. Late nights and six- or seven-day work weeks left me extremely satisfied creatively but often unintentionally neglectful of my personal and social needs.

I loved working in the fashion industry and creating exquisite gowns. I did not want to give that up, but I still wanted to move home. Knowing there would be no opportunity to walk into a position comparable to mine in New York, I began to formulate the idea of starting my own business. I did not move home to start a business; I started a business so that I could move home and permanently plant my roots in Louisiana.

After several years of building my savings, and a year and a half of planning, I put the plan in motion. I gave notice to Vera Wang and scheduled my moving date for August 31, 2005, the day my apartment lease expired. Spring 2006 fashion week was the week following my scheduled move, and a replacement for my position had yet to be found even though I had given notice back in April. There was no one to supervise my staff or to pick up my workload. Some of these talented sewers had worked with me in previous companies and had been with me for over seven years. I did not want to leave them without a supervisor or add work to the remaining staff. Vera agreed to put me in a hotel for the ten days between the expiration of my lease and fashion week so that I could continue to work with her on the upcoming show.

Little did we know what was about to transpire. Hurricane Katrina made landfall on August 29, 2005. My idea of home—New Orleans, Louisiana, and Pass Christian, Mississippi—appeared to be decimated. My mom and grandmother were both raised in New Orleans and grew up spending summers in the Gulf Coast community of Pass Christian. My parents and grandmother had both taken up permanent residence in The Pass years prior. The Pass and New Orleans: There was no other place I wanted to plant my roots. When the storm hit, my mom was with me in New York helping prepare for the move. My sister had picked up my grandmother and evacuated to Shreveport, Louisiana. My dad stayed close to the coast and ended up missing for four days. My furniture went into storage and my ten-day hotel stay became two months as Vera kept me on to work on the next bridal show.

It turned out that Hurricane Katrina delayed but did not derail my plans. My desire to be in Louisiana intensified. That fall, I flew home before dawn on the morning of the LSU-Auburn game in Tiger Stadium. I started a new chapter in my life with college friends and the exhilaration of game day.

The first several months home I spent living among the ruins in Pass Christian. I did what I could to help my family begin the long journey to recovery. When helping my mom sort through what could be salvaged, I came across my childhood art and sewing projects. I was heartbroken to see my entire body of childhood work ravaged by water, mold, rust, and mud. I became increasingly disheartened by the devastation and struggled to stave off the urge to give up. I began to question my plan to start a new small business. It all changed with a phone call. I was walking along the desolate path between my parents' house and my grandmother's house when my cell phone rang. My friend Naleah was on the phone. She emphatically stated, "I am getting engaged, and you ARE making my wedding dress!" There could have been no clearer message that I was supposed to start my business. I had met Naleah, a gifted dancer and Broadway performer, at a Bible study specifically for people in creative industries. There could have been no better friend to give me the encouragement—if not the flat-out push—that I needed.

Several months later, in the spring of 2006, I had office space, clients, and all of my belongings home from New York City. My vision of creating once-in-a-lifetime gowns in New Orleans was taking shape. The reason for my decision to focus on white and ivory was twofold. First, working in white and ivory allowed me to deal more efficiently with high-end wholesalers, stocking the same quality goods I worked with at Vera Wang. Second, a city of elaborate weddings, debutante balls, and Mardi Gras tableaus offers a great opportunity for making elegant, one-of-a-kind gowns in white or ivory. I was prepared to create a desirable product in a city with an appreciation for artistry and craftsmanship. With more manageable overhead, I could offer couture gowns at the price of an off-the-rack designer gown; the same gown could cost four times more if custom-made in a New York designer's workroom. I wanted to give potential clients the option of buying unique, custom gowns while keeping sales revenue in my home of New Orleans.

I had become aware of brides and debutantes flying to New York or other major cities to purchase expensive designer gowns. These factory-made gowns ultimately cost thousands more once the costs of travel and accommodations for several fittings are factored in. With these gowns being mass-produced, there is no guarantee no one else will have your gown. I wanted to offer the opportunity to invest in the garment, not travel expenses, and have a gown truly unique to the client. I have brought clients from across the country to New Orleans. I have worked with clients from Los Angeles, New York, Atlanta, Dallas, and Houston. Louisiana clients have come from all corners of the state. One client with local ties traveled from London for her gown. With other major fashion centers so far away, creating a quality fashion house in New Orleans is worth the effort. I can offer quality couture garments while sharing my industry knowledge and gown expertise with clients, student interns, and talented design employees. New Orleans's dynamic artistic and entrepreneurial community provides additional motivation for perseverance and success.

I dressed my first client nine months after Katrina. I was a well of emotions as I reflected on the event: a culmination of successes, trials, and dreams fulfilled. My friend Naleah radiated as she walked down the isle in my very first Suzanne Perron couture gown. She introduced me at the reception as "someone doing something beautiful in a city in need of healing."

The Couture Process

WHAT IS COUTURE?

Couture is the art of custom designing and making garments for a particular client. The design is unique, and the one-of-a-kind garment is hand crafted precisely to the client's measurements with labor-intensive techniques. A more exclusive term, *haute couture,* literally translates into "high dressmaking." The Englishman Charles Frederick Worth initiated the tradition of haute couture in Paris in the mid-nineteenth century. Worth gave his clients luxurious materials and meticulous fit. A couturier elevates dressmaking to an art form. A couture gown is made of the highest-quality fabrics and is sewn with great attention to detail.

The term *haute couture* is legally protected in France. Only members of the Chambre Syndical de la Haute Couture satisfying very specific criteria may use the term in any way. Criteria include designing made-to-measure garments for private clients, maintaining a Paris workshop of minimum size, and presenting a collection to the Paris press twice a year. Membership in the Chambre Syndical is highly selective, and participating design houses must demonstrate the utmost in design and quality. These well-defined standards have governed haute couture only since 1945.

In the United States, the word *couture* is used loosely. Companies manufacturing a range of goods—some not even related to garments—label their products as "couture." Many designers designate their high-end collections as couture even though they are produced in quantity, in standard sizes, and in factories. Thus the term *couture* does not always refer to hand-made, one-of-a-kind garments in the United States.

There are few true couturiers in the United States. *Prêt-à-porter,* or ready-to-wear, prevails. In ready-to-wear, garments are mass-produced in a range of standardized sizes. Ralph Rucci's couture house, Chado, is an example of true haute couture in this country. Rucci views garments as potential works of art and dedicates a large amount of his business to creating intricately detailed, made-to-measure clothing. He has succeeded to such a level of excellence in both design and construction that he has been invited by the Chambre Syndical de la Haute Couture to participate in the Paris couture shows.

My custom gowns are made in the couture tradition. Each gown is a unique design. Each is made to measure and sculpted to the individual client. We use high-quality fabrics and time-intensive hand-sewing techniques. We work with

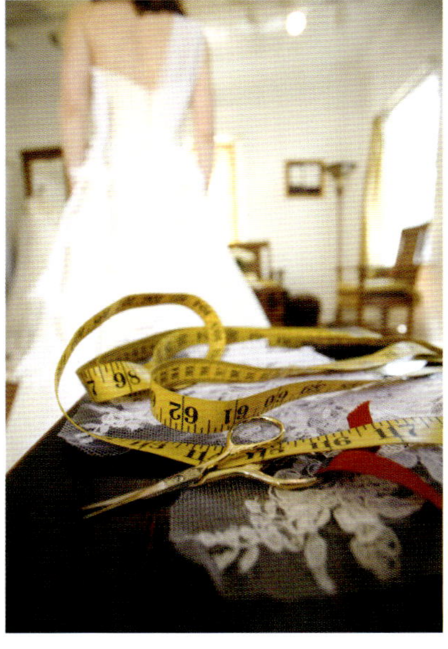

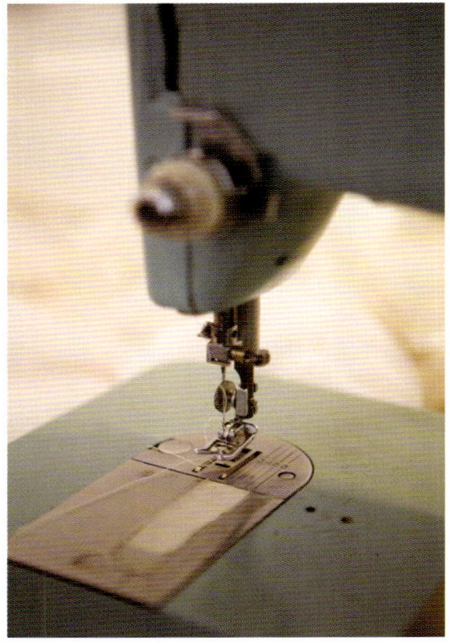

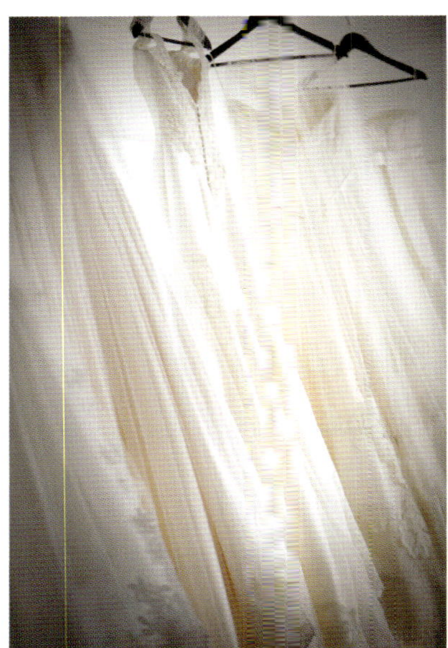

Workroom supplies at hand for fitting (BB)

Home sewing machine with precise controls (BB)

Gowns hanging from ceiling-height garment hooks (JC)

many of the same luxury fabrics as Vera Wang, Carolina Herrera, and other New York design houses. We are committed to the same perfection in construction and handwork seen in Paris couture while avoiding the exorbitant—often five- to six-figure—price tags of haute couture.

Technology, mass production, and a decreased appreciation for skilled craft have made the practice of couture sewing and gown making a dying art. There is less motivation to design, sew, and produce original garments when overseas mass manufacturing provides quality garments at reasonable prices. The work of skilled artisans is becoming rarer. Like the great plasterers and woodworkers from generations ago, fewer people are learning the craft of couture gown making.

THE DESIGN STUDIO

The design studio, or atelier, is a workroom for an artist or craftsman. Our workroom is stocked with more threads, needles, scissors, tape measures, and other supplies than can be listed. Pin cushions carry pins of various sizes for every need. Rulers and curves of many widths and shapes abound. The three most important pieces of equipment are the cutting table, the sewing machine, and the iron. Large cutting tables must be wide enough to accommodate bridal fabrics, which are usually 60 inches in width. For proper and accurate cutting, the fabric must be laid flat on the table. The table must also be quite long, as a back panel of a gown with a train can be more than ten feet in length.

We work with both industrial and home sewing machines. An industrial machine can be more difficult to control but is excellent for the straight, fast stitches of crinoline assembly. Home sewing machines give more speed and stitch control for fine sewing and often come with a greater variety of stitches. Professional steam irons are necessary to provide a consistent and continuous steam.

To keep the workspace clear, gowns are suspended from ceiling hooks. The high storage accommodates the length of the dramatic trains and the circumfer-

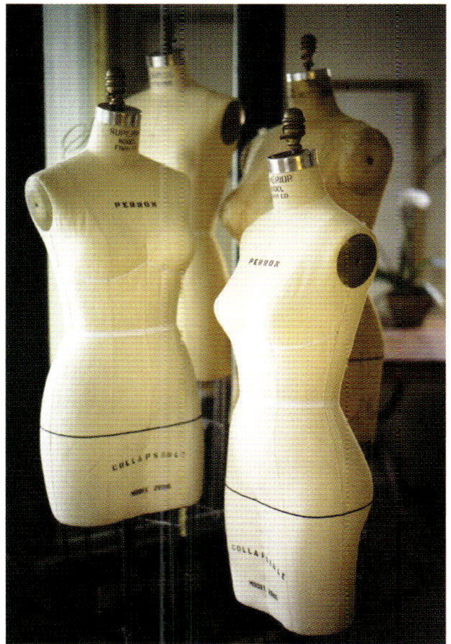

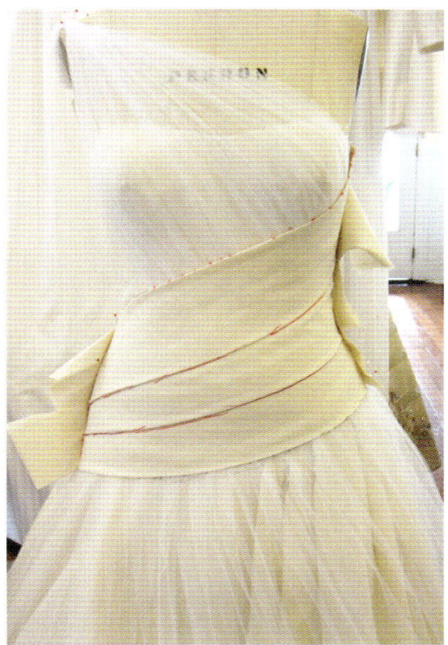

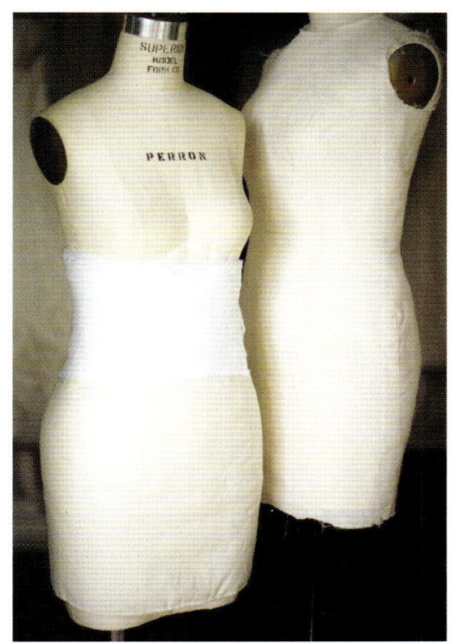

Various-size mannequins (JC)

Gown muslin draped over a mannequin, perfectly shaped to the client's measurements (SP)

Mannequins with padding and muslin covers to correspond to client size (JC)

ence of grand ball skirts. Keeping the dresses away from the floor also helps them stay clean and wrinkle free. We make sure the workroom is clean at all times, as the slightest bit of dust or dirt can leave a mark on pristine white fabric. Lipstick, other makeup, and colored nail polish can scar and permanently damage the luxurious material. We even take care not to wear dark-colored garments that could fuzz or pill onto white fabric. Constant hand washing is also crucial in keeping the white and ivory fabrics pristine.

MANNEQUINS

A mannequin used in the design studio is called a dress form. An atelier will have a number of dress forms in a range of shapes and sizes. Standard dress forms are shaped to specific industry niches including eveningwear, sportswear, and athletic wear. Eveningwear dress forms are sculpted to better correspond to the desired close fit and defined shape of evening and bridal gowns. Dress forms used in the design process are different from display mannequins. Our dress forms are very utilitarian. The canvas-covered, hand-sculpted paper mâché form sits on a metal stand adjustable in height. It is fashioned so that the shoulders can be collapsed and released to move garments on and off with ease. The outer finish of the dress form allows for pinning into it. Centers, natural waist and neckline, side seams, and armholes are marked with seams or tape.

The first step in the construction phase of a gown is to create a mannequin to the client's measurements. Having a dress form matching the client's measurements is essential for achieving ideal proportion and fit. The properly shaped dress form allows for multiple fit checks without the client present. The customized dress form also allows for safe steaming, pinning, and sculpting of the garment bodice to the perfected shape. If the client's measurements do not correspond precisely to one of the stock dress forms, a new dress form covering is made. We begin with the dress form closest to the final desired body shape. We create a muslin base to fit the dress form closely. Quilt batting and felt is layered over the muslin base. The batting is layered in varying thicknesses until the desired body circumference is achieved at each measurement point. An outer muslin covering encases the batting and yields a clean, durable, consistent base on which to work. Another advantage to working with the muslin covering is that it can be adjusted during the process if the client's weight changes.

THE FOUNDATION AND SKIRT CRINOLINE

The bodice foundation and the skirt crinoline provide the inner support structure for a couture gown. The finished product looks only as good as the base that supports it. The shape transfers from the inside out.

A bodice foundation resembling a corset is constructed of lining, canvas, organza, and boning. The foundation is molded to the body and shapes the torso. The previously mentioned mannequin is key to creating a successful foundation. The structure of the foundation can help sculpt and define a client's waist and bustline. This inner structure also provides support and encourages good posture. The canvas used is thin yet sturdy and stiff. The thinness prevents bulk. The sturdiness supports the boning and gives control. Cotton plain-weave canvas is responsive to steam and is therefore preferable to canvases of manmade fibers. Paper patterns developed for the cutting and sewing of foundations are well marked and must be very accurate. When creating such a precise fit, we have a slim margin of error. Support layers are precisely cut, marked, framed, and stitched.

Several types of boning can be used in the foundation. Flat metal stays, spiral boning, and Rigilene have replaced the bone, wood, and baleen stays of days gone by. Flat metal stays provide the most strength. These rigid steel strips are used with full-figured clients and where support is of maximum importance. The metal stays are used only in the foundation where the body does not have to bend. Spiral boning has strength coupled with flexibility and is used in places where both support and movement are needed. Rigilene is a sew-thru boning made of nylon. It has the most flexibility and the slimmest profile, as well as the least strength. These characteristics make Rigilene the ideal choice when smoothness of the figure is the goal, not support. With comfort being of utmost importance, all boning and foundation work is separated from the body with lining and interfacing.

A-line crinoline suspended from basic canvas gown foundation (JC)

Carefully drafted patterns used to cut and mark foundation pieces (JC)

Roles of Rigilene nylon boning (JC)

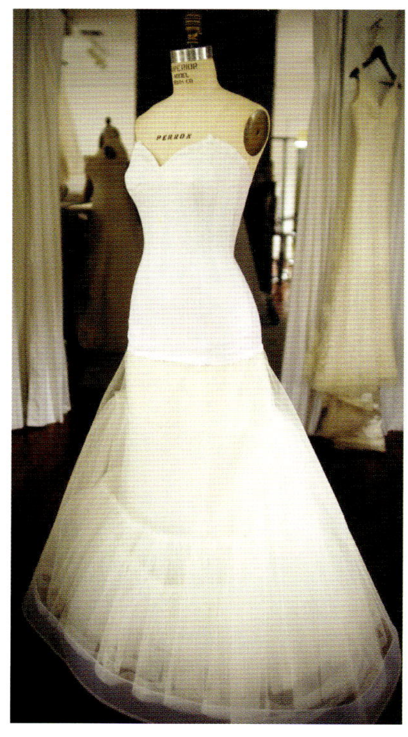

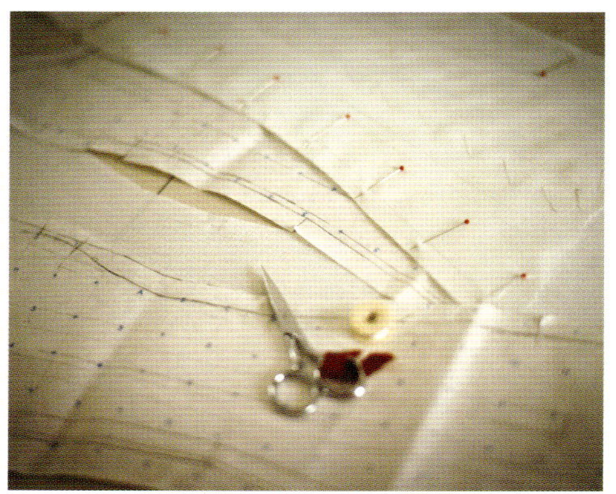

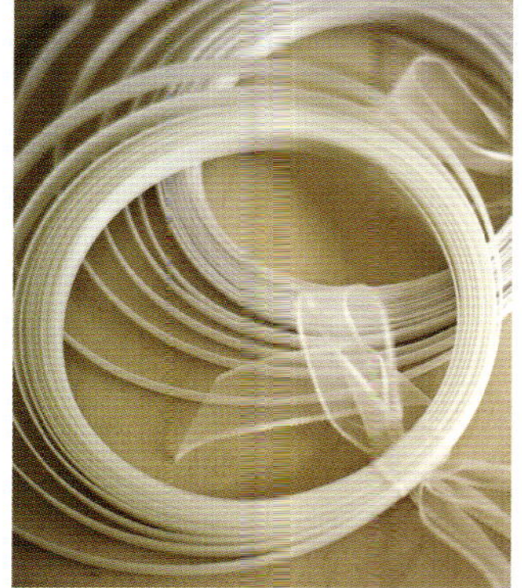

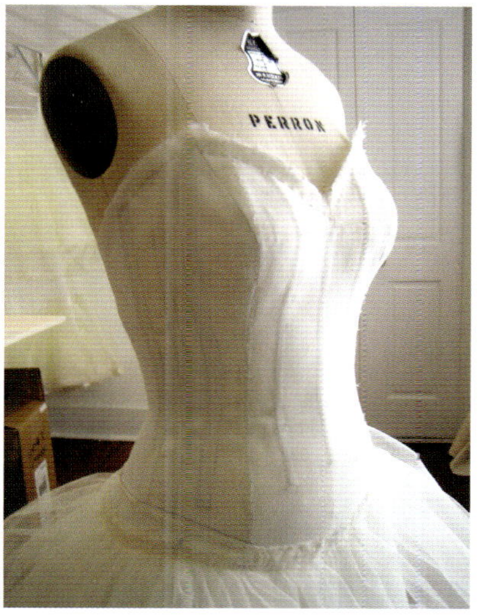

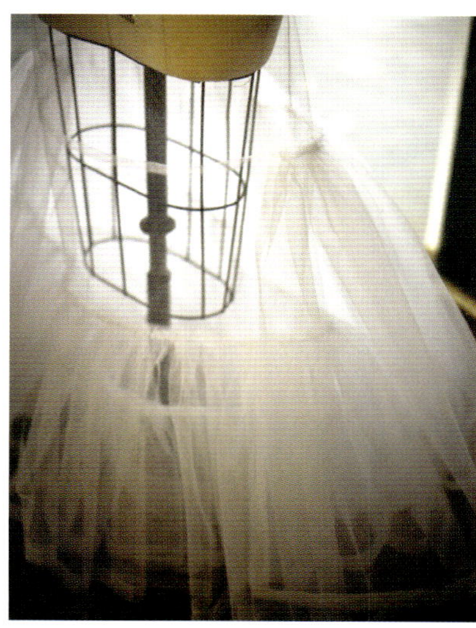

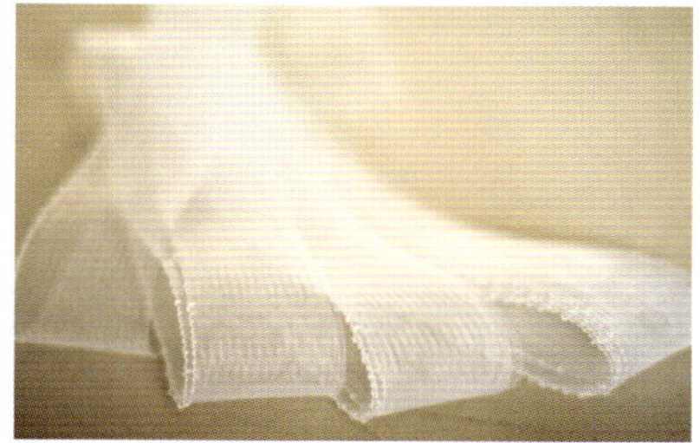

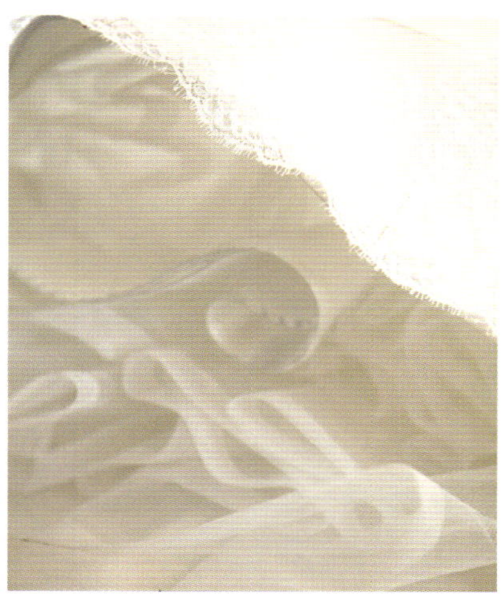

Ball gown crinoline with high hip fullness, attached to foundation (JC)

Gathered crinoline tiers to support skirt shape (JC)

Nylon horsehair braid (JC)

Layers of hemmed crinoline visible under lace gown skirt (BB)

The crinoline that supports the skirt shape will generally fall into one of three categories: A-line, trumpet, or ball gown. The crinoline is suspended from the bottom of the canvas foundation. Basing off of the stock patterns of these three shapes, we adjust and tweak each crinoline to correspond precisely to the gown design and the proportions of the client. Tiers and rectangular ruffles of crinoline are cut using the pattern pieces as guides. Each tier of the crinoline is prepared separately, with some tiers up to 15 yards long. One skirt crinoline can take as many as 45 yards of tulle and crinoline. Vertical seams are stitched and pressed open. The heavy crinoline is stiff and scratchy, so steps are taken to ensure the wearer's comfort. The hem edge of the crinoline is turned twice to conceal any rough and scratchy edges. The hem edge of any soft tulle layer is simply a cut edge; soft tulle does not scratch. The upper edge of each ruffle is gathered and attached to the tiers that make up the base. The hem of the lowest tier is finished with horsehair braid, a nylon banding that gives body and volume. Crisp satins and stiff fabrics easily float over the hard crinoline gathers. Lighter fabrics calling for a softer silhouette have layers of soft tulle covering the heavy crinoline layer. Attention to the subtle effects of this layering impacts the aesthetic of the final garment. An inside slip lining separates the crinoline from the body. Horsehair braid in the lining hem gives the inner slip shape and keeps the lining and crinoline away from the body. It is imperative to reduce the chances of lining and crinoline falling between the legs.

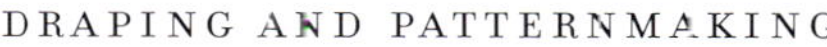

DRAPING AND PATTERNMAKING

Draping and patternmaking are two integral parts of the design process. Draping is sculpting on the mannequin with fabric. Draping can be esoteric, fluid, and tactile when an aesthetic effect is the goal. Draping can be less free-form when technically accurate fit is the goal. A gifted draper is an artist in her own right. Blocks of muslin are marked with grain lines and pinned to the mannequin. By manipulating the fabric on the mannequin, the draper creates the first three-dimensional interpretation of the sketch created for a client gown. The muslin

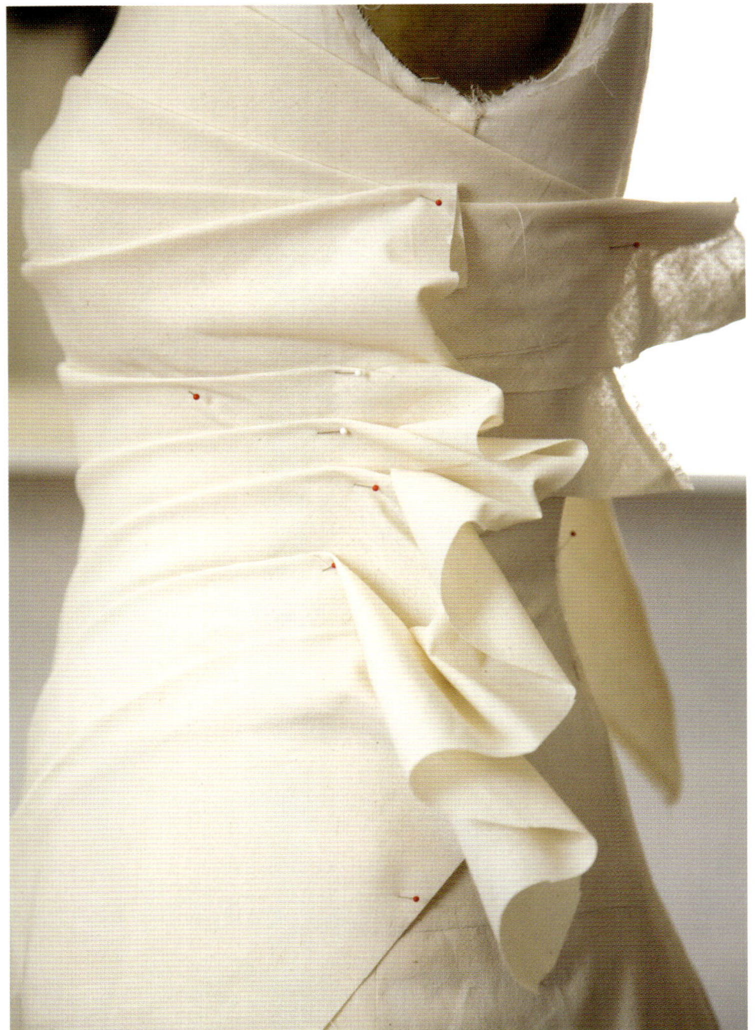

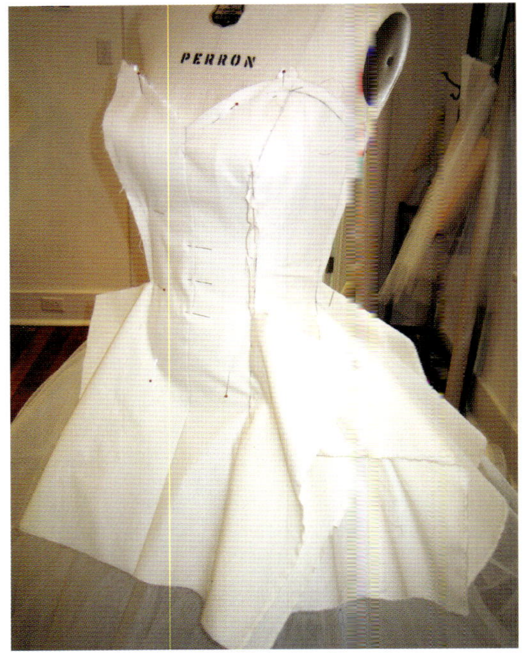

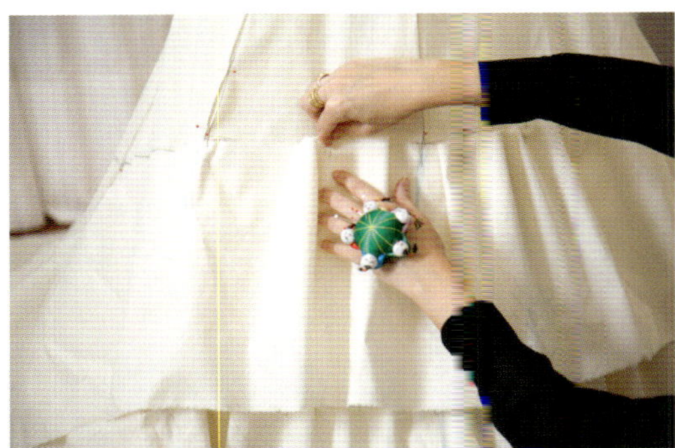

Draping for visual aesthetic (BB)

Draping to precisely and properly fit a bodice (SP)

Muslin pieces pinned to see ruffle proportion (BB)

is cut, folded, pinned, and marked until it captures as close a representation of the sketch as possible. Design details such as ruffles, pleats, and flounces can be pinned on the form while draping to achieve pleasing proportions. In fashion, there is always room to break the rules. An experienced draper knows the technical rules of draping and also how to break them effectively.

Pattern drafting and patternmaking more closely resemble architectural drawing. The use of various-shape rulers, curves, and fine-point pencils is necessary for precision and accuracy. With few exceptions, free hand lines are not appropriate. Pattern drafting is creating the shapes of garment pieces using mathematical and geometric applications. Ruffles, pleats, and other rectangular pieces are easily fashioned through drafting. Patternmaking is creating the shape of new garment pieces by manipulating an existing pattern block on paper. Additional fullness can be added by slashing and spreading the pieces. Darts can be moved by pivoting dart-equivalent fullness. Seams can be moved or eliminated through pattern manipulation.

Although a garment can be created through either draping or patternmaking, most use a combination of the two. Fabric draped and marked on the mannequin

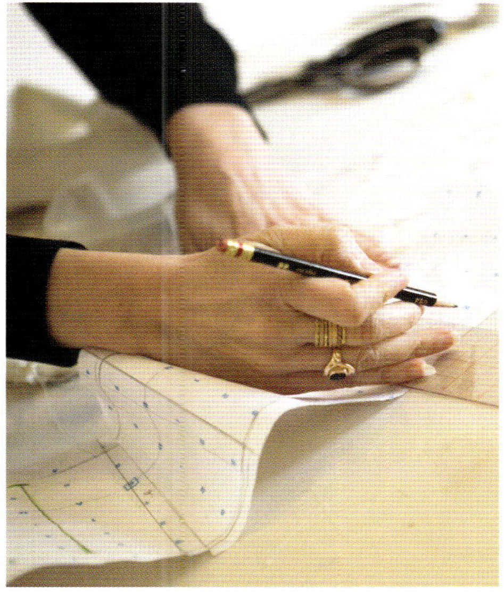

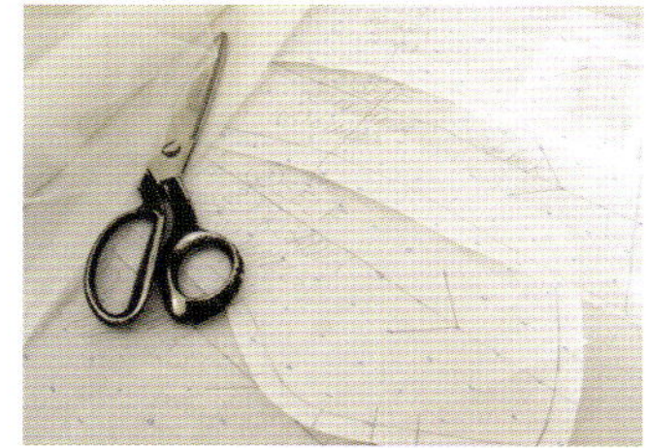

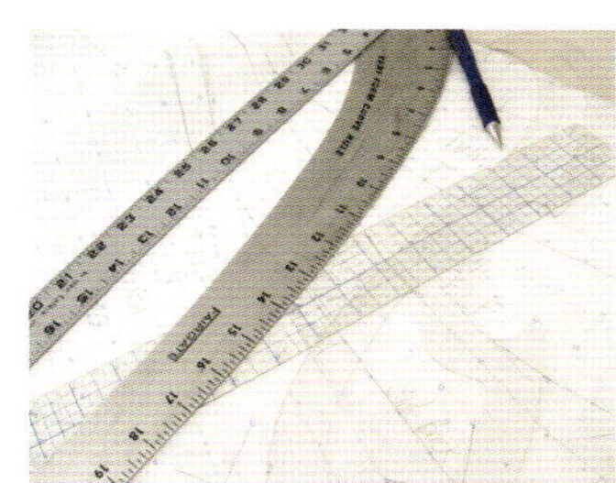

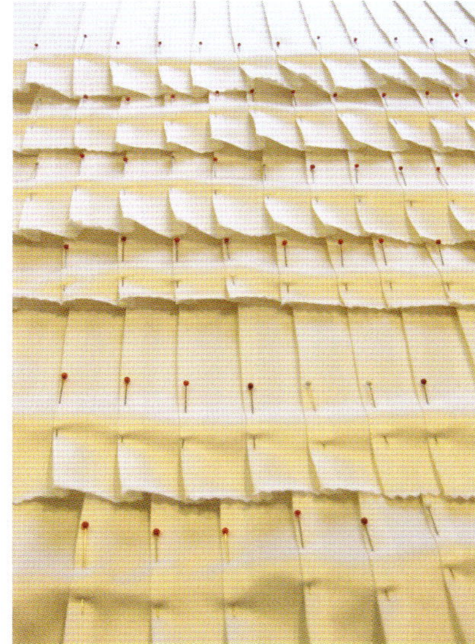

is unpinned, flattened out, and transferred to paper by flat pattern techniques. The end result is a pattern—a readable set of sewing and cutting lines on paper. The pattern pieces convey information such as the name of the piece, how many to cut, and what fabric to cut. Grain line, hem allowances, and other details are marked on the pattern. Decisions on interfacing and layering must be made in the patternmaking stage in order to properly label and cut a garment. Although the consumer only sees the outer layer, the under layers impact the finished look of the fabric. Many layers are often framed and worked as one to create a specific desired effect. Interfacings such as organza, tricot, lining, and other textiles are used on the unseen or "wrong" side of the fabric to create the desired weight, body, and opaqueness. The layering allows for the color adjustment of translucent fabrics and the camouflaging of seam allowances.

FABRIC MANIPULATION

Fabric can be manipulated, shaped, and steamed to create textural interest and design. Sculpting fabric provides three-dimensional elements in both the garment itself and in appliquéd design elements.

Pleating is a fabric manipulation process whereby two opposing creases in fabric cause the fabric to fold upon itself. Pleats are controlled by pressing, stitching, or steaming the fabric into place. There are several types of pleats used in garment design. Knife pleats can be used vertically to add the illusion of length. Ball gown skirt volume can be achieved or accentuated through inverted box pleating. Pleating can be very geometric and rhythmic with a clean, crisp look. Pleating can also be more fluid and less defined as in a technique known as mushroom pleating.

Pintucks and pleated bands are both controlled variations of pleating. In pintucking, very narrow pleats are stitched into the fabric and pressed one way, creating the illusion of fine lines drawn into a gown. Pintucking is one of the first techniques that became one of my signature design elements. Vertical pintucking is very elongating and adds visual and textural interest. In an attempt to create

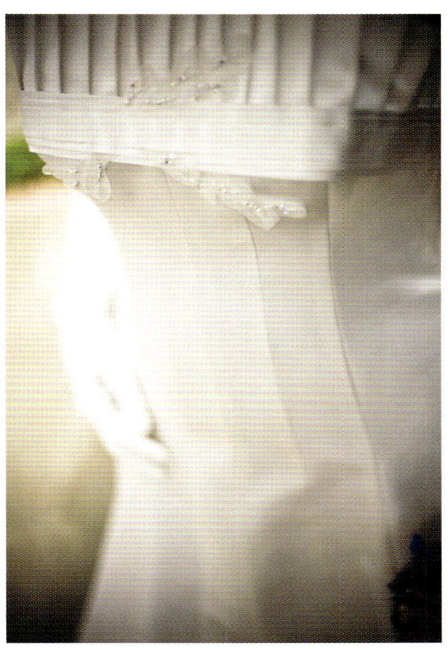

Drafting paper patterns for ruffles (JC)

Pattern pieces communicating grain, stitch lines, notches, and cutting information (SP)

Straight edges and curves, crucial to accurate patternmaking (SP)

Rows of sharply creased pleating (SP)

Vertical pleats, visually elongating (JC)

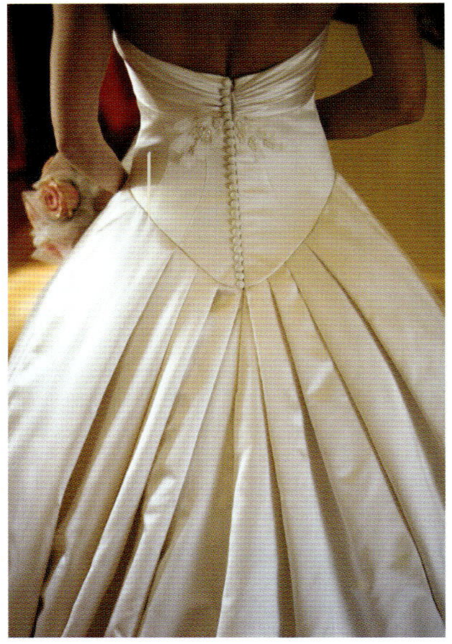

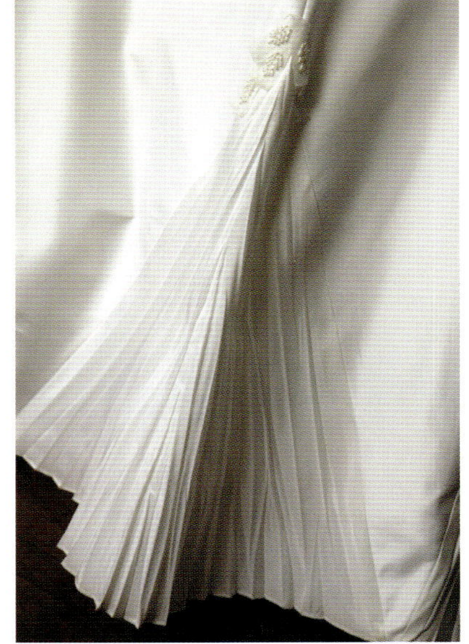

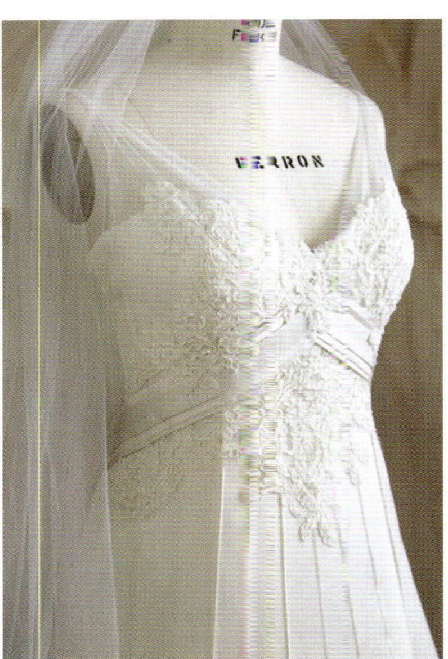

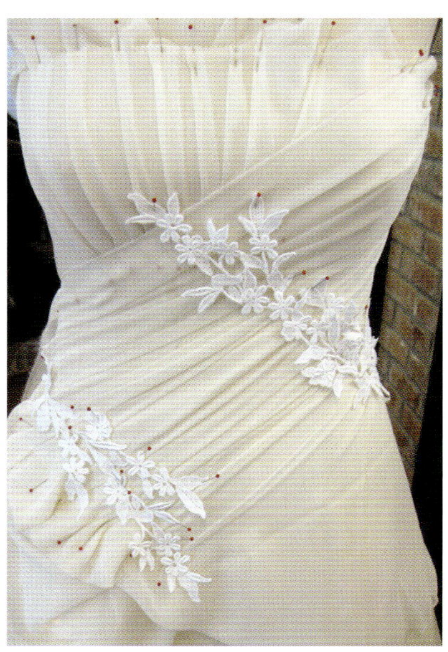

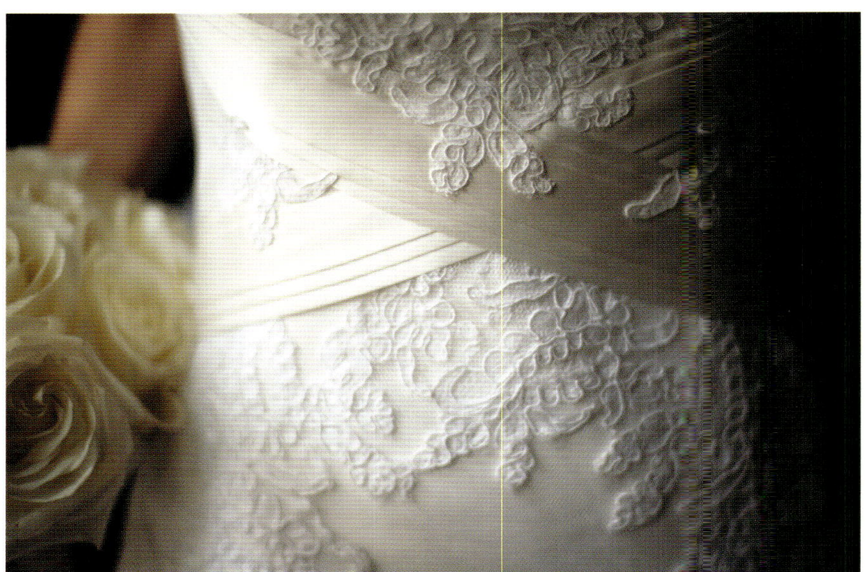

CLOCKWISE:
Pleats and inverted box pleats, adding volume to a ball skirt (JC)

Fluid mushroom pleating in a skirt godet (JC)

Vertical pintucking extending from empire line (BB)

Banded trim created by even folds (JC)

Soft, fluid draping of chiffon (SP)

unique banded trim on bodices and empire seams, I experimented with folding and pleating fabric to create textural interest. Rhythmic, even folds controlled by hidden stitches create beautiful banding that has become a recurring detail in my gowns. The parallel folds allow for additional visual interest when mitering.

Bodice draping with the gathering and folding of fabric creates directional interest and visual impact. Crepe weave fabrics such as chiffon, georgette, and charmeuse will create soft, fluid, romantic folds. Plain weaves with less give, such as satin or Mikado, produce a more architectural and controlled effect. Draping and gathering in taffeta creates a crushed effect. Draping over the bodice can camouflage traditional princess and side seams. Fabric draped on the bias grain will hug and mold well to the well-shaped bridal gown bodice. Draping can be incorporated into a design for the purpose of elongating the torso, defining the waist, or enhancing the bustline.

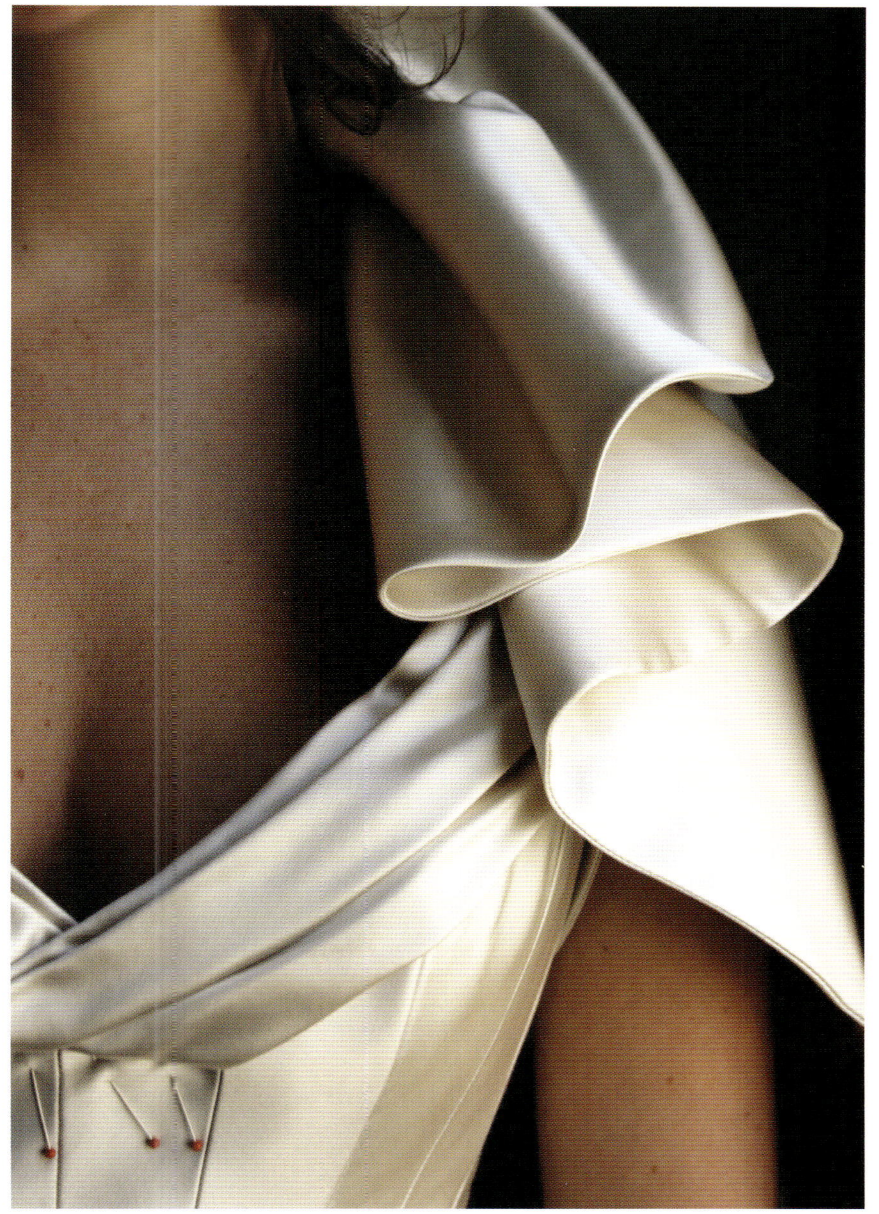

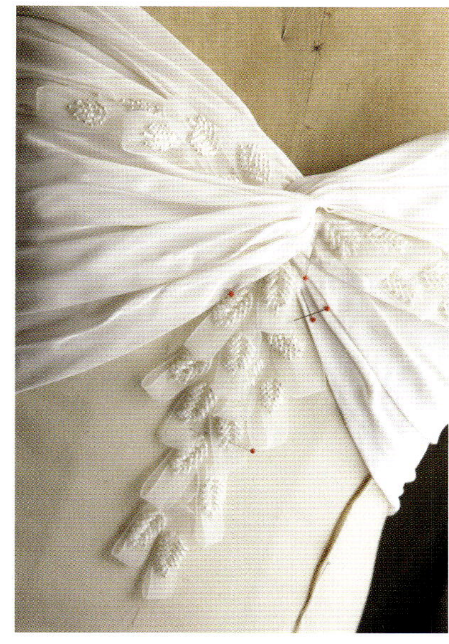

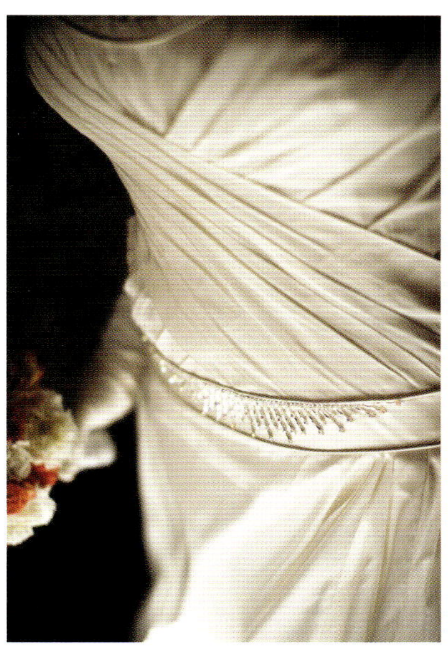

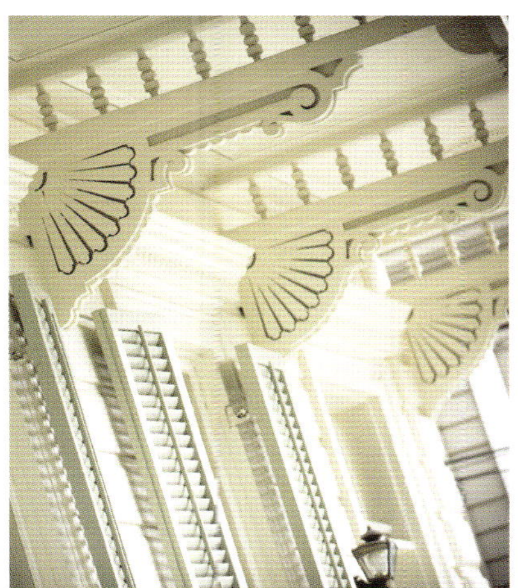

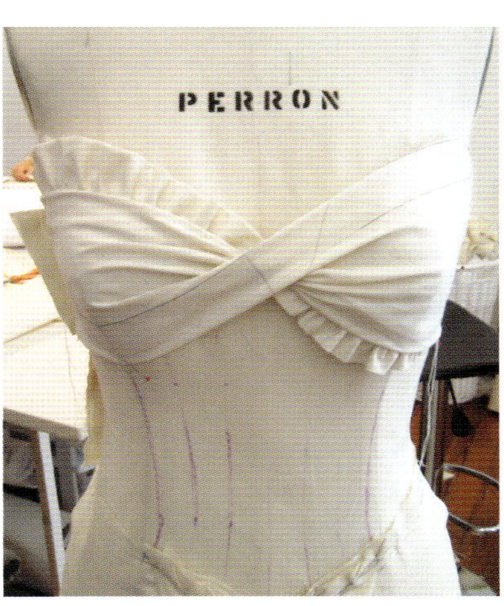

CLOCKWISE:

Controlled architectural folds created by satin (SW)

A more crushed effect with gathers created by taffeta (BB)

Folds molded to an hourglass shape (JC)

Bias draping molded to bodice curves, inspired by architectural detailing (SP)

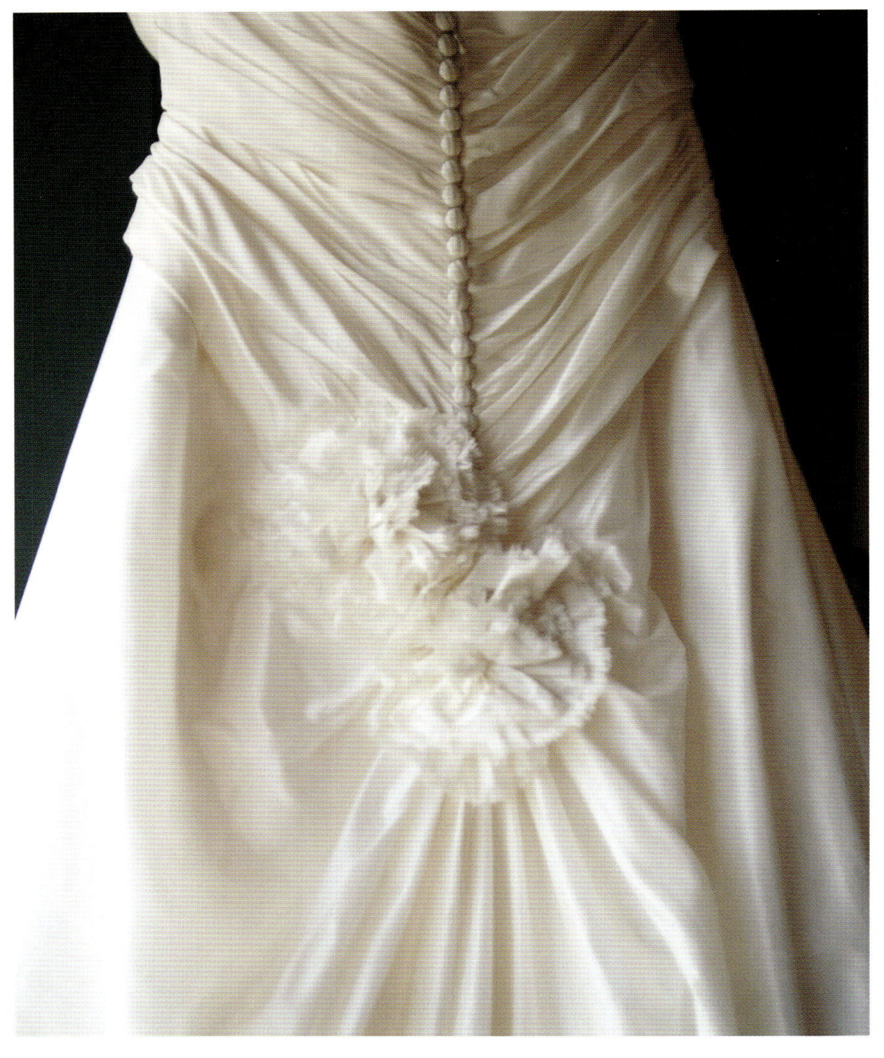
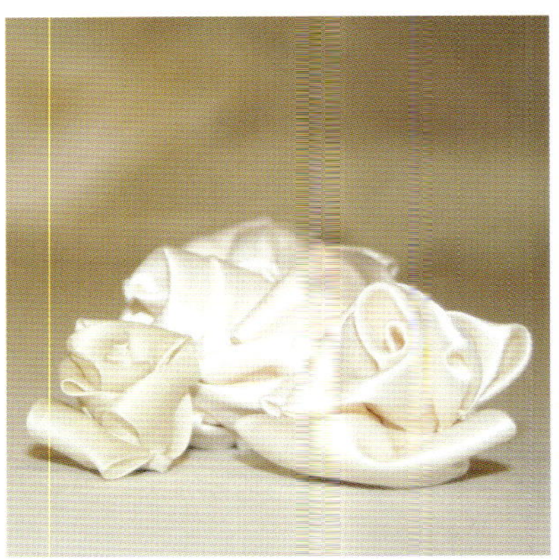
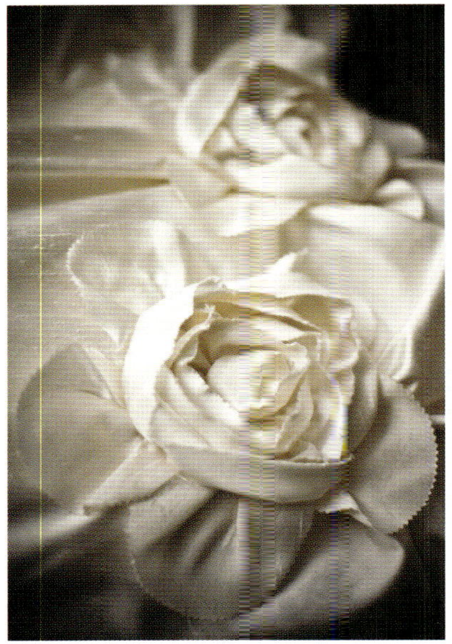
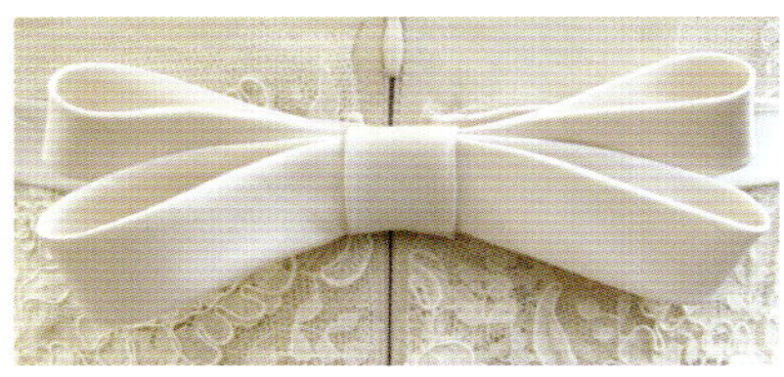
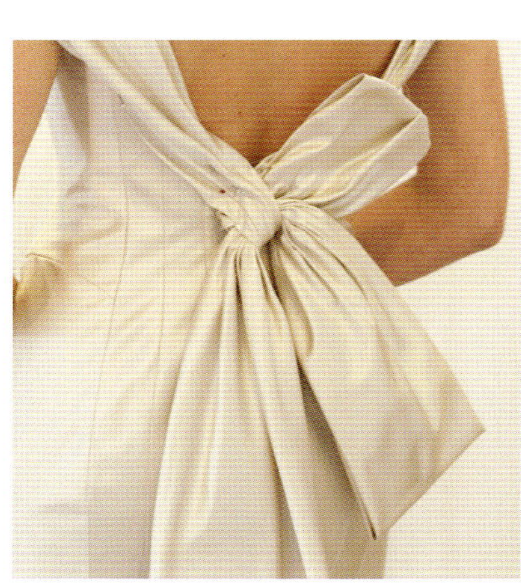
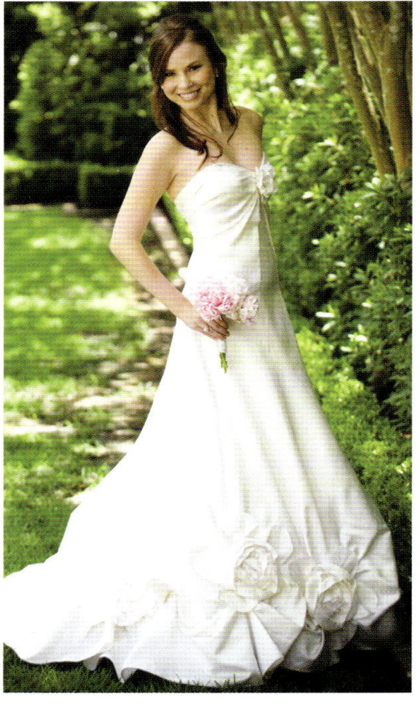
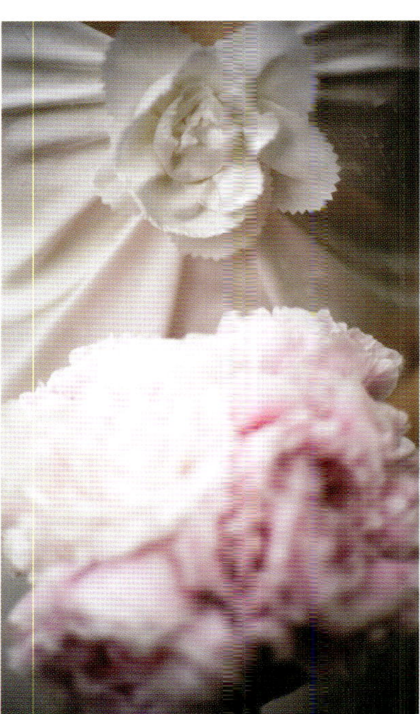

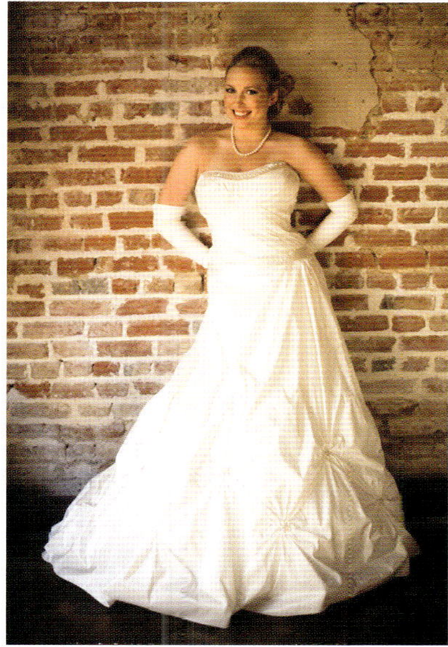

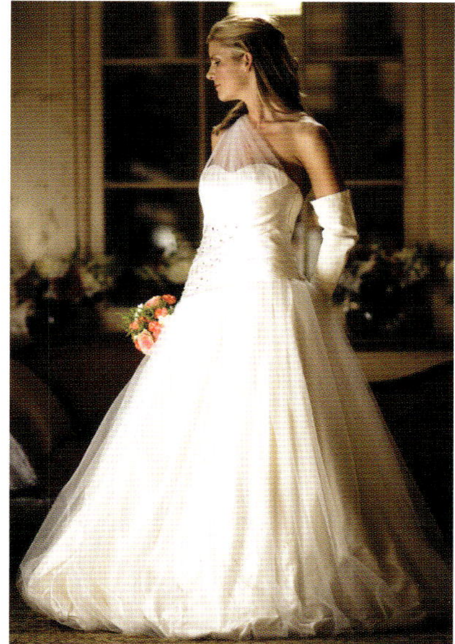

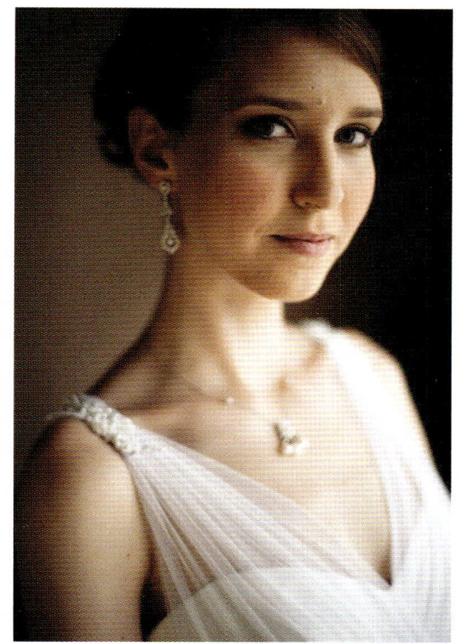

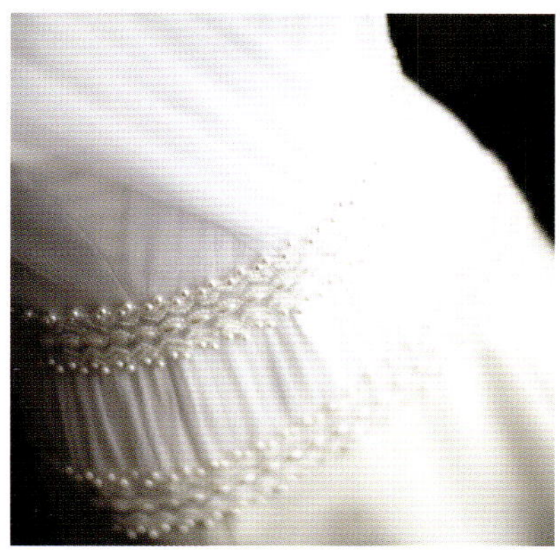

Pick-ups adding dimension to large skirt panels (JC)

Bubble-hemmed skirt with tulle adding another layer of volume (JC)

Strapless neckline softened with tulle draping (JC)

Sheer tulle allowing both over and under layers to be visible (JC)

OPPOSITE PAGE, CLOCKWISE:
Peonylike flower created by frayed edges (JC)

Folded bias edges sculpted into roses (JW)

Raw edges combined with pleats to create dramatic flowers (JC)

Flower motif on bodice (JC)

Draped hem echoing bodice flower (JC)

Free-form bow detailing (BB)

Structured bow (JC)

Adequate steam is a crucial element in creating beautifully draped bodices. The steam makes the fabric more malleable and is essential in helping to set the final draping in place. Great care must be taken when steaming draped bodices. As much as steam is an integral part of successful draping, improper steam and pressing can destroy draping.

Fabric can also be sculpted into three-dimensional design elements. Flowers, leaves, braids, and bows are a few examples of elements sculpted in fabric for gown design. Fabric can be twisted, folded, and gathered to form literal interpretations of flowers or artistic representations. Frayed raw edges may be incorporated to create flowers resembling peonies, carnations, chrysanthemums, or more ruffled flowers. Folded, clean edges create a look more like roses or camellias. Raw and folded finishes can be blended. Details adorning a gown's bodice can be repeated as hem or skirt detailing when properly proportioned. Multiple elements can be combined for visual interest. Braids of various widths, tension, and fabrics can be made to blend several elements of a gown together. Bows can range from traditionally structured bows to free-form asymmetric loops and tails. Fabric sculpting is an art of endless possibilities.

Fabric manipulation can go beyond intricate detailing. The skirt can be the focal design point of a gown when fabric is draped and manipulated for sculptural effect. Voluminous drapes, folds, and gathers can add dimension to large skirt panels. Fabrics such as tulle can add yet another layer for sculpting and volume. Tulle draped over the décolletage adds dimension and coverage while maintaining airiness. The translucency of tulle allows for under layers to be visible and create yet more depth and visual interest.

HAND BEADING

Hand beading is a labor-intensive, time-consuming process often reserved for use in couture garments. Beading can add light reflection, opulence, and depth. Threadwork layers detail to a fabric as brushstrokes of paint add design to a canvas. Bead-

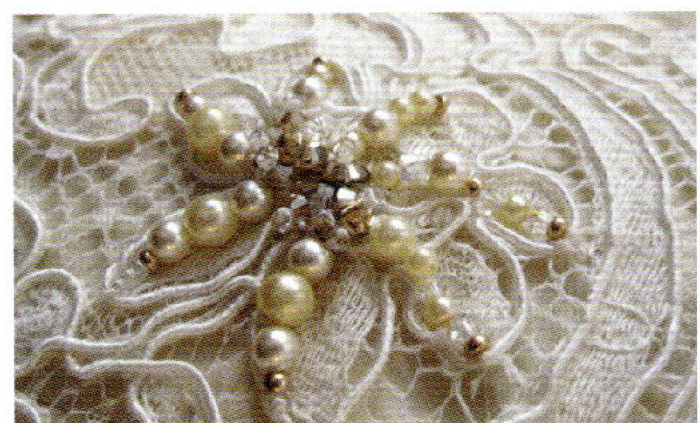

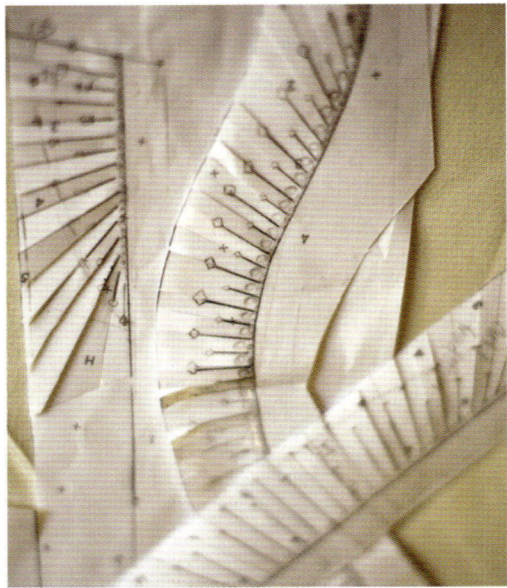

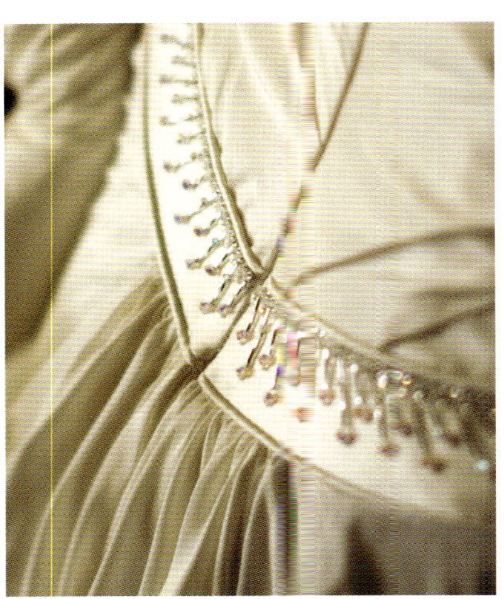

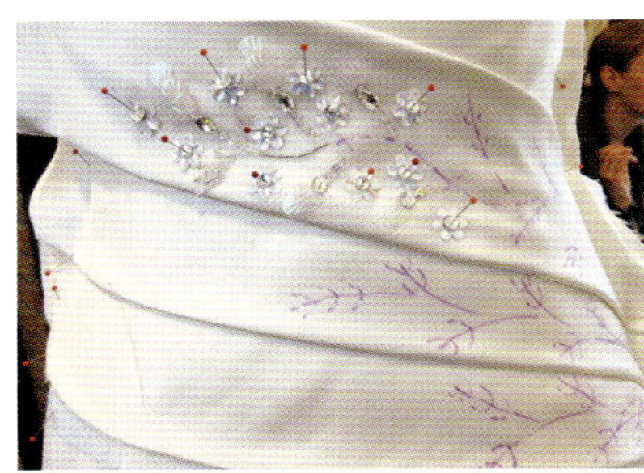

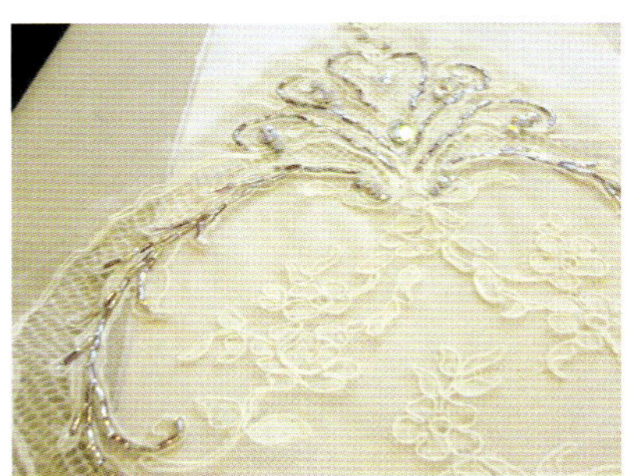

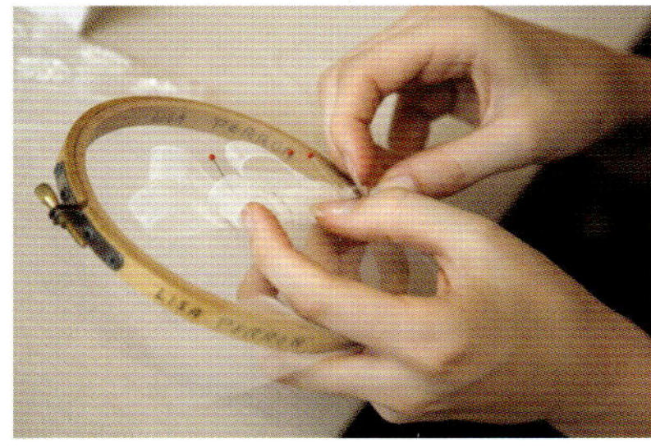

ABOVE:
Pearls, seed beads, and Swarovski crystals (SP)

Beading placement marked and pinned on actual garment pieces (SP)

Bugle beads and seed beads outlining the motif of hand-loomed French lace (SP)

Dimensional loop beading sewn on tulle (BB)

RIGHT:
Paper pattern developed for in-house beading (JC)

Hand beadwork on finished gown (JC)

ing can affect the mood and character of the garment. Pearls add dimension more than sparkle. They are appreciated up close and are ideal for the subtle detailing of bridal gowns and the romantic venue of a wedding. Swarovski Austrian crystal rhinestones add tremendous light reflection visible from a distance. The striking radiance of rhinestones has particular impact for a queen or maid under the stage lighting of a Mardi Gras tableau.

The cost of beading is determined by type of beads used, the density, and appliqué technique. The more fine the beads, the more dense the beadwork and thus the higher the cost. Beading with a single thread, stringing one bead at a time, and using limited beads per stitch is the most secure technique offering the most luxurious effect. Frequent knotting prevents excessive bead loss should a thread break. Chain stitches created on the reverse side with a tambour hook increases beading speed but presents the risk of losing multiple beads with one broken stitch.

Beading can be accomplished in the design room or by employing overseas beading resources. Beading can be sewn to the garment pieces before construction or directly on the fabric of the finished gown. Beadwork can also be completely executed on tulle and then hand stitched to the gown as an appliqué.

Overseas beading resources can vary in cost and quality. Beading houses in Paris such as Lesage are the ultimate in luxury beading; price tags can exceed six figures. India is an outstanding beading resource with an array of quality beads, sequins, and techniques for endless possibilities. The expertise and techniques developed in India over thousands of years are astounding.

When beading is done in house, we have complete design, time, and quality control. Specialty threads and needles are necessary for quality beadwork. Beading thread of strong, smooth, continuous filament is required to resist abrasion and tangling. Beading thread must pull through the fabric and beads effortlessly. Extremely fine beading needles are essential when using the highest-quality bugle beads, seed beads, and pearls. Beading needles are so thin that they bend easily and are not desirable for most other handwork. An embroidery hoop is useful to keep the fabric secure and smooth. It is best to bead with the fabric taut but not stretched in a hoop or frame. As with all handwork, stitches should be even and uniform with knots secure and well camouflaged.

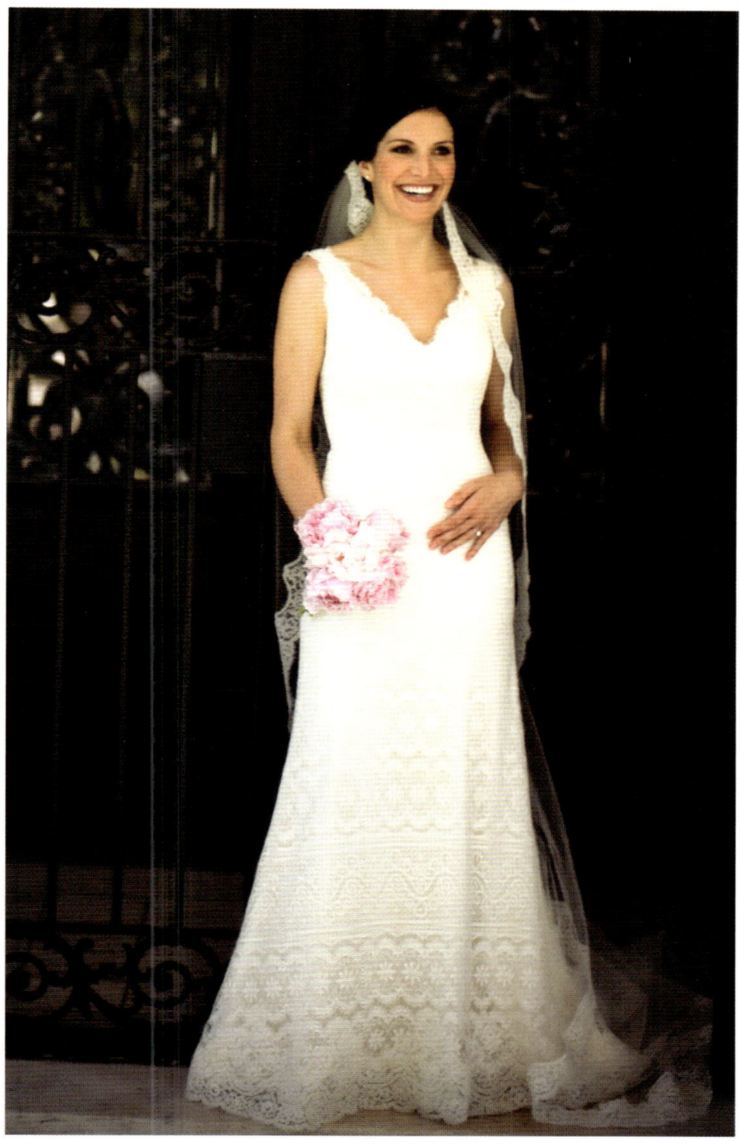

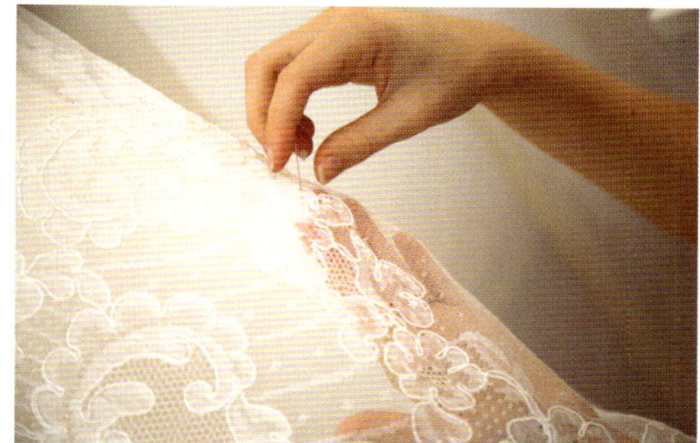

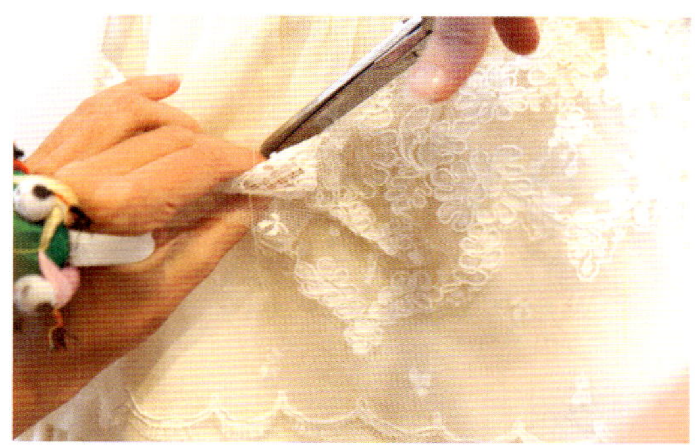

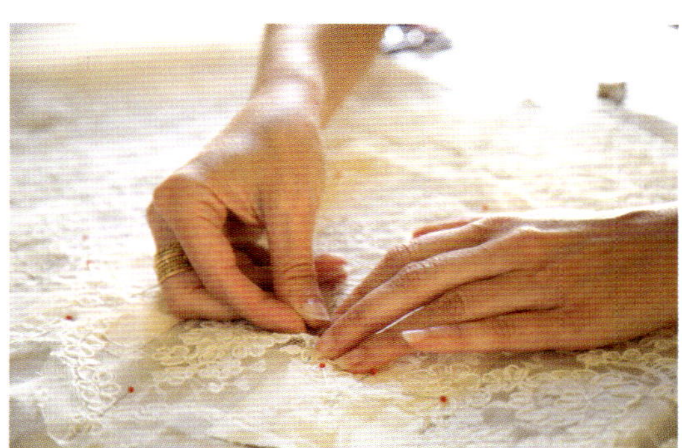

Romance and femininity, the essence of an all-over lace gown (JC)

Reembroidered lace appliquéd using cording as guide (BB)

Cutting lace through the netting base to reduce fraying of the cut edge (BB)

Hidden stitches following the motif of the lace in a lapped seam (BB)

LACE MANIPULATION

Lace is one of the most useful and malleable design elements when creating bridal gowns. Lace suggests romance, femininity, and luxury. The majority of re-embroidered Alençon and Chantilly laces we use are imported from specialty lace manufacturers in France. These manufacturers have been producing exceptional lace for centuries. Re-embroidered lace has a fine cord stitched in linear patterns to accentuate the motif or design elements of the lace. Re-embroidered lace has dimension and texture, and lends itself well to appliqué. Re-embroidered lace is easier to mend than Chantilly lace. The weight of the applied cording on re-embroidered lace creates a sturdy base for hand stitching where stitches are more easily hidden. Chantilly lace takes a finer hand and involves smaller, more intricate stitches.

Lace can be cut through the tulle base between motifs without fraying. Design elements such as flowers or leaves are best left intact to prevent fraying from a cut cord or within a motif. The tulle base allows lace to be stretched, eased, and

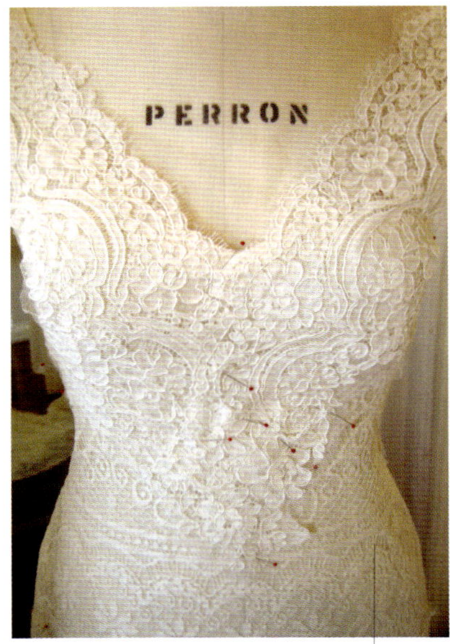

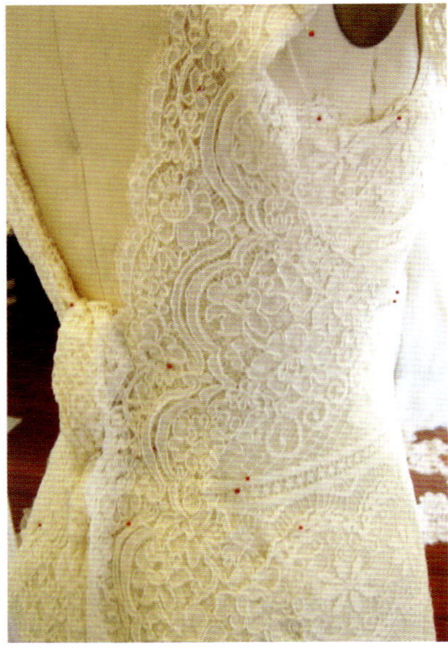

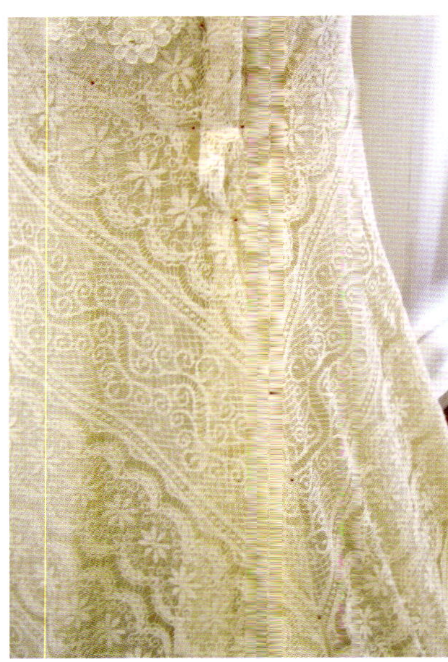

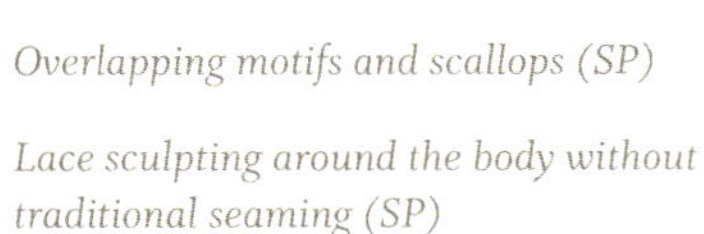

Overlapping motifs and scallops (SP)

Lace sculpting around the body without traditional seaming (SP)

Gown's skirt created from a single piece of lace and finished in a mitered seam (SP)

steamed into place to take the shape of the bodice or skirt with few seams. Hand mending is the technique used when seams or darting is necessary. Instead of mending in the straight line of a traditional seam, motifs are overlapped to follow the pattern of the lace. Many very small, hidden stitches along the lace's existing design motifs camouflage both the stitches and the seaming of the underlying structure. Lace is best used when sculpted in continuous pieces with as few seams as possible. The beauty of lace is diminished when interrupted with princess and side seams. The same properties that make lace malleable also make it delicate. Some sort of support or structure under lace is often helpful to protect the lace from stretching or fraying.

Galloon or scalloped laces make beautiful borders on gown necklines and hems. Galloon refers to lace with a scalloped border on both selvages. The imported scalloped lace is generally loomed in straight panels about five yards in length. Less expensive synthetic laces of man-made extruded fibers can be produced in much longer continuous lengths. There are also variations of lace that are circular. The circular patterned lace is quite a rare find and much more expensive. The straight borders must be manipulated to take the shape of the curved hem of a gown. Narrow laces can be shaped into a curve with the use of steam. Wider laces are curved to the hem shape by cutting, lapping, and mending out wedges of lace opposite to the scalloped edge.

The same principles of lace manipulation to create a curved gown hem apply when creating a lace finish on veils with rounded shapes. Lace can be beautifully manipulated into straps or sleeves where the openness of the lacework keeps the silhouette looking light while at the same time providing coverage.

VINTAGE GOWN DESIGNING

Some brides are eager to wear the gown of a mother, grandmother, or great-grandmother. Many of these vintage gowns are made of marvelous lace of exceptional

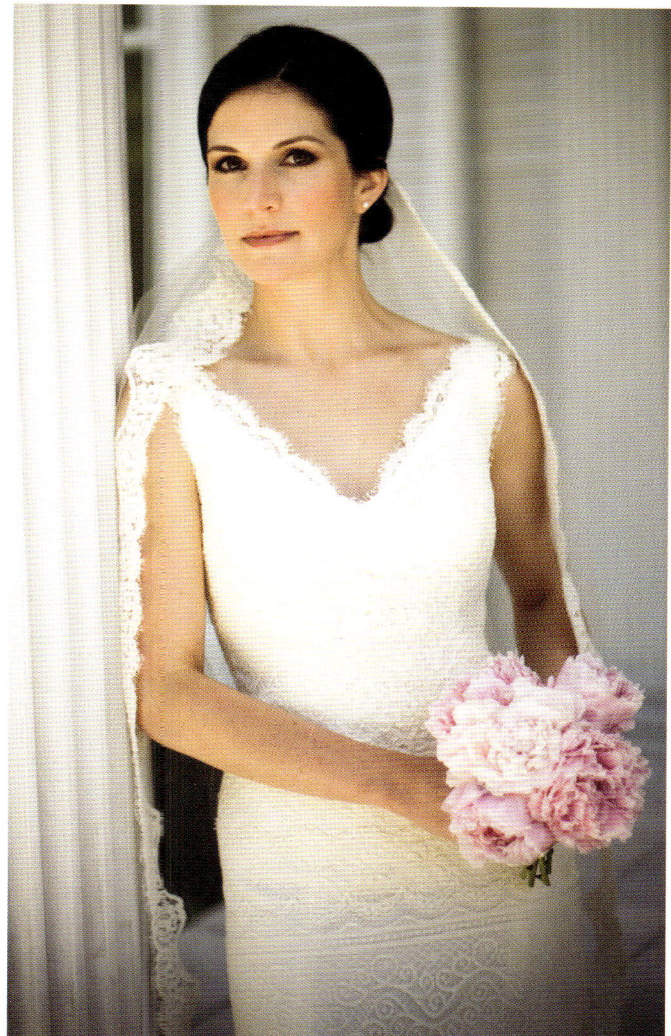

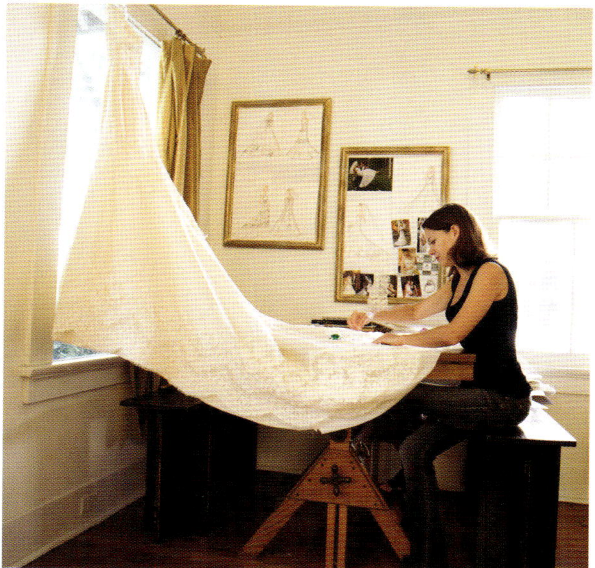

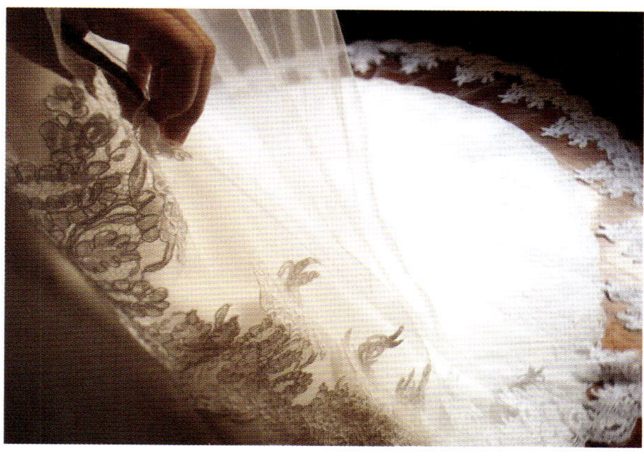

craftsmanship no longer seen today. A very skilled and creative seamstress is necessary to preserve the integrity of the original garment and textiles. Working with vintage gowns calls for extreme care. The fibers of the fabric can be fragile, and there is a finite amount of material to work with. There is little room for error.

The smaller frames and shorter proportions of women decades ago often present a challenge for the modern-day bride-to-be. Many vintage gowns are short waisted and have high bustlines and modest necklines. Maintaining a balance between the design integrity of the original gown and the design and fit needs of the new wearer requires much planning and consideration.

A new foundation and inside gown are often made to the current bride's specific measurements. The new inner gown provides support for the irreplaceable vintage outer fabric. With the fit perfected on the inner gown, designing with the elements of the heirloom piece begins. If the vintage piece is taken apart to be resewn, the stitching of each seam is painstakingly opened so as not to disturb any decorative stitching or damage any intricate lacework. Rubbing off the shape and pattern of the original pieces of the garment onto muslin allows for experimental cutting and draping without subjecting the vintage garment to damage. Reducing

Beautiful neckline border made of galloon or scalloped lace (JC)

Manipulating a straight panel of border lace to take the curve of the skirt hem (BB)

Curving lace to the shape of the veil and skirt hem (JC)

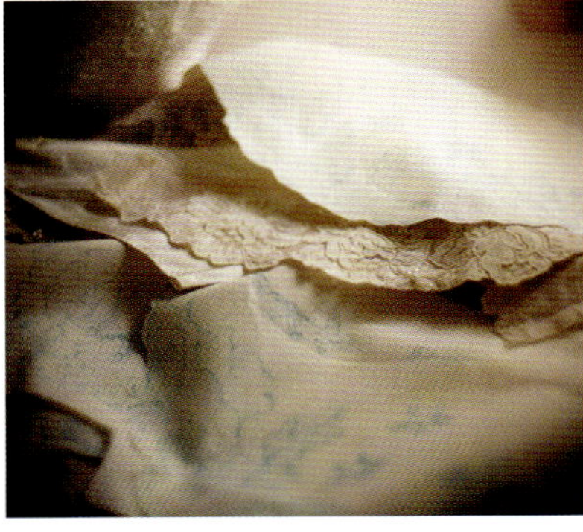

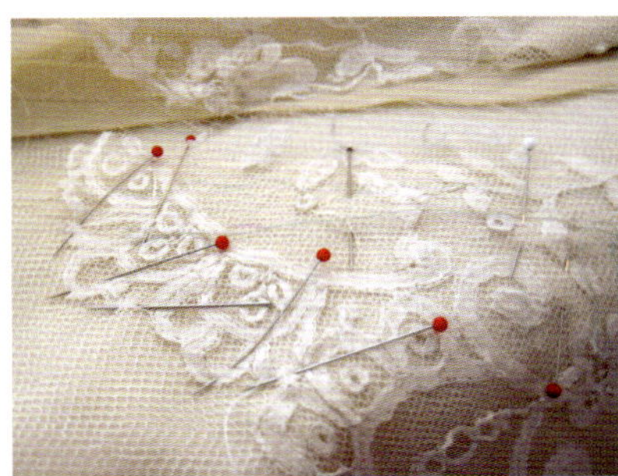

ABOVE:
Vintage lace pattern rubbed off onto muslin for design experimentation (JC)

Vintage lace carefully thread marked and pinned for sewing (BB)

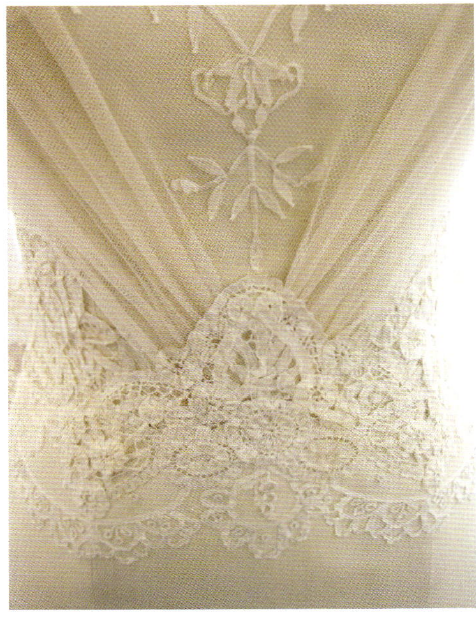

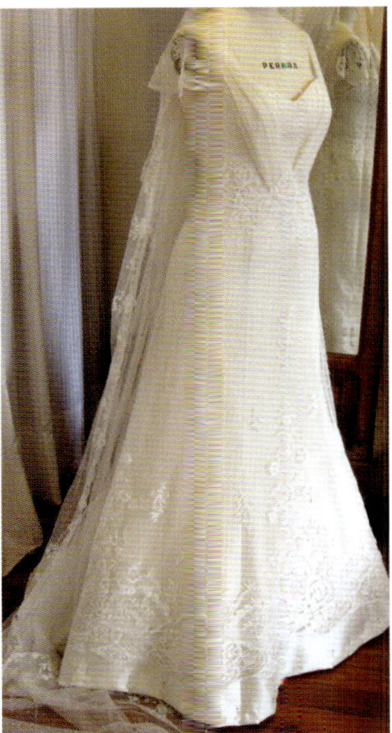

RIGHT:
Original vintage bodice lace placement maintained but carefully adjusted and elongated to create a longer-waisted bodice (SP)

A completed gown of vintage lace over a new inner foundation and base (SP)

the handling of the vintage piece during the design process requires more steps but yields a better outcome. Special care is taken to support the delicate vintage pieces. Backing the fragile pieces with tulle or organza provides stability without changing the aesthetic. Long hand-construction processes including thread marking of seam lines, hand basting of seams, and hand framing of layers are implemented in reassembling the gown. In time, the vintage piece takes the shape of the current wearer's dream dress.

Some clients may wish to incorporate part of a vintage gown or pieces of heirloom lace into their own gown or veil. When a family gown is not in condition to be reworn, pieces of lace can be lifted off for use in a new silhouette. Heirloom collars, yokes, and other shapes may also be incorporated into new silhouettes. These pieces can be worked into the shape of bodices, hemlines or other detailing. Color presents one of the greatest challenges of mixing old and new. The textiles' original hues of ivory or white take on subtle hints of pink, brown, green, or gray with age. The vintage pieces can be carefully lightened in a bath of sodium perborate or sodium peroxide. Layering new fabrics of varying shades of ivory can help blend with the color of the lightened vintage elements.

PRESSING AND FINISHING

Proper pressing sets a quality garment apart. From the first time the iron touches the fabric, great care is taken. A professional gravity-feed steam iron is essential in crafting dresses. Consistent steam and heat far exceed that of a home iron in both quality and quantity. A Teflon shoe over the iron's face plate eliminates scorching on even the most delicate of fabrics. A gown is constantly pressed during the construction process. Fabrics are pressed before they are cut, before framing, and after framing. Seams are pressed closed before being pressed open or one way. Care is taken not to allow the seam allowance to leave indentations on the face

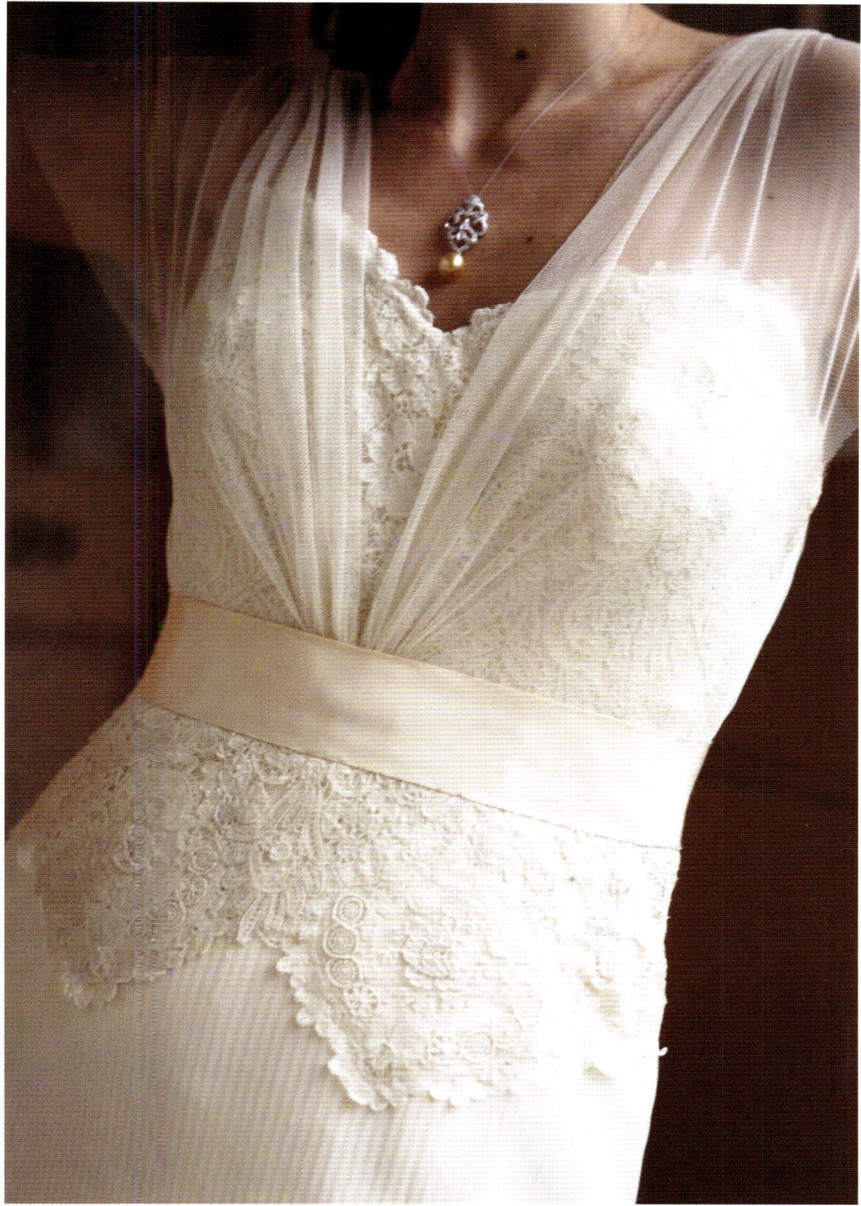

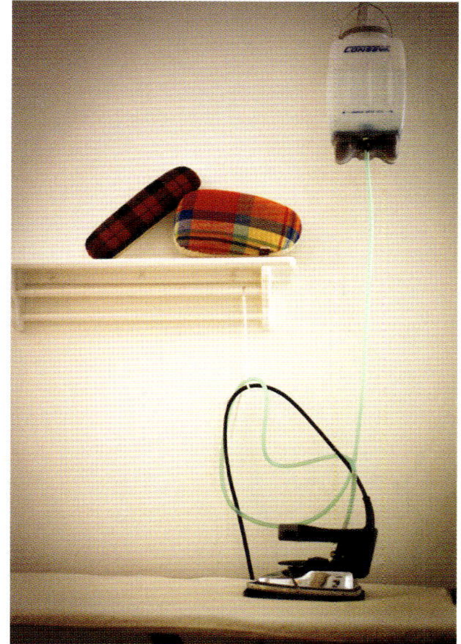

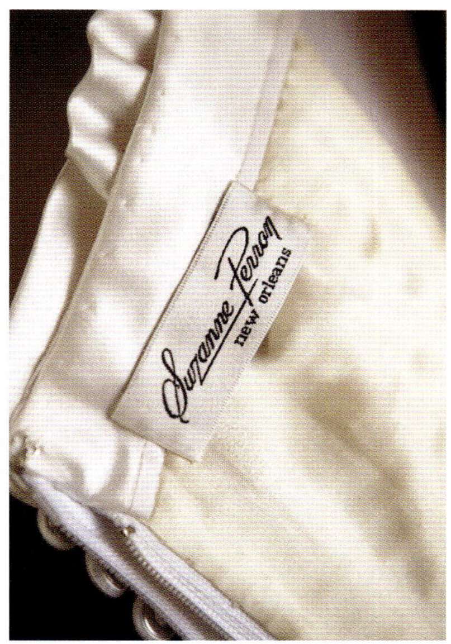

of the garment. Seams can be pressed on a sleeve roll, a pressing ham, or sleeve board. Strips of cardboard can be used to prevent cut edges of seam allowances from leaving indentions on the face.

Hand stitching is orderly and clean. Handwork and tacks are invisible where possible. Basting and thread marks are removed without leaving marks or damage. Hook-and-eye closures are securely stitched. Linings and facings are neat and secure. Hems are carefully hand stitched without catching the face or creating puckers.

When dancing, a good dancer makes the most difficult steps look effortless. The same holds true for a gown. A finished gown looks effortless: not over worked, not over pressed, and all the supporting stitches as well as supporting layers and structures are invisible.

A gown bodice made of vintage lace collars and yoke pieces (BB)

Tools for a flawless finish: proper equipment and adequate steam (JC)

Some of the unseen details including facings and linings finishing the inside of the gown (BB)

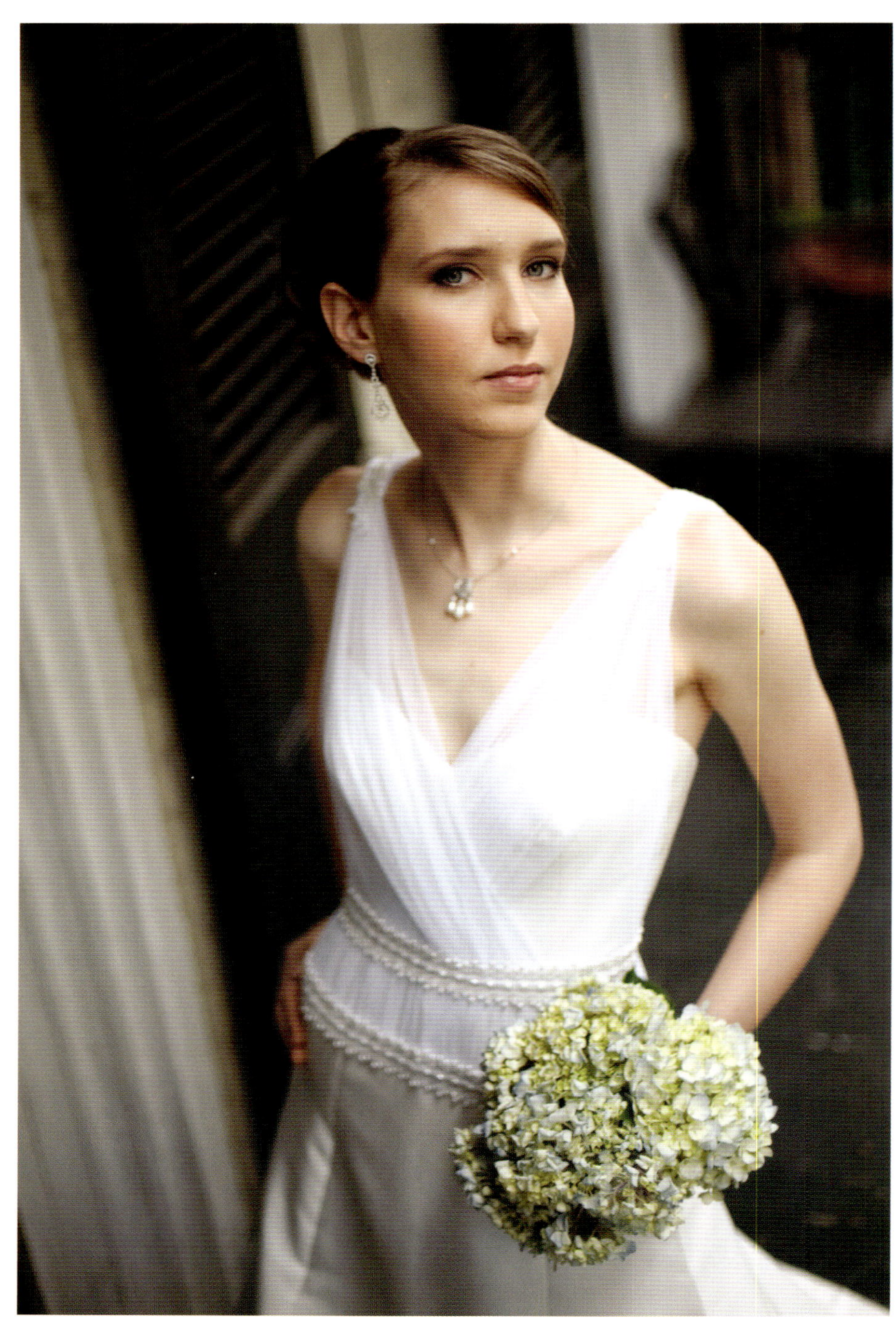

The Client Experience

CONSULTATION

The initial phase of the couture design process is the consultation. The consultation is scheduled at the design studio well in advance of the event, generally six to eight months before. This window can be as short as six weeks, schedule permitting. Clients are welcome to bring friends and family members to share in the experience, and their involvement is valued. Each consultation is as unique as the finished product. The more information a client shares, the more specific a gown can be created to her. The dialogue between the client, friends, and family provides a glimpse of the client's personality. The goal is to glean as much information from the client as possible in a short amount of time. The more I feel I know a client, the better I can create for her. Paying attention to how a client dresses and carries herself gives insight into what type of gown she would be most comfortable in. General conversations about interests, hobbies, activities, schooling, and career can help further increase an understanding of who the client is. Gaining insight into a client's sense of style is crucial. A client seeking out a couture gown generally has developed an individual sense of style and a realistic idea of which silhouettes will be flattering.

I first like to discuss basic event information. Understanding the event is an important part in formulating the perfect gown. The type of function, geographic location, venue, time of day, and time of year dictate what type of gown is appropriate. A debutante gown for a fall presentation does not need to be as elaborate as a gown for a ball on Mardi Gras night. An evening cathedral wedding may call for a grand and formal ball gown, whereas a garden wedding on a spring day may call for a more light and airy sheath. For a wedding, the groom's choice of attire is an important consideration. If the groom's preference is tails, the formality of the event is reinforced. If the groom has a penchant for white linen, color and texture choices for the bride should be less formal.

As the conversation brings the event into focus, we begin to narrow the limitless possibilities of a custom design. Some clients choose from existing sketches and give me complete artistic liberty. Others come in with defined ideas, an organized collection of magazine tear sheets, and specific fabric preferences. I encourage clients to start a file of pictures of gowns or design elements that they like. It is also helpful for them to include pictures of what they do not like. A client does not have to choose one silhouette. In a custom gown, design elements from several gowns can be blended into one unique creation.

With a custom gown, special accommodations can be made. If a client has a particular fit need, it can easily be addressed from the beginning. Modesty elements such as straps or sleeves required by a venue can be made part of the original design. Incorporating all or part of a family heirloom gown is another option best dealt with from the start. A gown can also be designed to work with a family veil or even to complement sentimental or heirloom family jewelry.

The initial consultation concludes with measurements. Couture, or more specifically haute couture, is the art of custom designing and making garments for a particular client. The design is unique, and the garment is crafted precisely to the client's measurements. With fit being of ultimate importance, the measurements are much more inclusive than those used to order from a size chart at a traditional retailer. As few as four measurements may be used to order a dress at retail, while the custom measurement chart includes a minimum of two dozen measurements. Unlike a retailer ordering a gown by choosing the size closest to your largest measurement, a couture gown is made specifically to each and every measurement, including torso and gown length. A couture gown is designed and sculpted to fit perfectly to each and every measurement.

Designers often reference their muse. A muse is a source of inspiration. A designer's muse may be a model, an actress, a client, a historical figure, or anyone else of interest to them. A designer may gain inspiration from a single muse for a collection, a season, or a career. My muse constantly changes. The client becomes my muse. I find my inspiration through the client. The goal is to create a gown complementary to the client's personality, style, and body type.

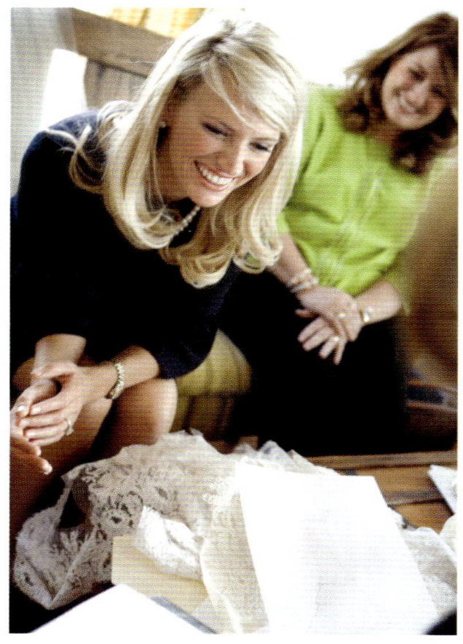

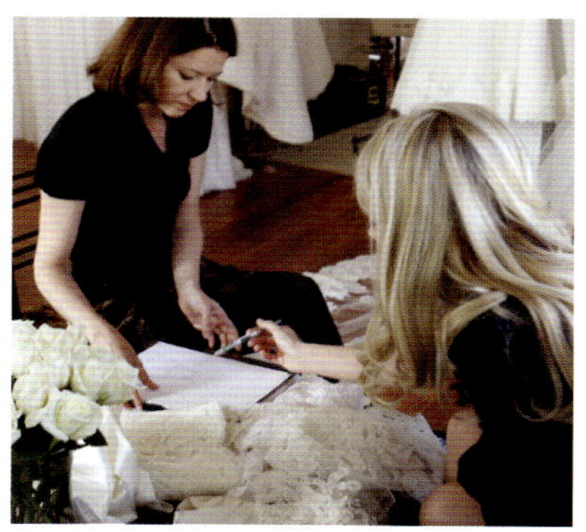

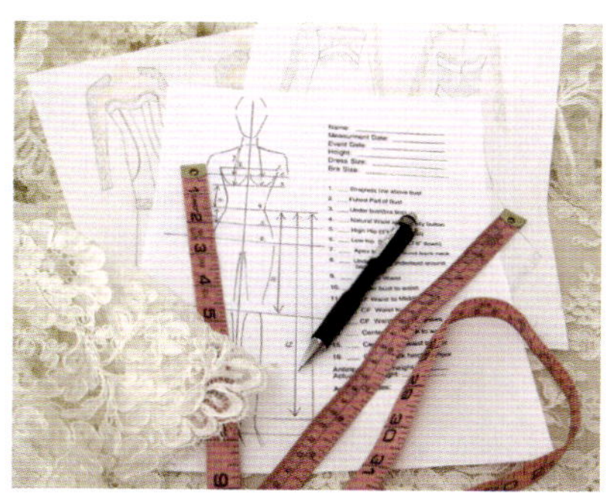

Bridal client Jolie and her mother meeting with me to discuss wedding gown design (BB)

Designer and client reviewing gown options and fabric choices (BB)

The detailed chart used for recording client measurements (SP)

SKETCHING

Ideas begin to take shape through pencil put to paper. Sketching is a quick way to explore various concepts and design ideas. Working in pencil creates a very fluid interpretation. Soft, quick lines of developmental drawings allow the concept to take shape. There are many styles of sketching. Quick idea sketches known as thumbnails put brainstorming to paper. The thumbnails are small renderings several to a page to allow for many ideas to be explored and viewed at once. Impressionistic drawings may communicate a mood with little indication of what the garment actually looks like. Clean linear drawings called flats communicate all construction details with less emphasis on aesthetics. Flats are drawn as if the garment is flat on a surface. In the design room, sketches that communicate both mood and detail are most effective.

Sketching can be done during various stages of the process. During the initial consultation, ideas may be communicated by sketching in front of the client. When ideas are readily flowing and the parameters for design have been narrowed, sketching with the client is ideal. Immediate input and reaction from the client is valuable. The overall shape of the garment is lightly penciled with long, fluid strokes. As the silhouette takes shape, the pencil strokes become more defined and the details are layered in.

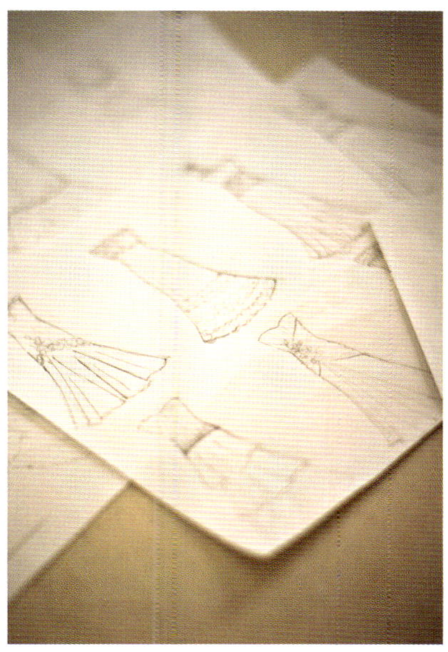

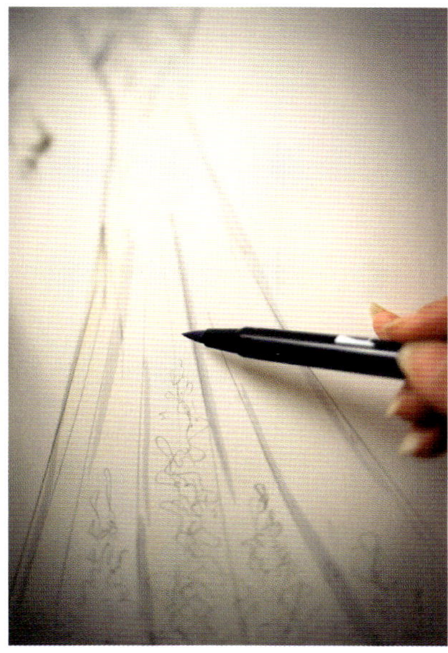

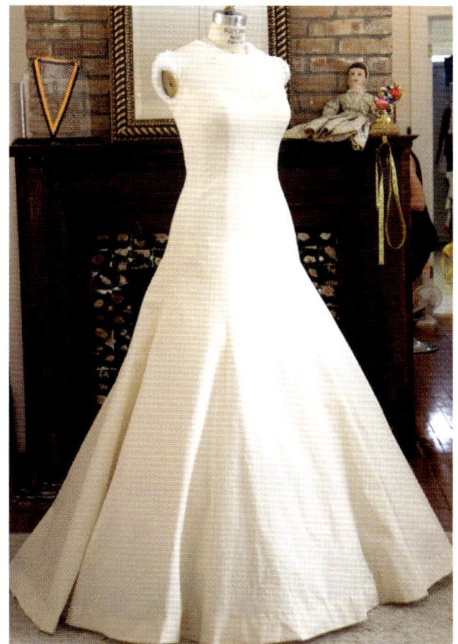

Not all gown designs take shape quickly. In fact, most gown designs evolve over time. I may mull over the event details and client preferences for some time, allowing design ideas to take shape. I may invest time doing additional research and fabric sourcing to supplement a client's folder. Sketching may take place over several weeks after the consultation. Several variations are then shown to the client for input. In some cases, the gown design is achieved through draping fabric directly on the mannequin, not through sketching. For very sculptural designs, draping precedes sketching.

Sketching is an important communication tool for a designer. The freehand drawings are not intended as finished work. The gown is the ultimate finished work. The sketch or sketches are ideal keepsakes for a client.

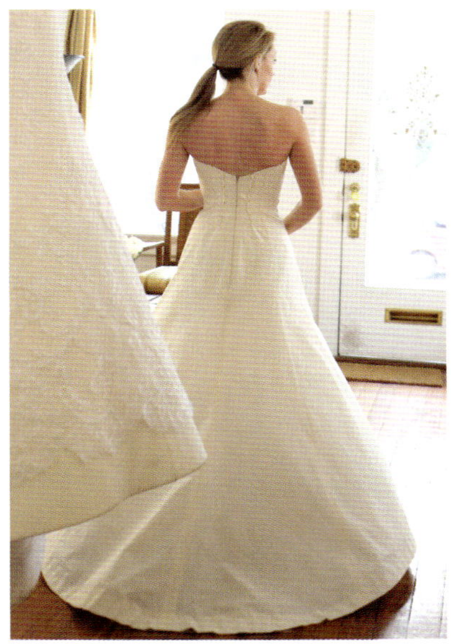

Thumbnail sketches allowing for quick design development (JC)

A sketch that is more fluid and showing less detail (JC)

Basic gown prototype of muslin (BB)

A bridal client modeling muslin sculpted to her measurements (BB)

MUSLIN FITTING

The creation of a couture gown involves the development of a prototype made of muslin. Muslin is an inexpensive, plain-weave cotton fabric. The term *muslin* also refers to the muslin garment itself. Muslin development adds time and labor to the design process, but ensures ideal fit, proportion, and aesthetics. Fitting a muslin on a client also reduces costly mistakes when working with the actual, more valuable fabric.

Developing a muslin specifically for a client is part of what sets the couture process apart. When buying a dress off the rack or from a traditional bridal retailer, the gown is premade to a standard set of measurements. A muslin-fitting stage is not part of the process. This contrasts our one-of-a-kind, custom garments sculpted precisely to the client's measurements and proportions.

Countless hours of work are invested between the sketch and the muslin fitting. Patterns are drafted. Fabric is draped and redraped. Multiple muslins, or parts of muslins, may be made during the design process in the pursuit of the perfect design. All of the inner structures are made. Yards of heavy crinoline are

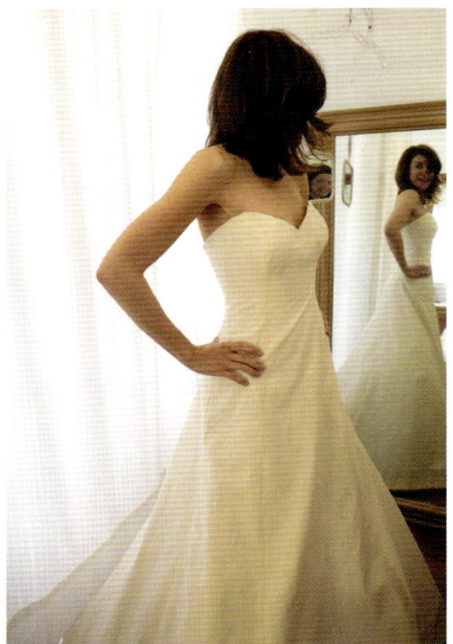
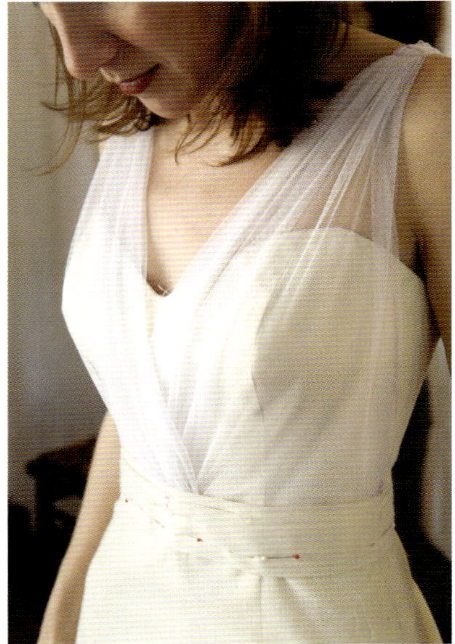
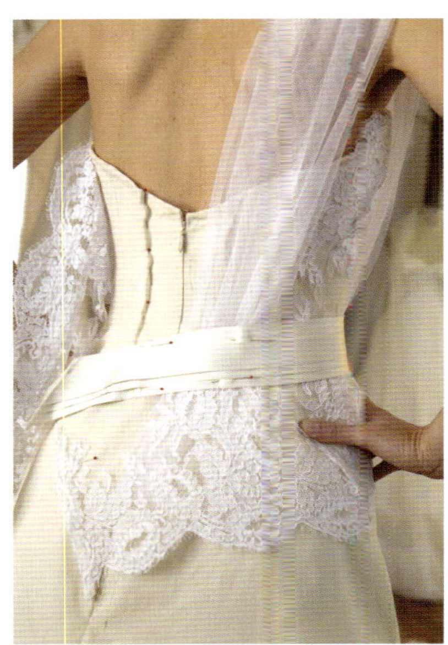
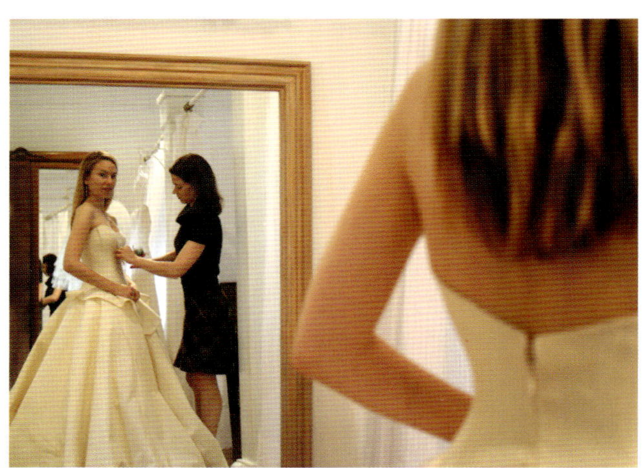
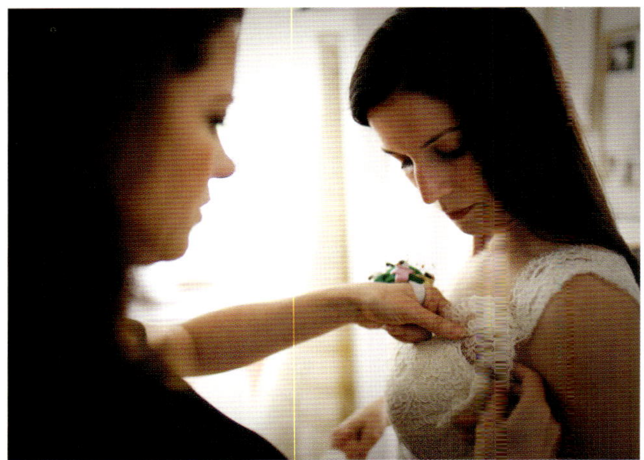

CLOCKWISE:
A client viewing the first three-dimensional shape of her gown (BB)

Experimenting with design detail on the client's muslin (BB)

Adjusting back details on the muslin (BB)

Pinning lace detailing in place on the client (JC)

Minute fit adjustments pinned during fitting (JW)

cut and gathered into tiers of varying lengths and widths to create the desired skirt shape and structure. The muslin garment floats over the intricate inner structures, showing the client the first three-dimensional version of her gown.

While some muslins are near perfect from the beginning of the fit process, others continue to evolve during the fitting. The muslin serves as a rough draft. This malleable prototype gives the client and designer a canvas on which to work. The muslin fitting allows for adjustments big and small. The muslin fitting allows the designer to easily address any weight changes of the client. Design elements can be experimented with. The shape of the skirt can be adjusted for maximum flattery. Seam lines, details, and style lines can be literally drawn or pinned in place. Details such as lace or pleating that are hand basted on prior to the fitting can be moved, adjusted, or removed. Length can be changed to accommodate various heel heights. Strap length and width can be adjusted to the client for the best fit, comfort, and appearance.

Other details such as veil design and bustling are addressed in the muslin fitting. The muslin fitting is an excellent time to experiment with bustle place-

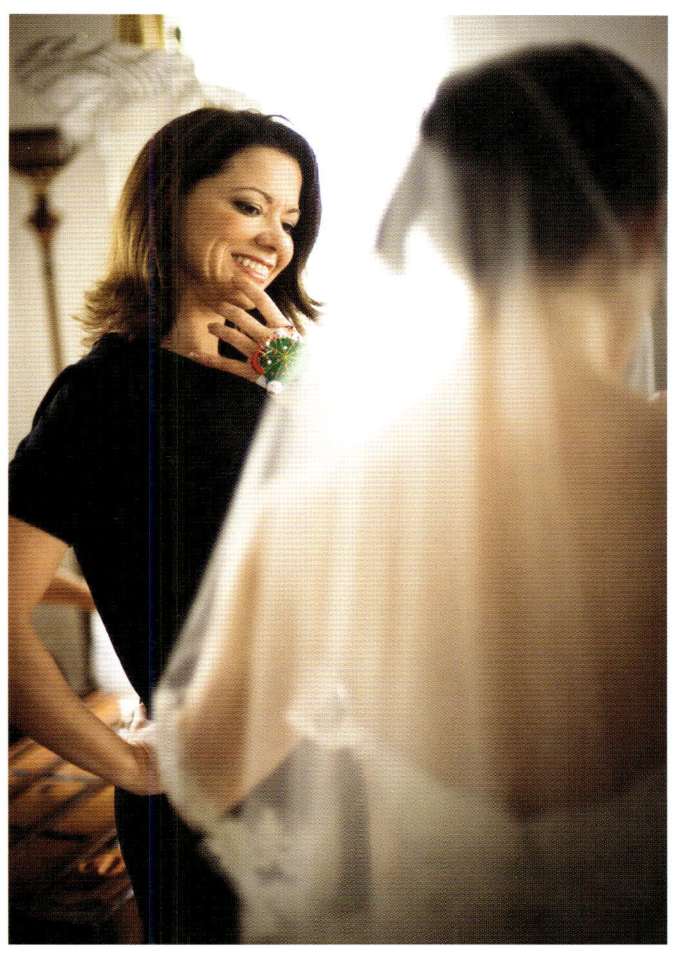

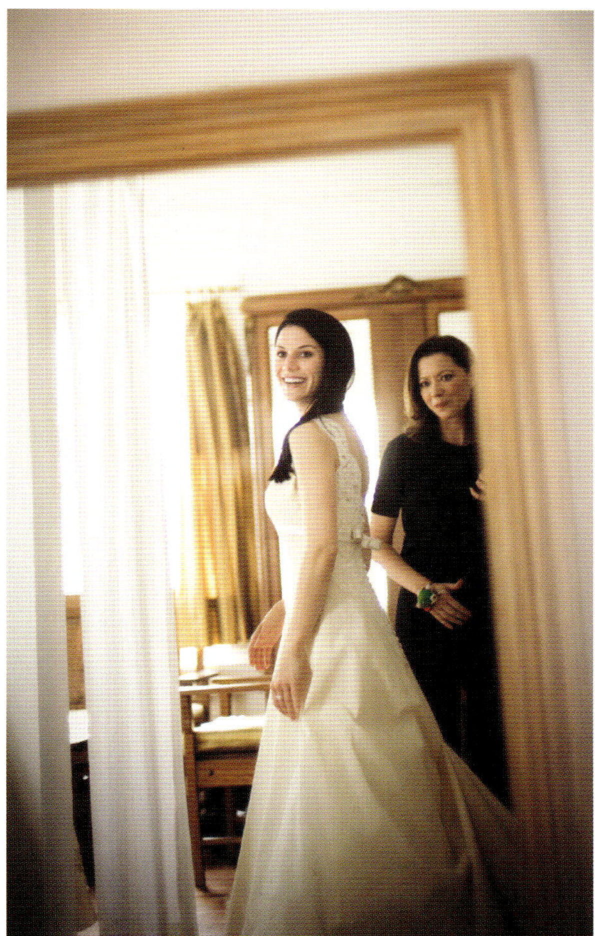

ment. A variety of bustle options can be pinned, draped, and tied in muslin with no worry of creasing, damaging, or tearing the actual garment. Some silhouettes bustle more attractively with an inside French bustle, while other gowns drape and show off details better while bustled on the outside. In the muslin stage, the skirt and train shape can also be slightly adjusted to correspond to the most appropriate bustle shape. The client walks, moves, and sits to ensure comfort, proper fit, and length. Once the muslin is satisfactory to both client and designer, working in the actual fabric commences. The more perfect the muslin and the more perfect the fit, the more perfect the finished product. A well-executed muslin can truly communicate what the finished product will look like. I have had clients say they would get married in their muslin.

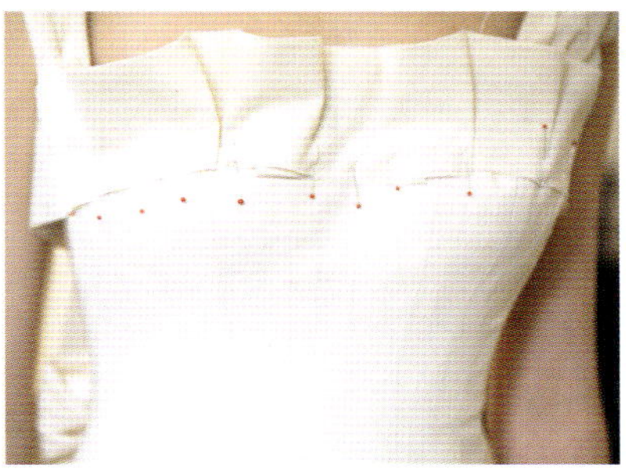

Discussing veil design (JC)

Checking the side view of the bustle placement (JC)

Pleat detail adjusted and repinned during the fitting (BB)

GOWN FITTING

The last step in the process for the client is fitting the gown constructed in the actual fabric. The muslin layer has been replaced with the new, more luxurious outer fabric. The inner foundation and crinoline from the muslin fitting stay constant. Between muslin fitting and final fitting, numerous couture sewing techniques have been employed. Layers of fabric, under layers, and interfacing have been cut, pressed, and assembled. Meticulous hand sewing, framing, thread mark-

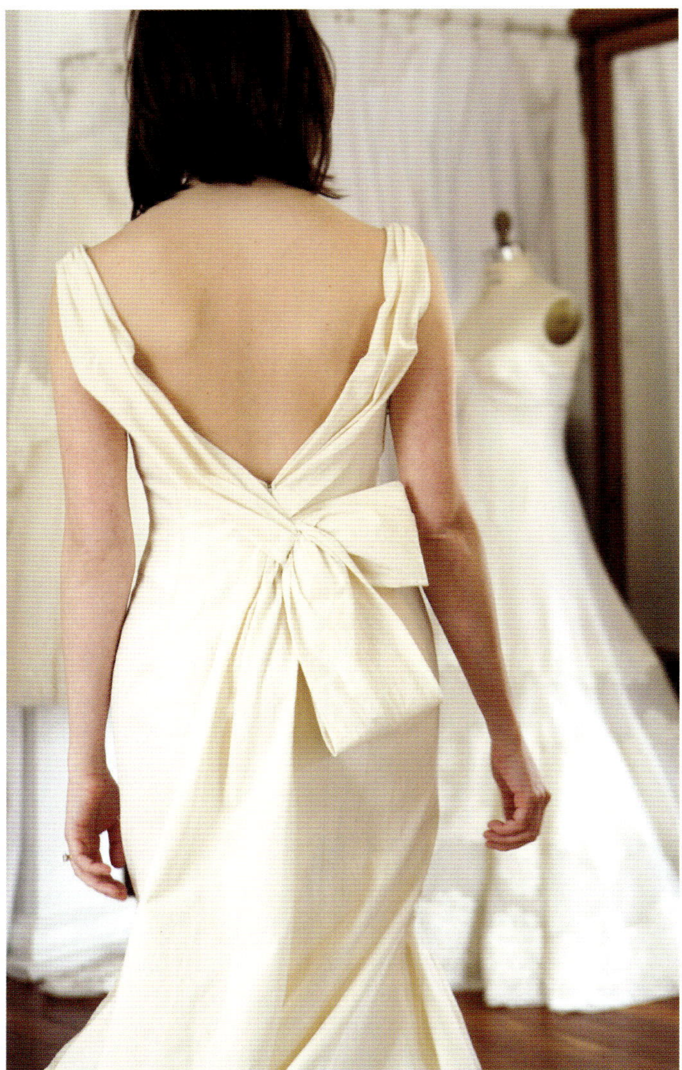

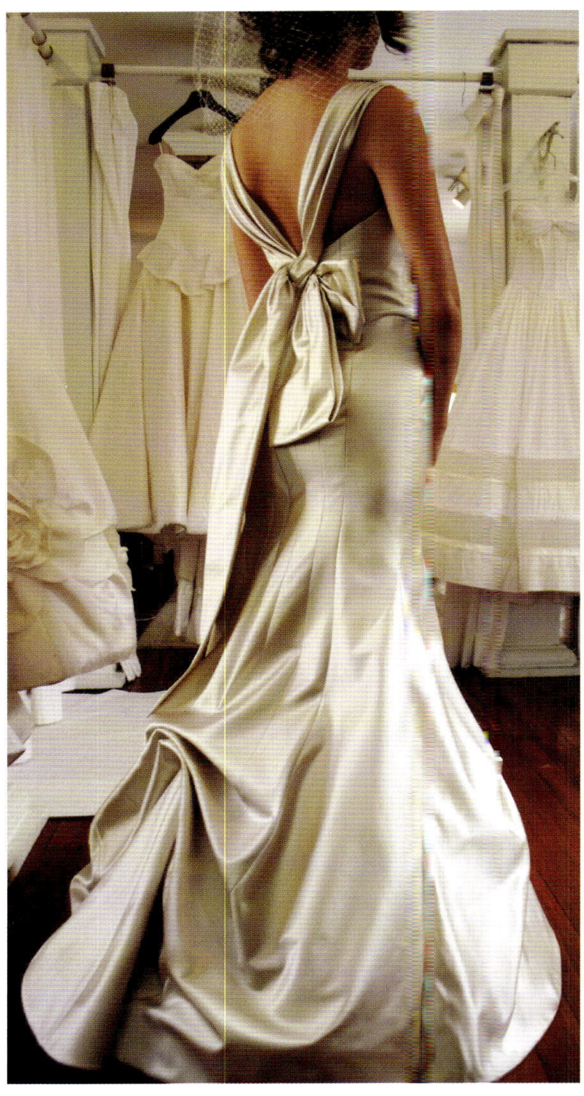

A near-perfect final muslin (BB)

Gown constructed in Italian silk satin for final fitting (SW)

ing, machine work, and appliqué have occurred. All of the hidden details—from seam finishes to organza stays to neckline facings to hemming—have been executed. The final gown fitting will have the hem hand basted with additional hem allowance to accommodate for any adjustments or for heel height. If a gown has shoulder straps, they too may be basted in place to allow for final placement.

Having worked from the client's previously perfected muslin, the designer makes only minor modifications and design changes, if any, at this fitting. Working out all of the design details and fit corrections in the muslin keeps the final garment from being overhandled. With a muslin prototype as a guide for the finished product, the luxurious and often costly outer fabric can be cut once, stitched once, and pressed once. The less the fabric is handled, the more pristine the final product. Even the finest of needles can leave subtle marks if seams need to be moved. Any fit alterations must be carefully pinned and skillfully sewn. Shoulder straps may be adjusted. A perfect hem length is finalized.

The final fitting can serve as a dress rehearsal. Some clients will schedule a hair and makeup trial run to correspond with the fitting. Friends and family are

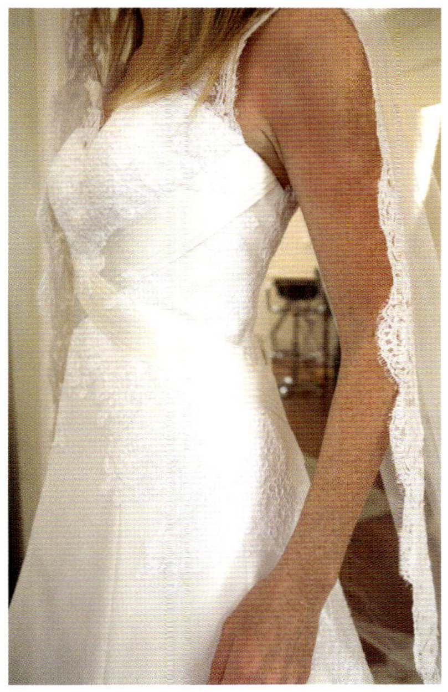

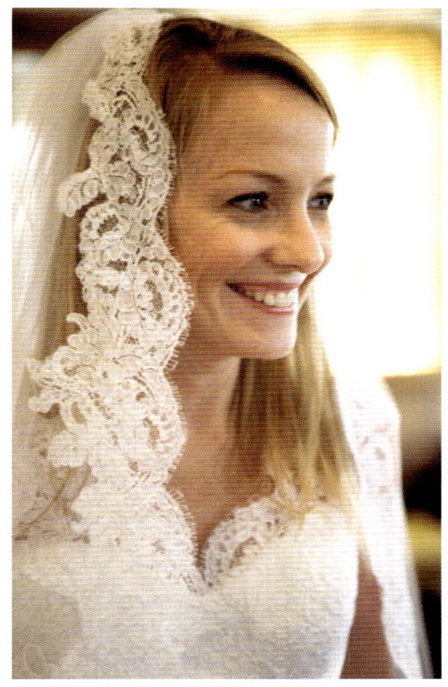

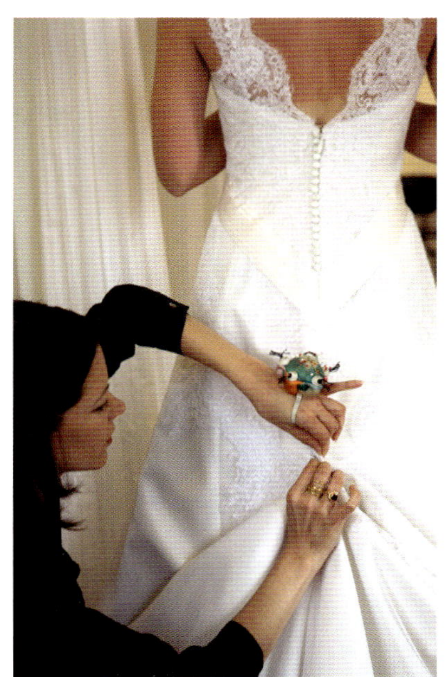

welcome. It is essential for the client to be in the shoes she will be wearing for the event. Jewelry and other accessories can be styled on the client at this time. For bridal clients, the completed veil is paired with the gown. If the bride chooses to have a blusher on her veil, this is the ideal time to practice with it. The father of the bride may take this opportunity to learn how to maneuver around a full bridal skirt, veil, and blusher. With the buttons, loops, ties, or hooks of the bustle in place, the client and her attendants are shown how to bustle the gown. The client can practice walking, turning, and dancing.

After the gown fitting, the painstakingly precise handwork of the hem and other intricate detailing is completed. The gown receives a final pressing and steaming. It is carefully inspected for any imperfections or wrinkles. When all is satisfactory the gown is packed and covered in an oversized garment bag and ready for transportation.

The muslin of a finished gown is archived with the paper pattern and other developmental work. With the finished gowns no longer a part of our inventory, the muslin serves as our record. A library of patterns and muslins is a valuable resource.

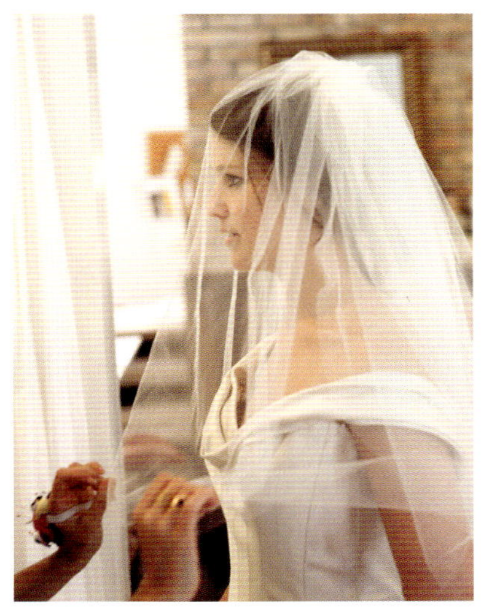

Final gown pristinely finished and perfectly fit (BB)

A lace-appliquéd veil to complete the wedding-day look (BB)

Demonstrating how to bustle the gown (BB)

Practicing with a blusher (SW)

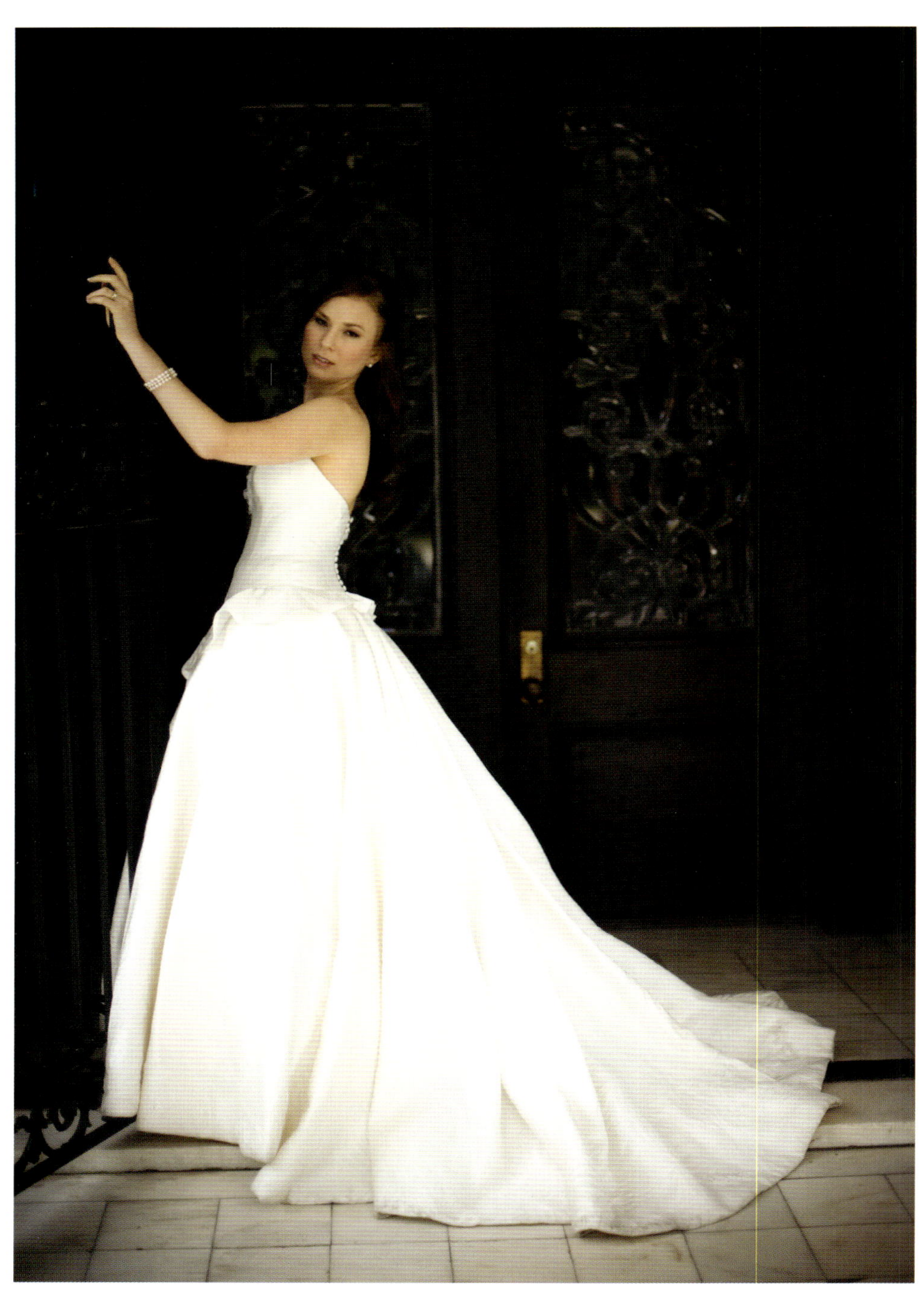

The Gowns

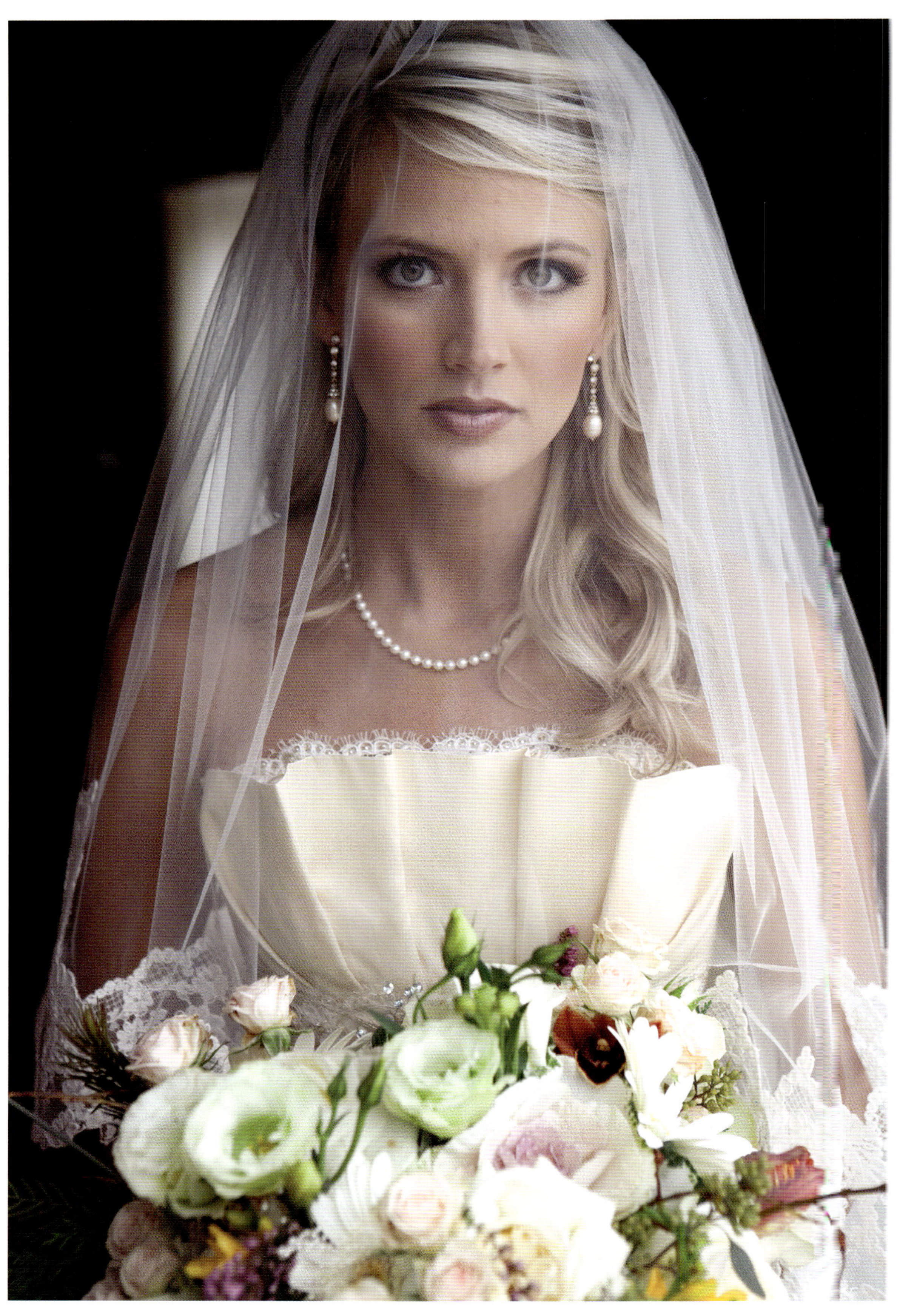

Jolie, Bride

A statuesque bride dressed in golden hues of ivory commands the eye of far and near in a dramatic gown created to reflect her vision. A three-tiered skirt, an elaborate train, and a sinuous trumpet silhouette were part of that vision. Jolie was specific in every detail: the shape of the skirt, the hues in the beading, and the depth of the bodice pleating. Jolie's gown was a true collaboration between client and designer.

The bodice is sculpted with a dozen vertical seams. The seams extend into deep pleats framing the neckline. Three perfectly shaped tiers are gathered below the knee and fall generously to the floor.

An exhaustive search of all of my fabric sources yielded three choices of dark ivory. One option was a rich silk double charmeuse. Another fabric in a dark ivory hue was a weighty duchess satin. The final option was a raw silk dupioni suggesting the hues and striations of corn silk. The last option prevailed. The raw silk offered the richness of color and desired lightness in weave conducive to the elaborate tiers of the skirt. Ivory lace plays beautifully against the color.

Two galloon laces with pronounced borders were combined to decorate the gown. An elaborate, wide Alençon lace with a large scallop repeat was of the perfect scale to work with the generous ruffles and expansive train. A more narrow scalloped lace with a smaller repeat was appliquéd around the empire line and knee seam. Peeking from behind the elongated pleats of the crumb catcher is yet another border of lace.

Light reflection was crucial to this creation. Hand-sewn crystals of golden shadow and crystal-transmission lochrosens accent the imported floral appliqués. Threads of gold and silver intertwine with beading to create vines of foliage accented by dimensional blossoms of tulle. Crystals cluster to make dimensional centers. Silk organza is shaped to create delicate petals. The scallops of the hem lace are further accented with golden shadow bicones and antique-ivory Swarovski pearls.

Dozens of silk-covered buttons finish the entire length of center back. The pleats of the front crumb catcher are repeated along the top of the back bodice. The back vertical seams allowed for the painstaking shaping of the sculpted silhouette.

The theme of three is repeated in the veil. Three tiers of illusion are individually adorned with unique borders of lace. The longest tier of the cathedral-length veil bears the most generous border and is adorned with crystals and elaborate floral embroidery.

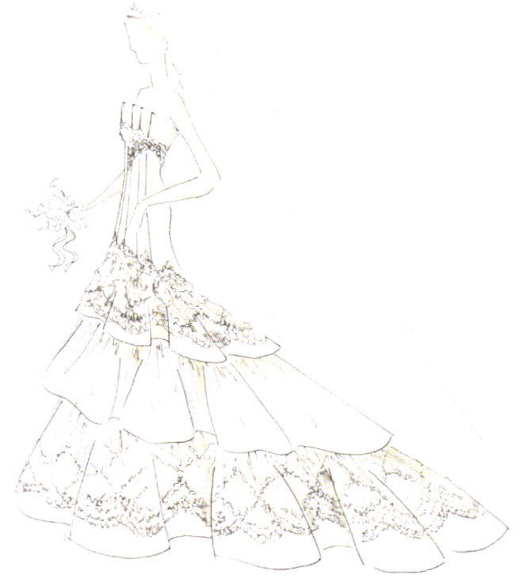

Sketch of Jolie's gown

OPPOSITE PAGE:
Pleated crumb catcher with lace peeking beyond (BB)

CLOCKWISE:
Lace and sketches (BB)
Pinning lace ruffle (BB)
Appliquéing embroidery (SP)
Dimensional tulle flowers (SP)

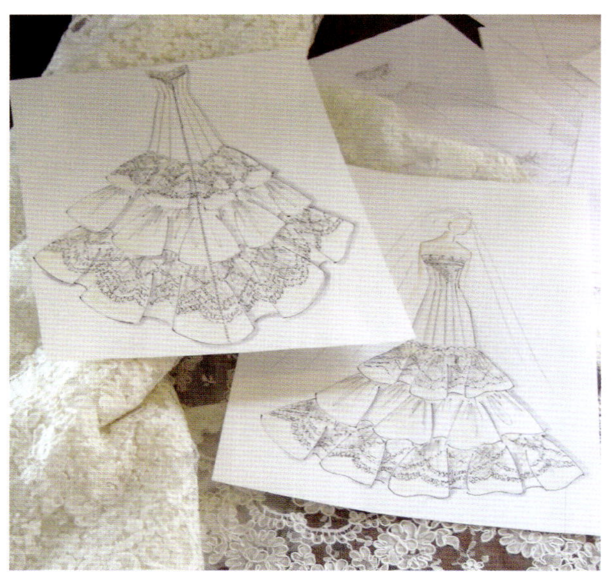

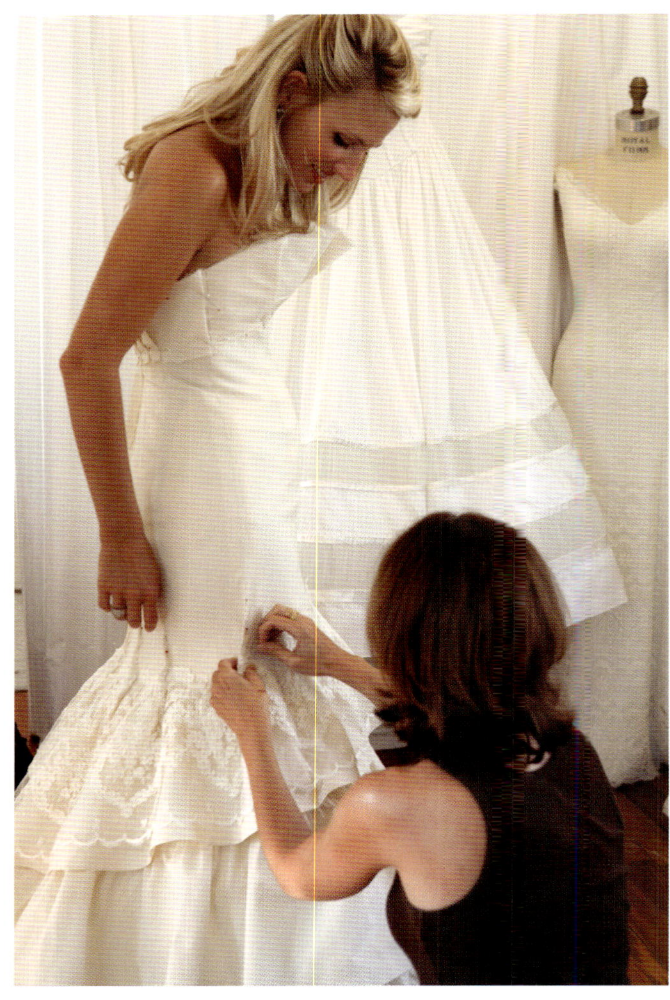

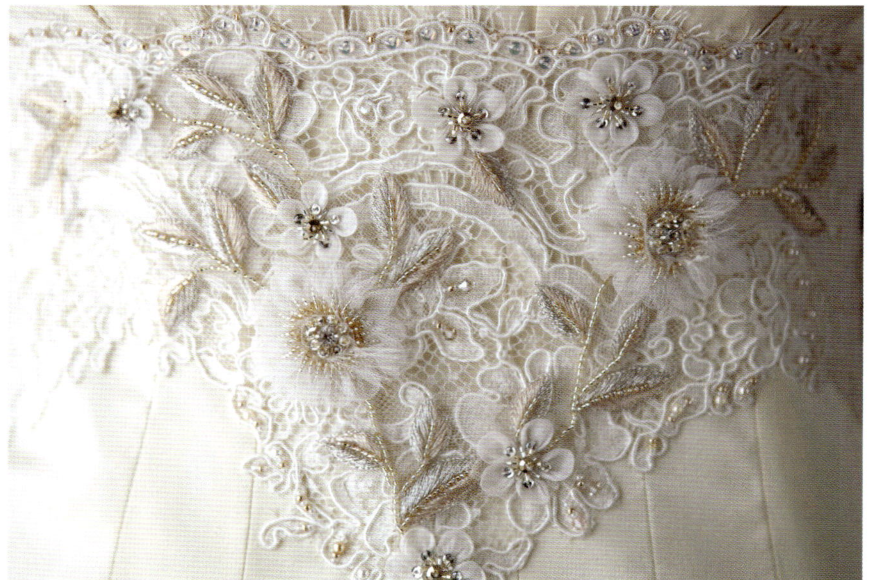

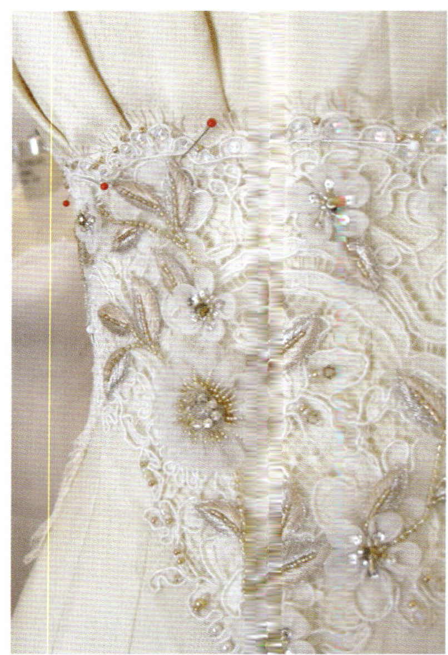

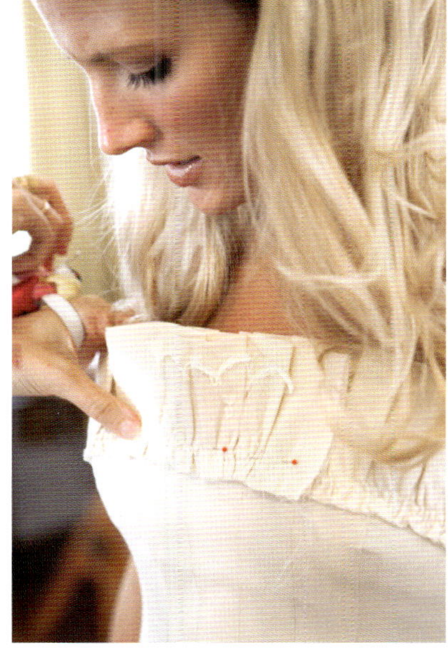

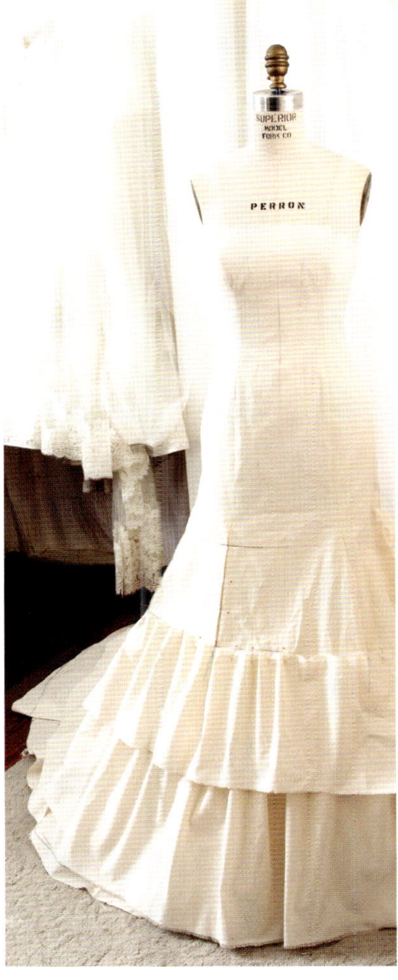

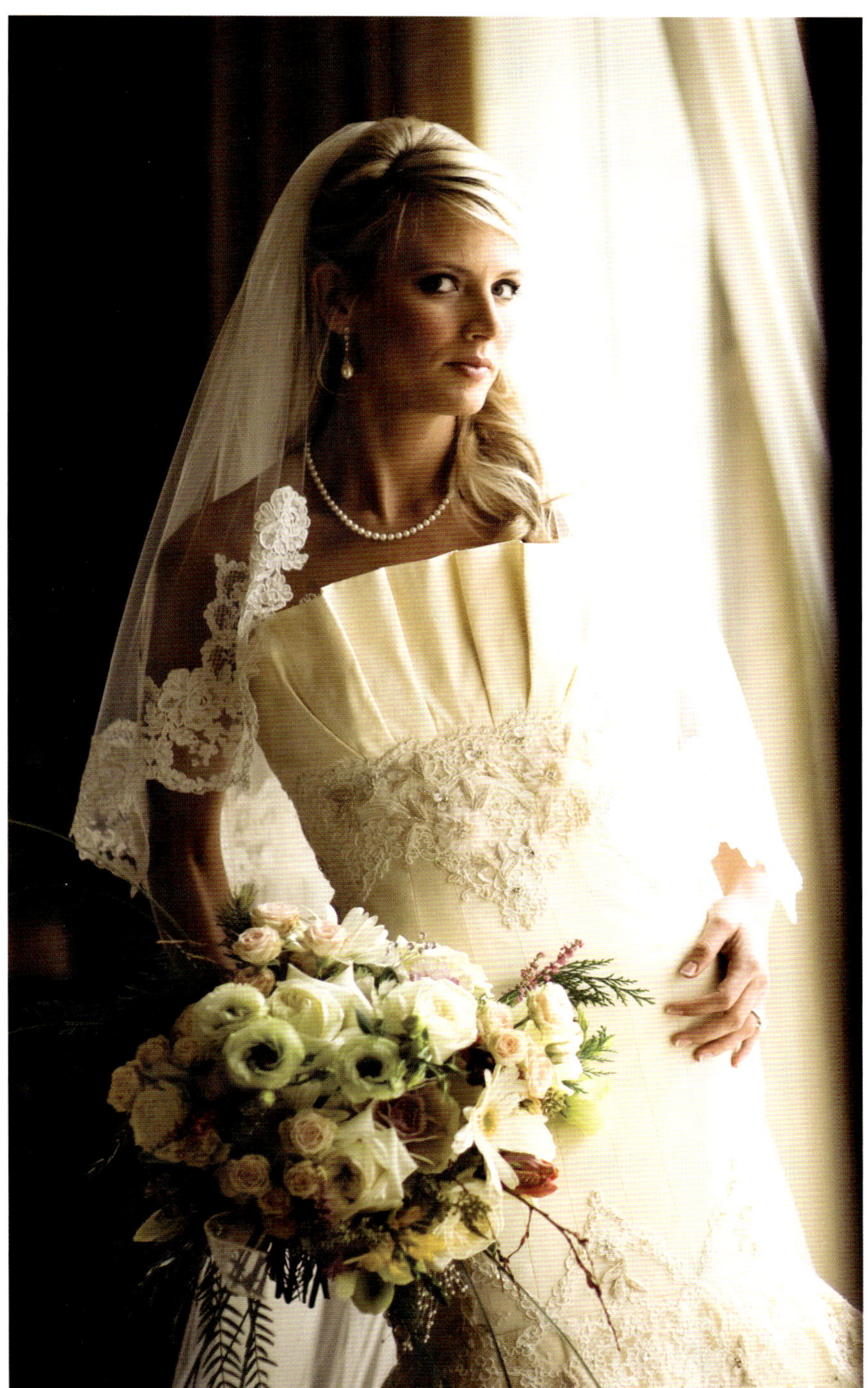

CLOCKWISE:
Bodice ruffle detail (BB)
Shaped midriff with lace appliqué (JC)
Developing gown shape in muslin (BB)

Back train (JC)
First of three tiers (JC)

OPPOSITE PAGE:
Full-length silhouette (JC)

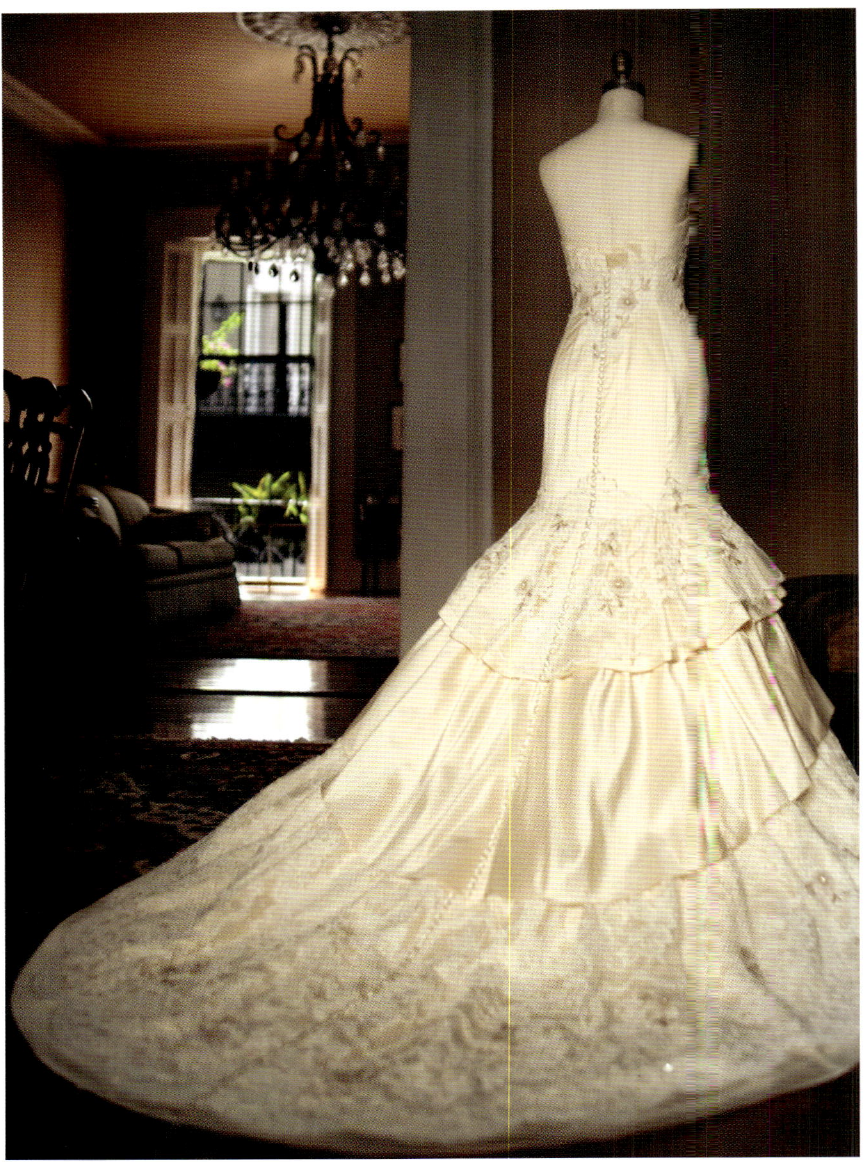

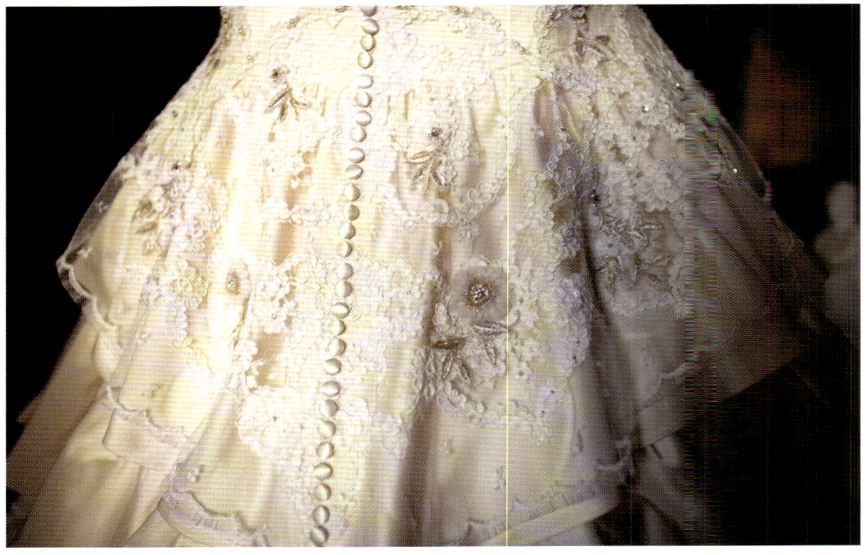

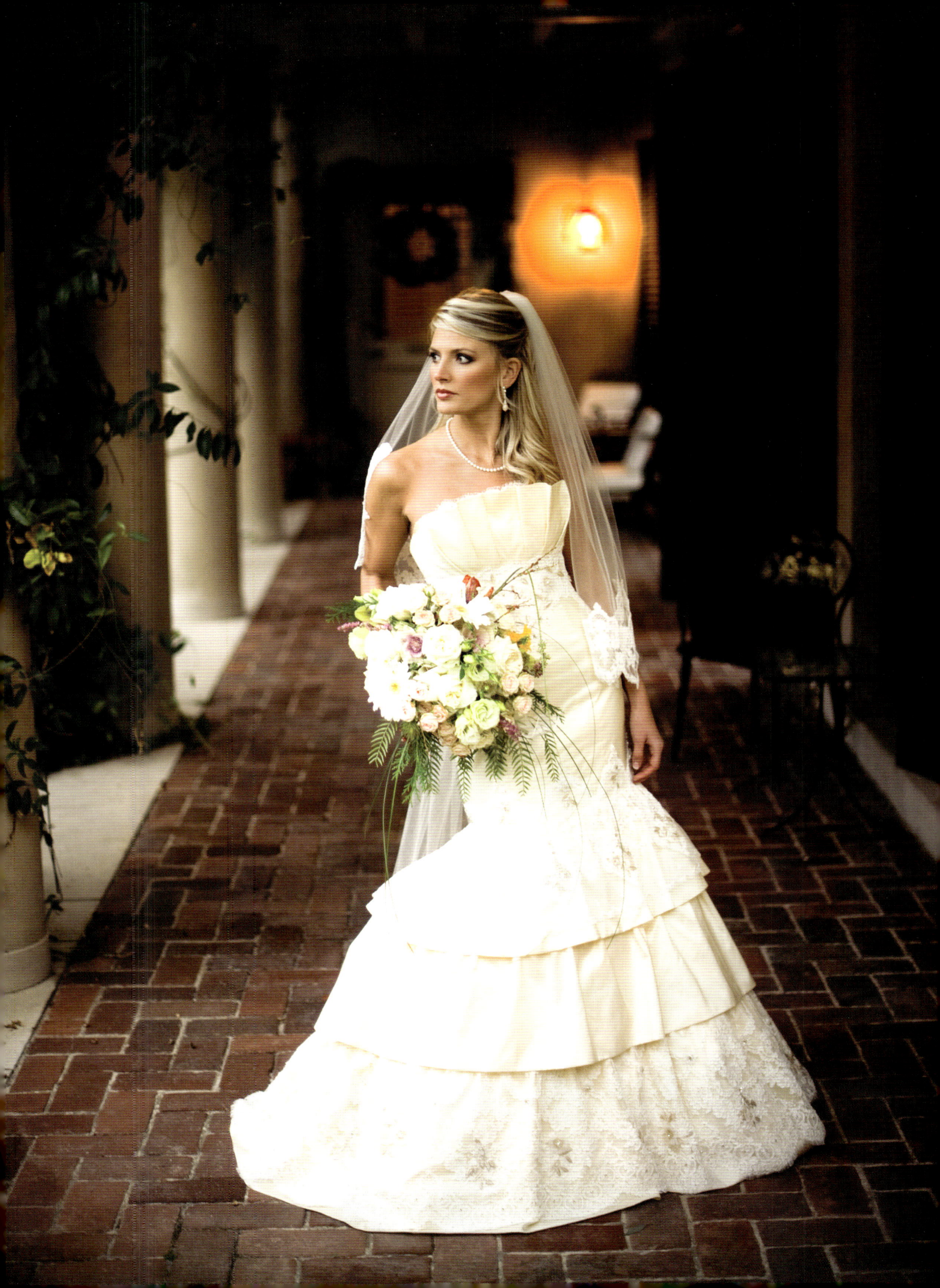

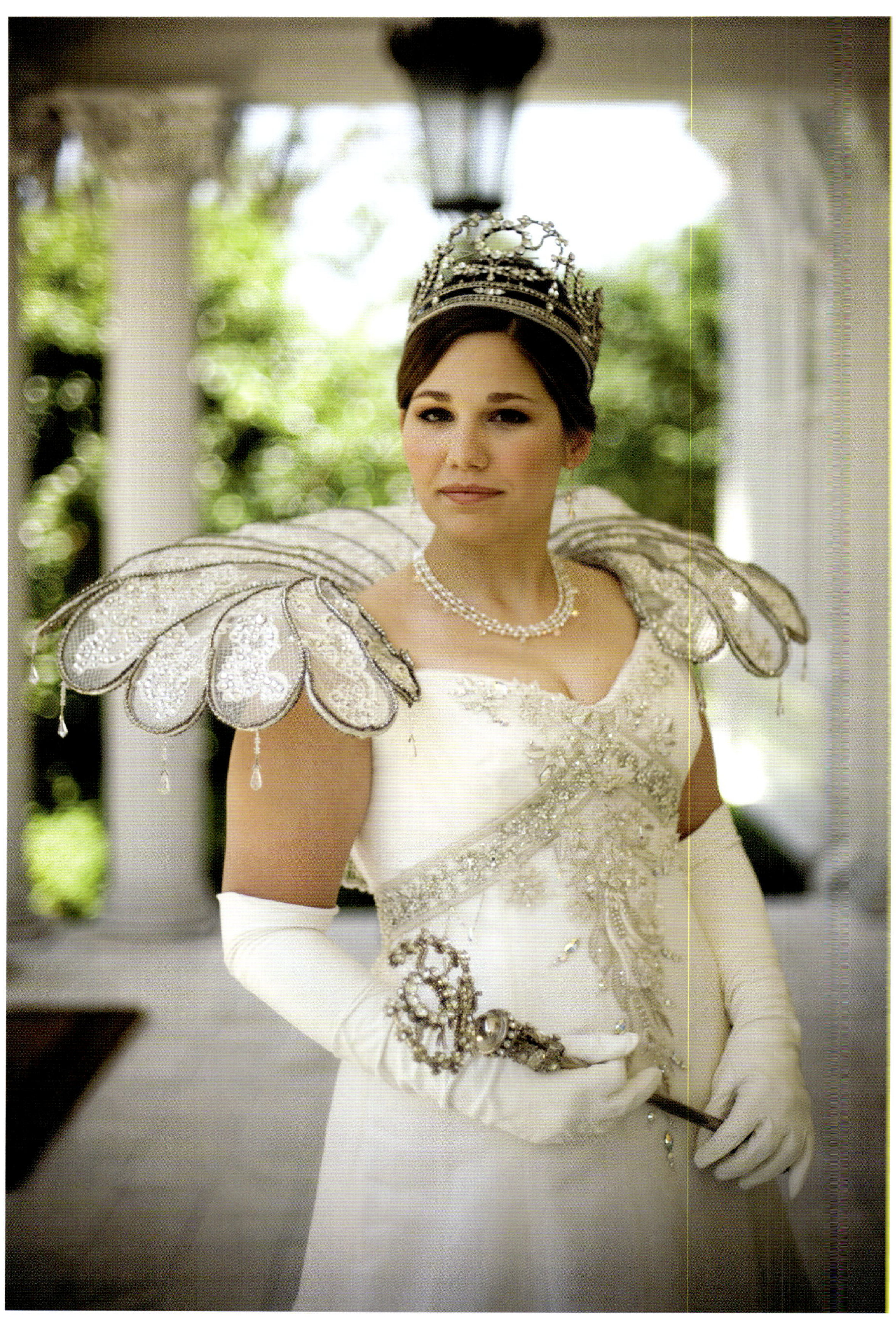

Jackye, Olympians Queen

Jackye reigned over the Krewe of Olympians, a Mardi Gras organization dating back to 1904. Jackye stepped gracefully into the long line of royalty wearing a traditional Medici collar and a couture gown of tulle and satin. The inspiration for the gown came from a magazine tear sheet of a wedding gown with vertical seams, an empire waist, and tulle straps. To elongate Jackye's figure, the empire seam became an inverted V and tulle was draped to create an opposing V neckline. Silver was the adornment of choice as dictated by the organization's dark navy mantle and train, encrusted with silver stones and appliqués.

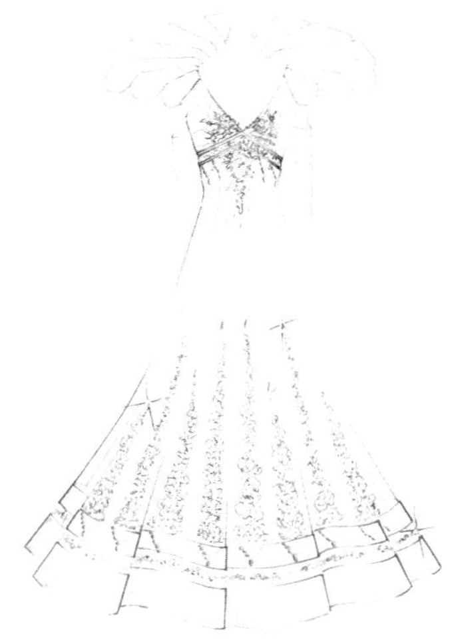

Sketch of Jackye's gown

OPPOSITE PAGE: *Queen's portrait (JC)*

Sixteen blocks of tulle were embroidered in India using the same resources available to the couture designers of New York's fashion industry. Two different blocks of embroidery were developed. Each block was embroidered eight times. The embroidery consists of exquisite threadwork, bugle beads, pearls, rhinestones, and fabric-twisted flowers. The leaflike scrolls at the bottom of the embroidery resemble the leaf motif of the traditional Olympians mantle. When the blocks arrived back in the design studio, they were cut and sculpted to fit the pattern pieces coinciding with each panel of the gown body. The embroidery was positioned vertically through the center of each panel shaped like an elongated isosceles trapezoid. The two embroidery blocks were alternated to create a high-low effect.

The pattern for the gown was developed by flat pattern and drafting. A fitted muslin was completed before we decided on the placement of the vertical seams. We divided the circumference of the gown equally and penciled precise lines onto the muslin, giving a proportionate representation of the finished product. We transferred the lines to the paper pattern and developed the sixteen vertical panels for the body. The tulle bodice was created by draping on the mannequin. Once the appropriate look was achieved three-dimensionally, the tulle was marked and made into a paper pattern.

Sewing with fabric as delicate as tulle requires special handling. Strips of tissue paper were used as under paper when machine stitching. The tissue prevents the tulle from getting caught in the machine or from puckering under the presser foot. The seam allowance was also marked on the tissue for extreme accuracy. Seam allowance accuracy is crucial to a fitted garment with multiple seams. The smallest seam allowance variance over sixteen seams can yield a garment circumference being off by a few inches.

The assembled beaded tulle panels float over a duchess satin princess-seamed gown. Metallic bands encircle the hem and outline the empire waist. Silver lamé

CLOCKWISE:
Beading approval sample from India (SP)
Assembling tulle panels with tissue stays (CP)
Marking vertical seams on muslin (BB)
Alternating heights of beaded godets (JC)
Sheer embroidery base (SP)

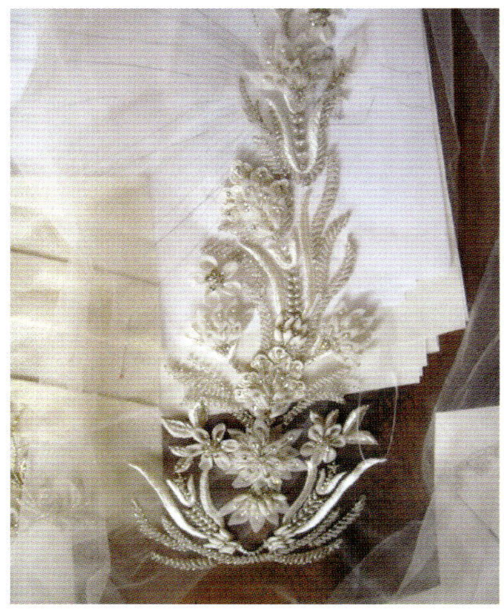

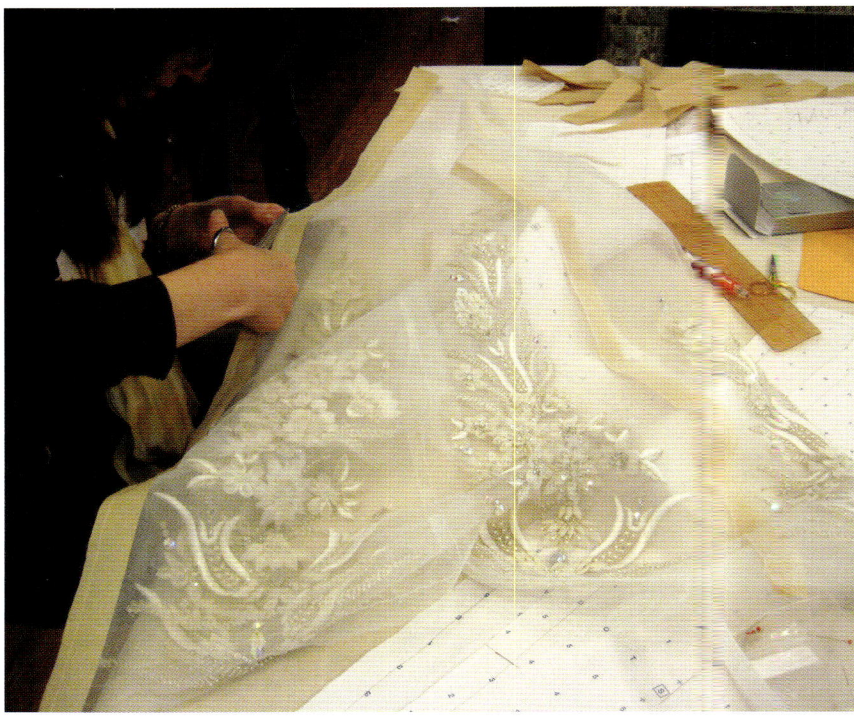

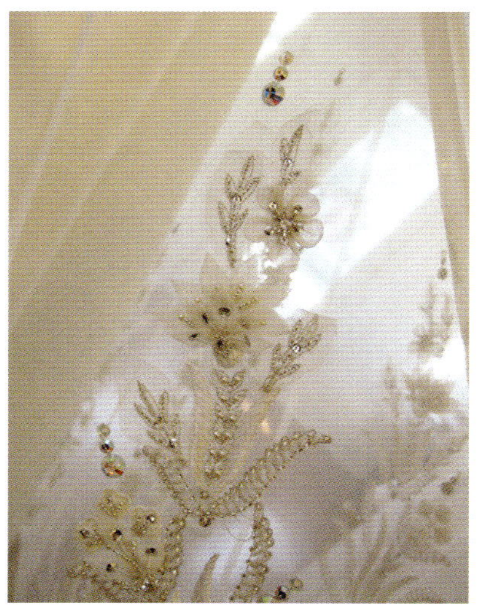

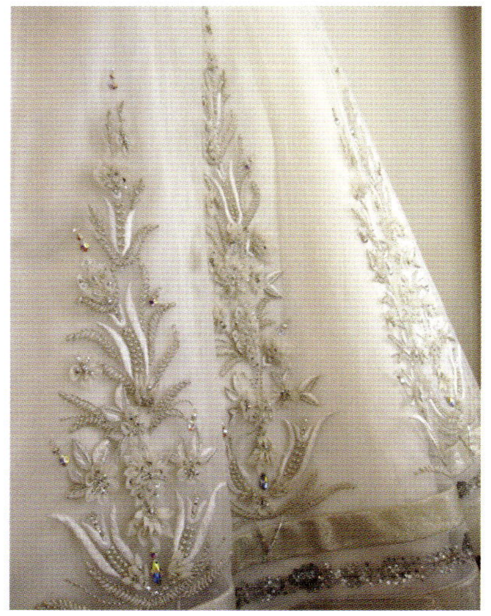

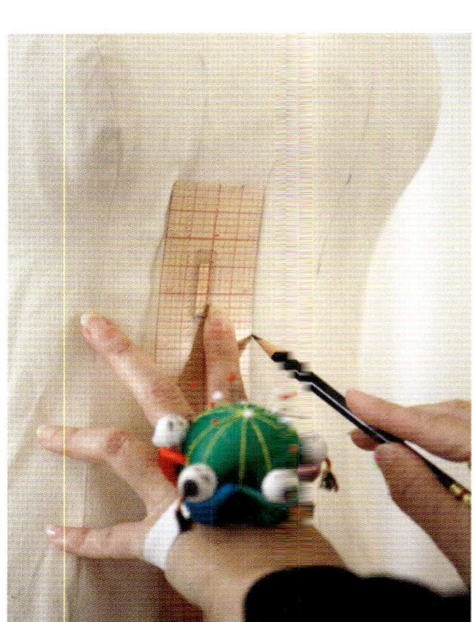

OPPOSITE PAGE:
Side view (JC)

was veiled with gold mesh to blend with the antique silver of the organization's mantle. Swarovski crystal lochrosens and navettes hand appliquéd in the design studio add shimmer. Bugle bead fringe finished with faceted crystal drops finish the empire line and hem with added sparkle.

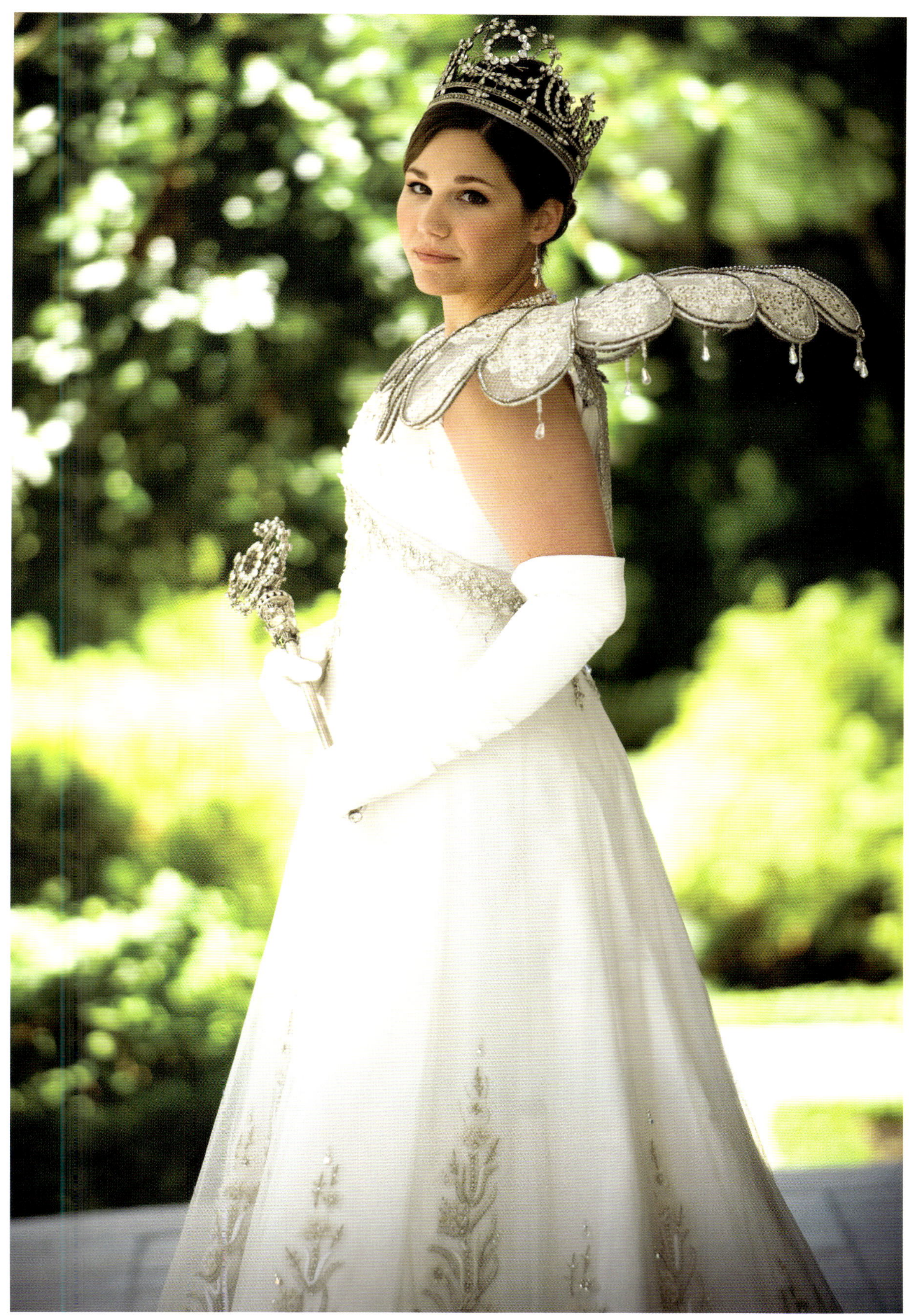

JACKYE, OLYMPIANS QUEEN

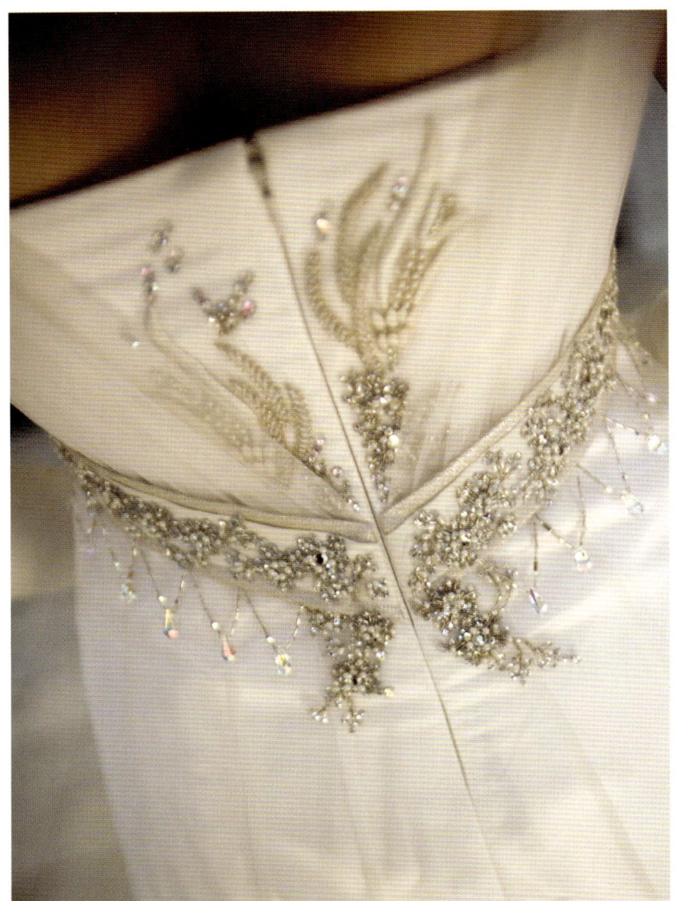

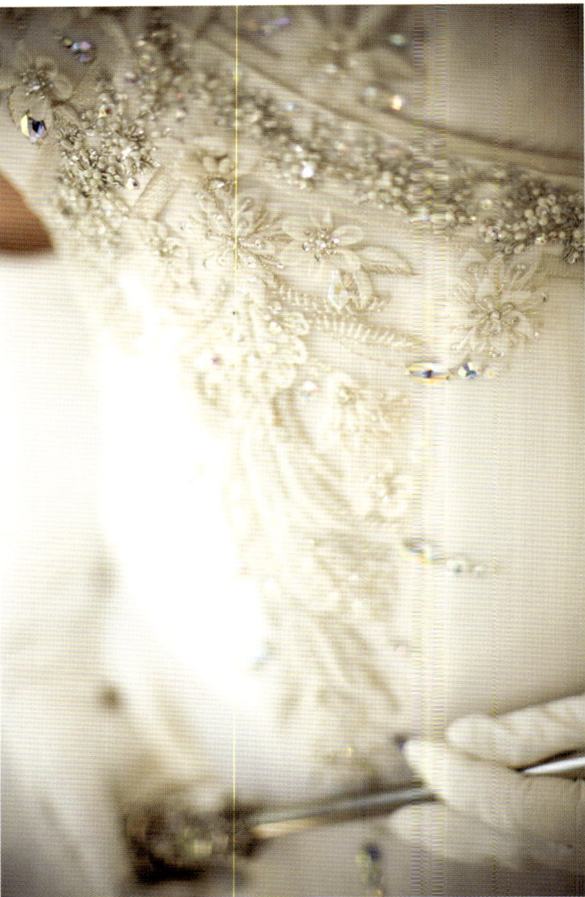

Back appliqué and tulle shoulder drape (JC)
Decorative empire band (JC)
Front beadwork (JC)

OPPOSITE PAGE:
Full-length silhouette (JC)

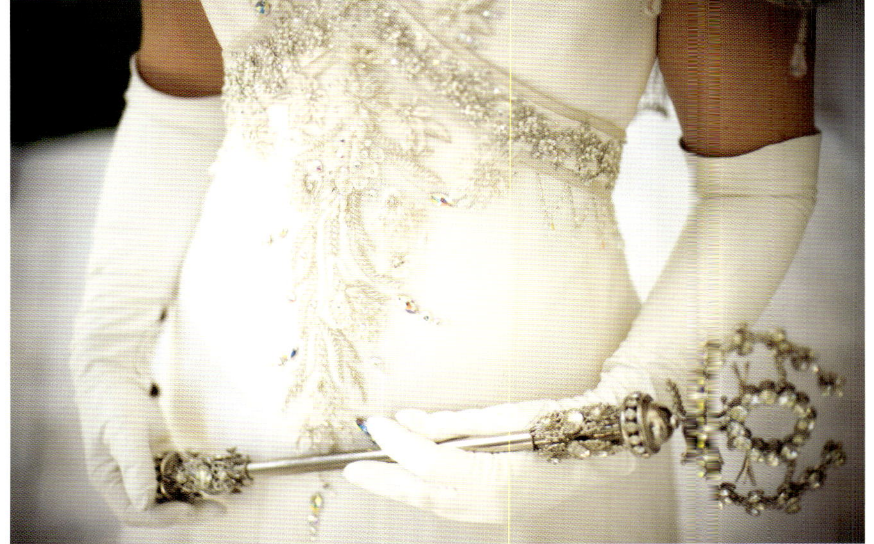

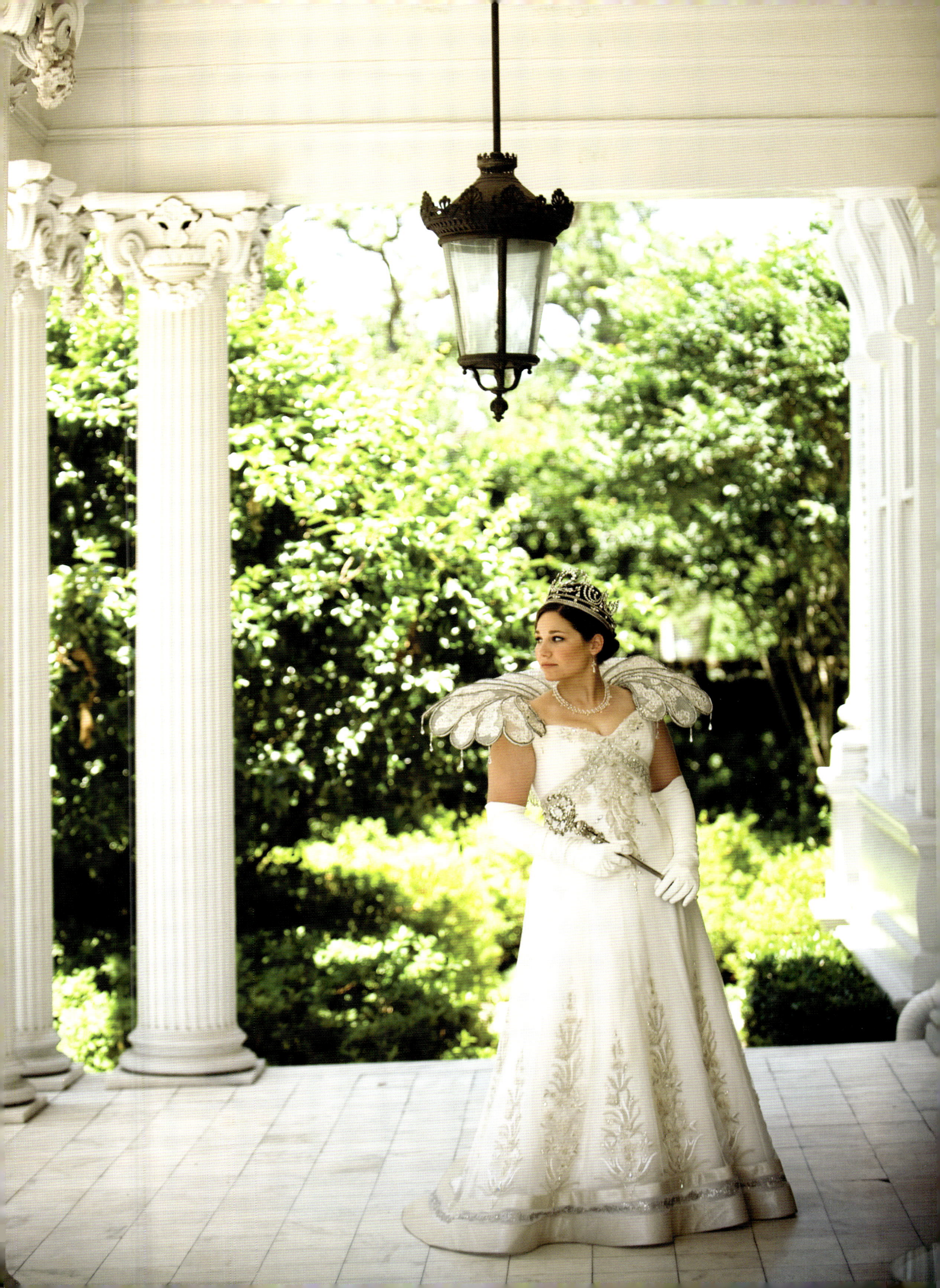

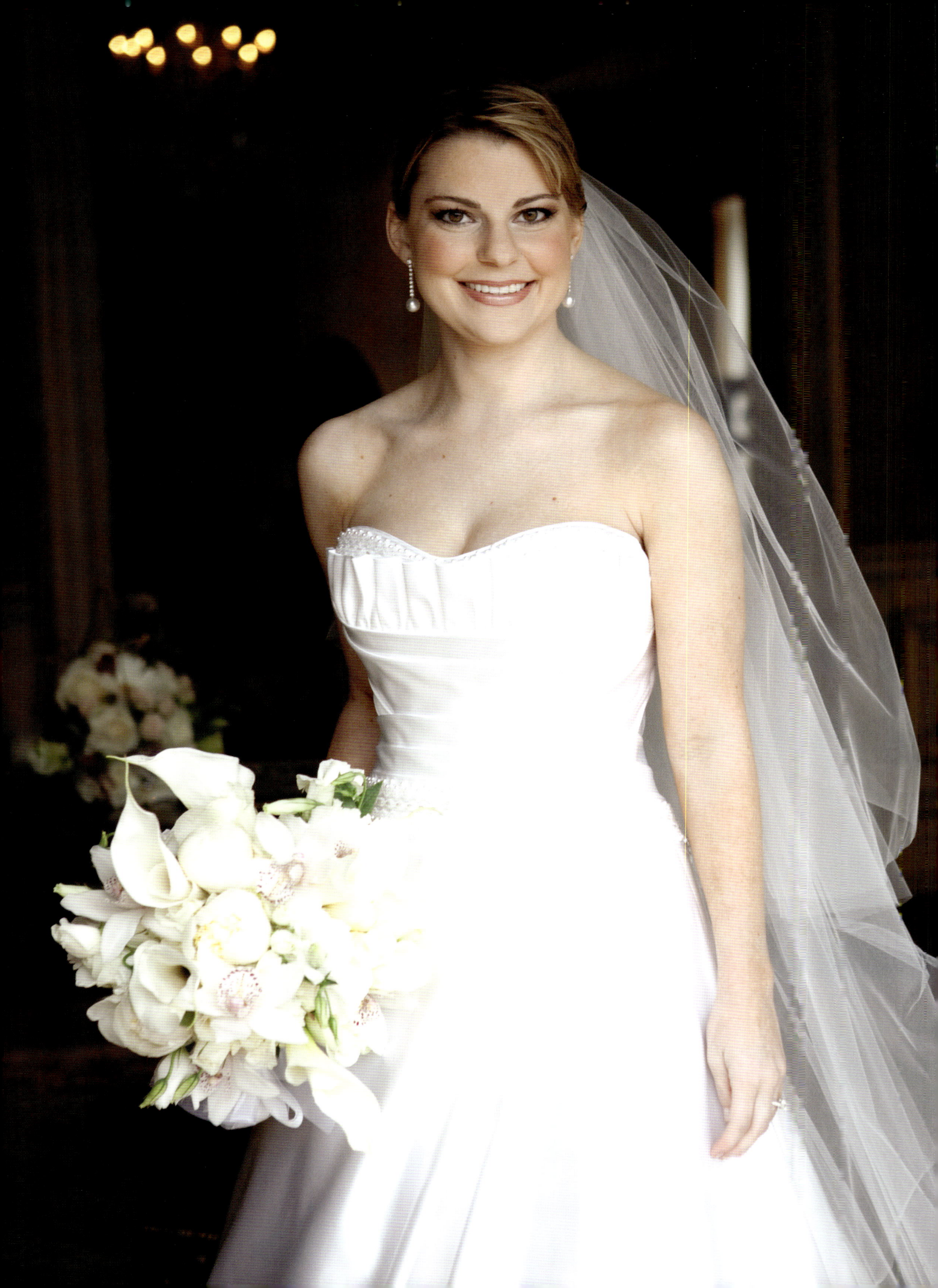

Shelley, Bride

Shelley envisioned a gown of luxurious white satin adorned with subtle touches of pearls and beadwork. Her preference for a strapless ball gown with a full A-line skirt provided ideal parameters in which to work. Her coloring was most enhanced with white, not ivory. Her narrow waist was easily accentuated through draping. Her décolletage was beautifully accented by the curves of a sweetheart neckline.

The formality of Shelley's wedding attire was dictated by both the grandness of location and the time of day. The Saturday evening ceremony was held at the Holy Name of Jesus Church on St. Charles Avenue. This neo-Gothic work of art claims the longest aisle in all of New Orleans. Its glistening marble floor, soaring stained glass windows, and vaulted ceilings resplendent with mosaics create a dramatic atmosphere. The grandeur of the event continued with a reception in the Ritz-Carlton Ballroom.

This gown concept did not come to life through paper and pencil. The concept was first realized through fabric draped, manipulated, and pinned on the mannequin. What is sketched on paper does not always translate into fabric, or to the body shape and form. Fabric must lead the design. Sketching is flat, whereas fabric draping is dimensional and full of life and movement. Draping is most successful when you follow what the fabric wants to do naturally. Working with a light hand and never forcing the fabric yield the most satisfying and artful results.

Figure-flattering lines and proportions were achieved in this gown through sculpting the fabric to mold and wrap the body. When building the final product in the luxurious silk satin, we shaped and hand appliquéd each band around the body, eliminating bodice side seams. The front folds continue around the side seam and fall gracefully into a dropped V at the back waist. Each layer camouflages the hand stitching of the previous band.

Gathered satin adds another layer of dimension and design interest to the gown. The clean, tailored linear draping is softened with the undulating ruffle detailing. Bias strips of satin were folded and lightly steamed to create a soft rolled edge. Two rows of long stitches along the cut edge, known as shirring stitches, were pulled to gather the fabric. We used steam to shape the ruffles. The bodice ruffle frames the face and brings the eye to the décolletage. The hem ruffle outlines the sweeping train and gently brushes the floor.

Finishing details include pearl trim, satin piping, and covered buttons. Pearls, bugle beads, and iridescent sequins combine in a geometric patterned trim. The

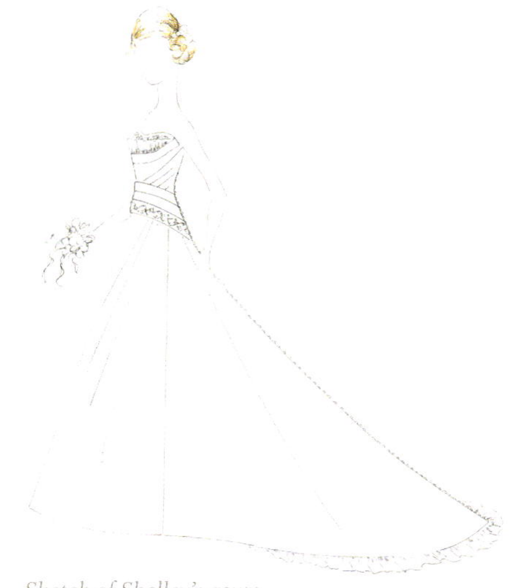

Sketch of Shelley's gown

OPPOSITE PAGE:
Formal bridal portrait (BB)

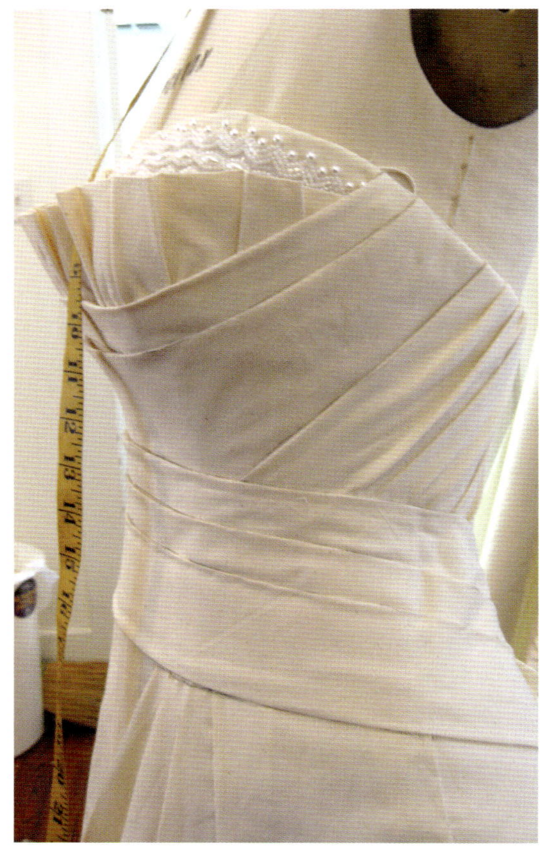

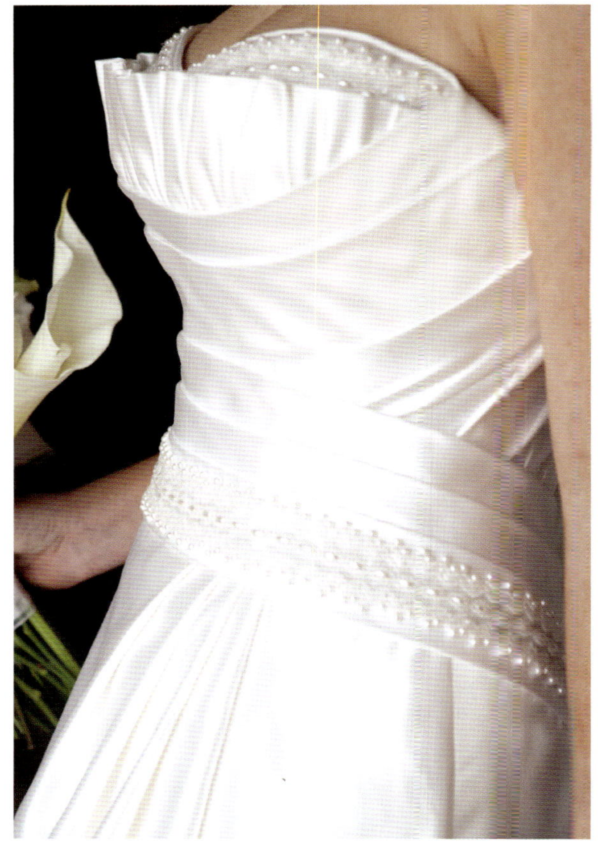

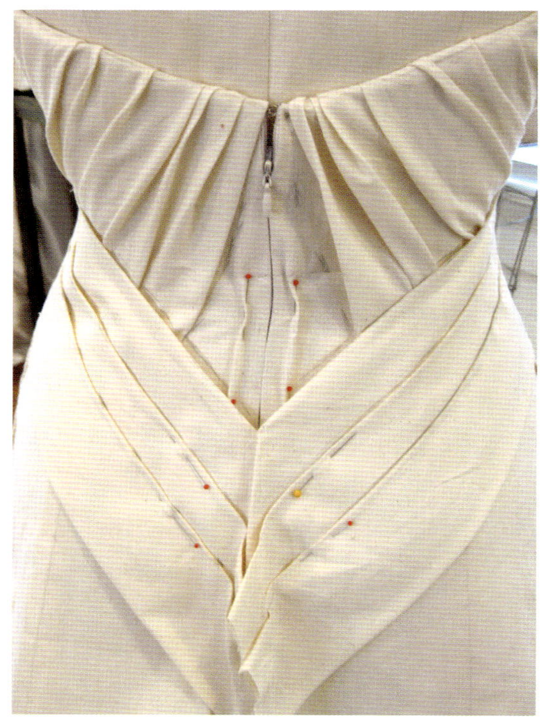

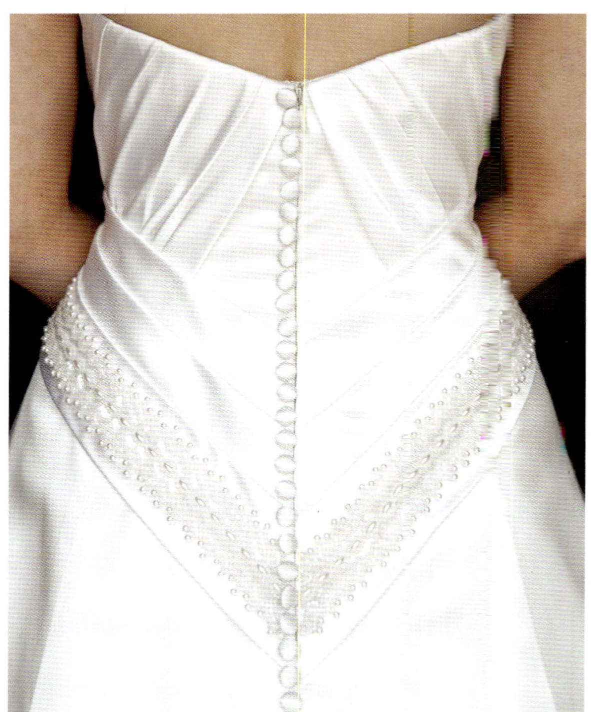

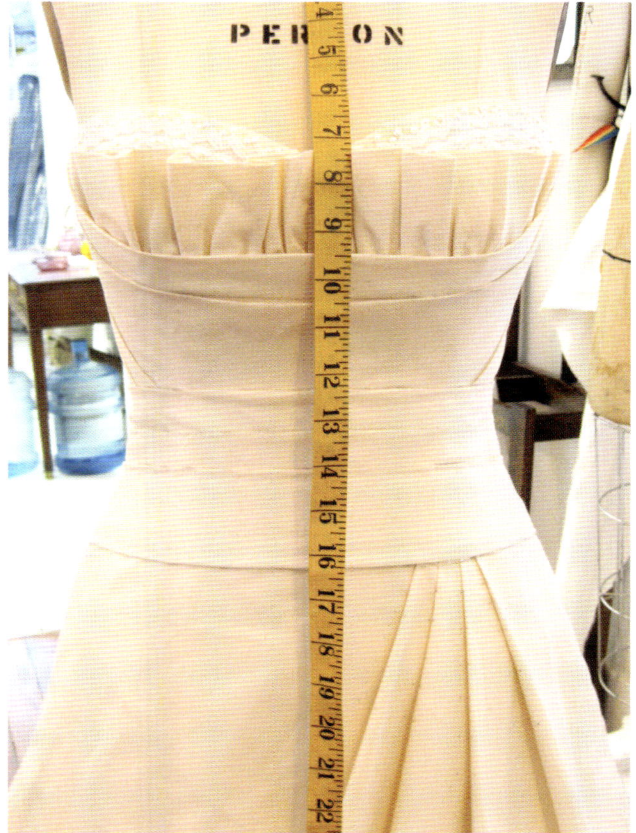

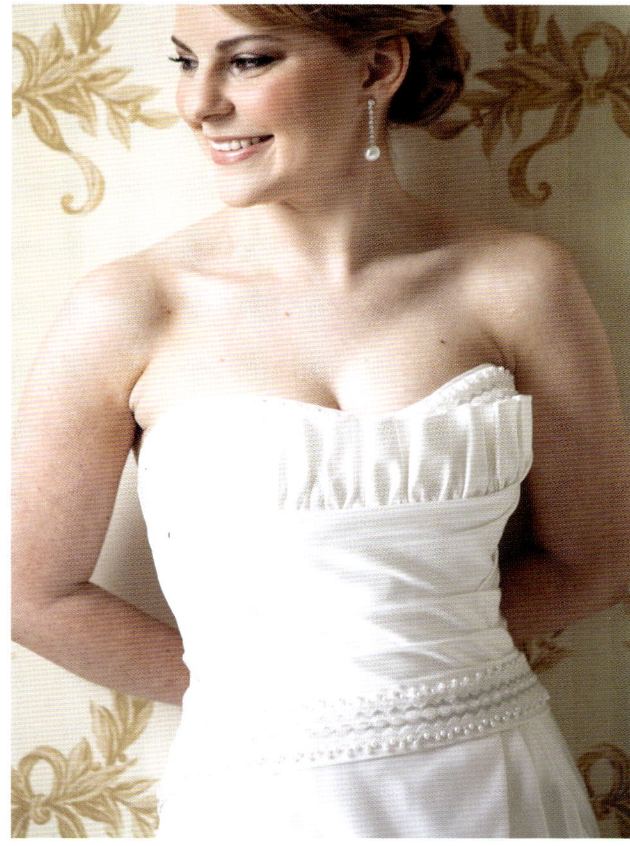

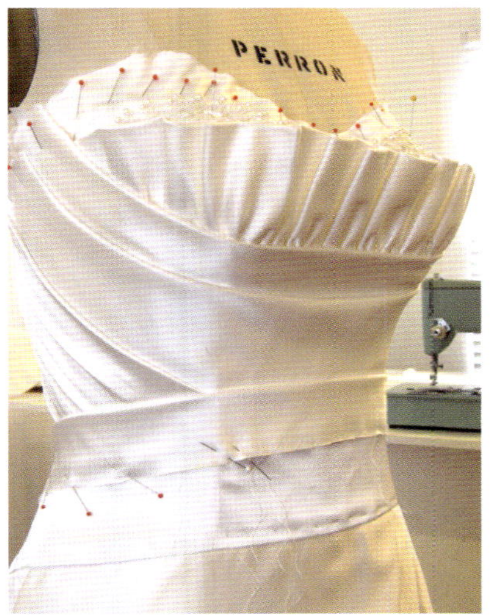

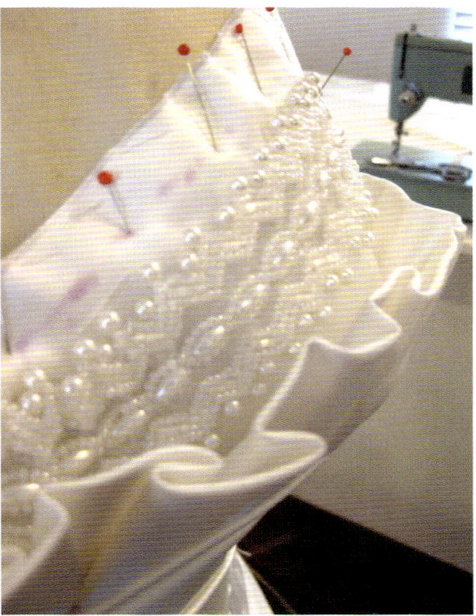

CLOCKWISE:
Front muslin drape (SP)
Finished front (BB)
Shaping crumb catcher trim (SP)
Building midriff in satin (SP)

OPPOSITE PAGE:
Muslin side view (SP)
Finished-gown side view (BB)
Muslin drape of center back (SP)
Finished center back (BB)

trim arcs with the sweetheart neckline and curves with the sculpted waistline. Satin corded piping is visible just beyond the beaded trim, adding definition to the front neckline. Satin-covered buttons follow the center back from bodice to train. A generous illusion cathedral veil with blusher floats over the gown.

Side view with button detail (BB)
Sculpted waistline (BB)

OPPOSITE PAGE:
Full length with ruffle hem detail (BB)

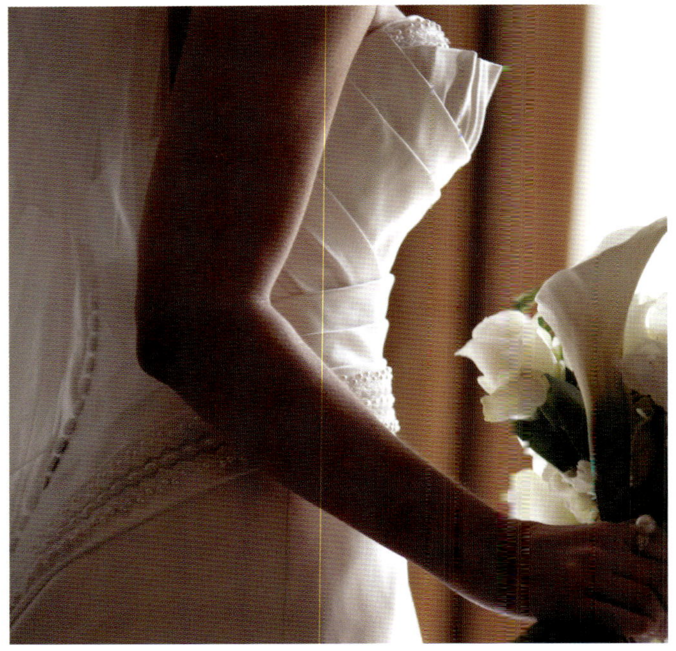

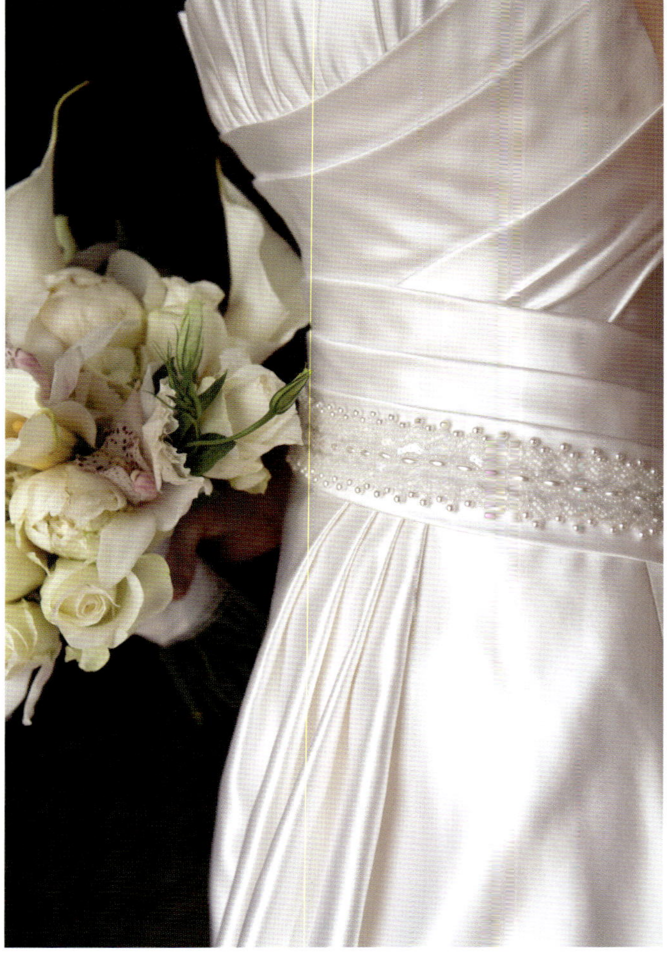

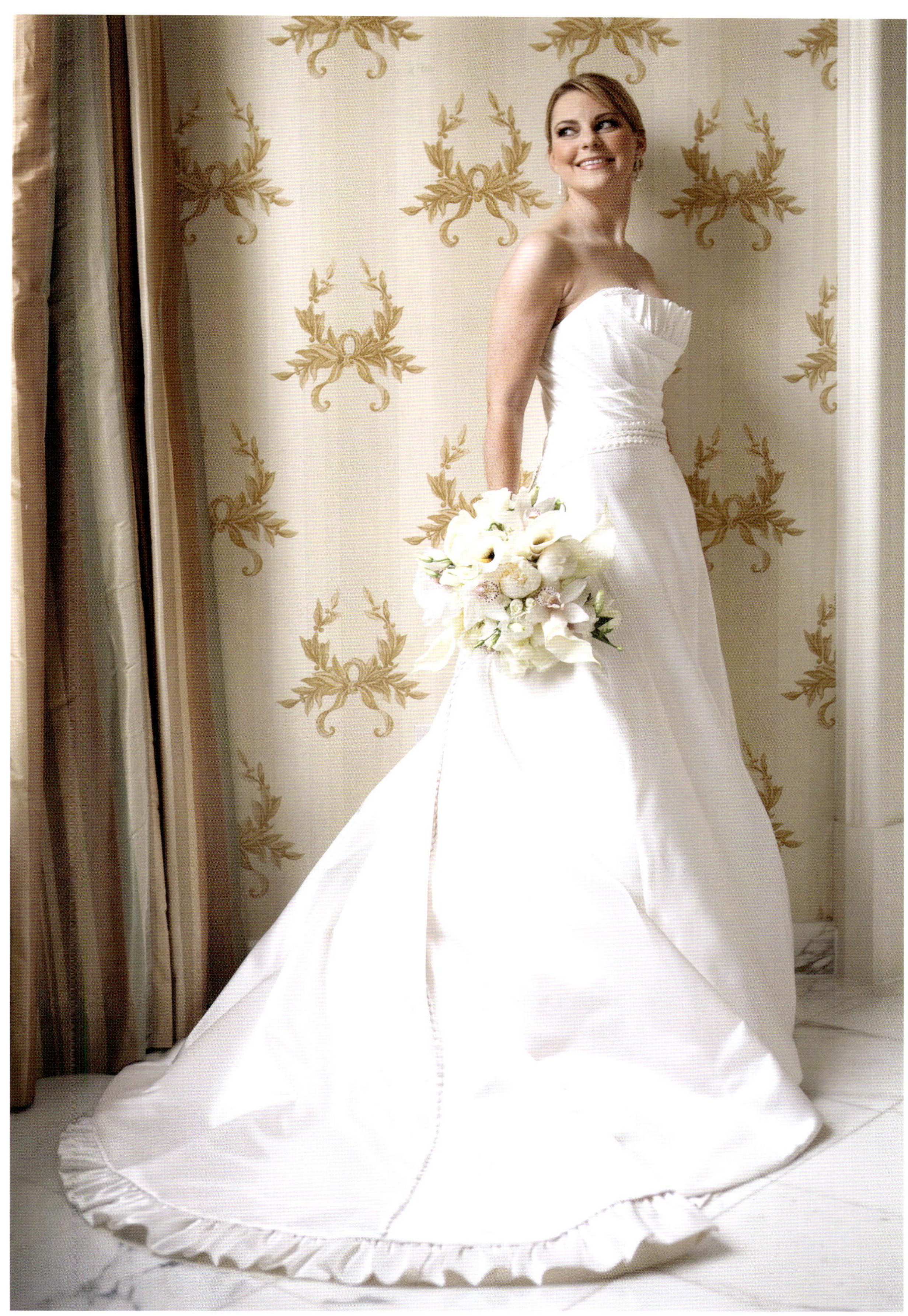

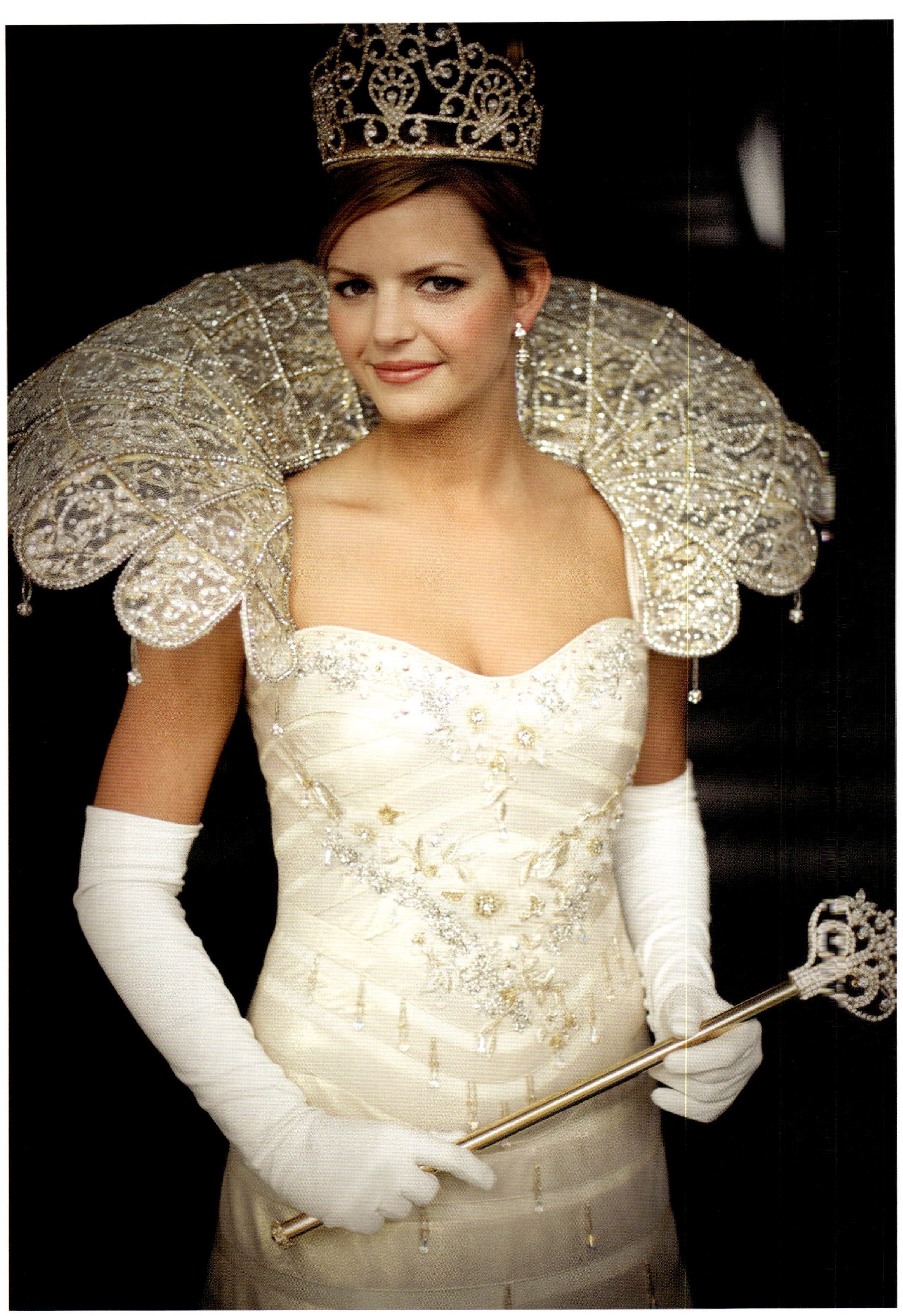

Emily, Athenians Queen

The Krewe of Athenians celebrated its one hundredth anniversary with Emily ruling as queen. The accomplished athlete was transformed from college coed to Mardi Gras royalty in this gown specifically designed for the occasion. The grand tableau staged at the Morial Convention Center was followed by the queen's supper at the New Orleans Country Club. Our creation brings a queen's gown from costume to couture. The color palette was chosen to coordinate with the organization's traditional gold mantle and collar. Emily's coloring and rich skin tones were easily flattered with warm golden hues. Emily's height provided the ideal frame for horizontal banding and a sculpted bodice.

The bias banding is the most unique feature of this gown. Metallic gold lamé was used to achieve a shimmering, opulent effect. The banding was created by cutting fabric strips on true bias. The true bias is at a forty-five-degree angle from the selvage. The bias of fabric is very malleable, allowing the straight strips of lamé to be molded into arches and curves. To create a band with perfectly parallel folds, we used a cardboard guide to press the folded edge. The cardboard was cut to the desired finished width. A different cardboard guide was cut to each band. The fabric was wrapped around the cardboard and pressed. The parallel bands were curved to the desired shape with a steam iron. The paper pattern for the gown provided the template for shaping.

The patternmaking of the gown was very intricate. Before using precise measurements to develop the skirt shape and band spacing, we pinned strips of muslin on the muslin prototype. The muslin bands allowed for a rough idea of the most aesthetically pleasing placement on a three-dimensional form with accurate proportions. The carefully drafted pattern was manipulated to sculpt the body without side seams. The goal was to create continuous bands, wrapping the body with perfection. Metallic tulle provided the base for the appliquéd bands. The sheerness of the tulle creates the floating effect of the gold lamé with light passing through the dress. The gown shimmered under the lights as if it were dusted with gold.

A princess-seamed, ivory duchess satin base provides the inside structure, while beading and thread work decorate the outside. Gold and silver leaf embroidery intertwines with sequins, pearls, and beads. Flowers of tulle and crystals add dimension. Petals of organza radiate from glistening centers. Light reflection was magnified by adding dozens of hand-sewn Swarovski crystal novettes and aurora borealis lochrosens. Fringes of bugle beads tipped with crystal-faceted drops circle the hem and add movement to the gown.

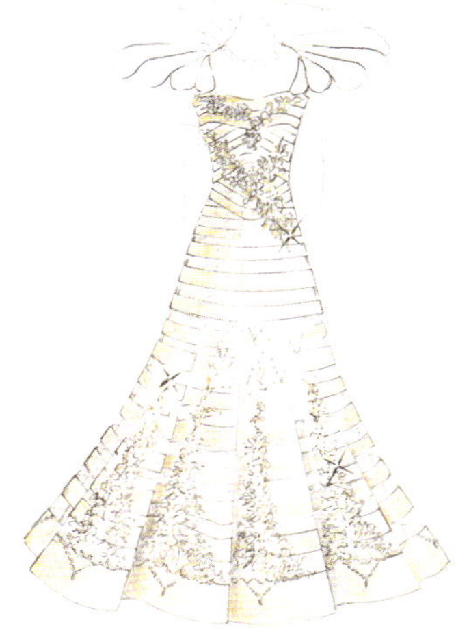

Sketch of Emily's gown

OPPOSITE PAGE:
Queen's portrait (JC)

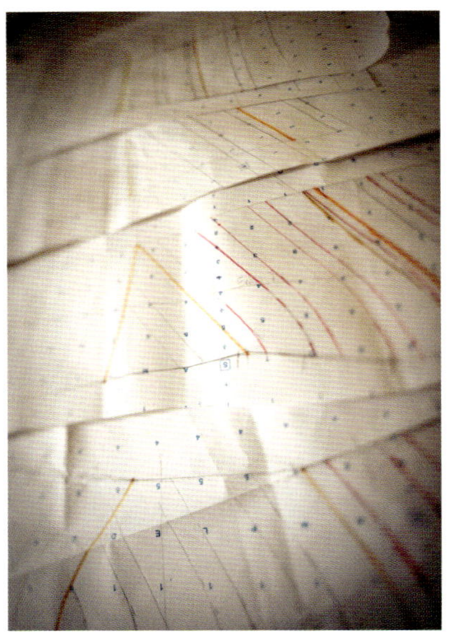
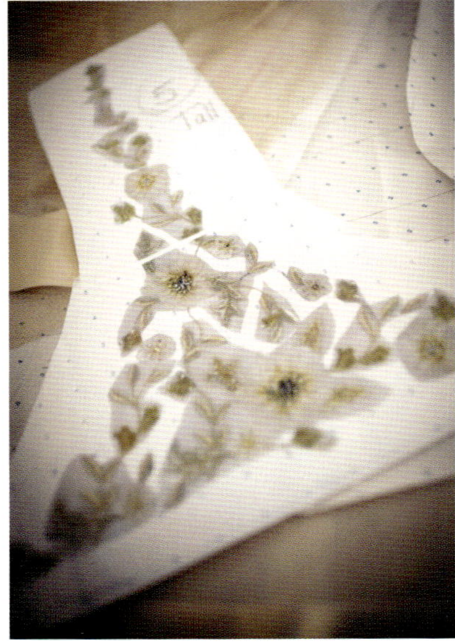
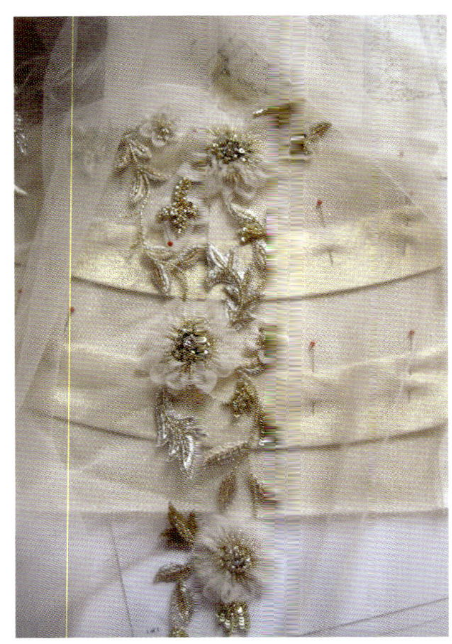
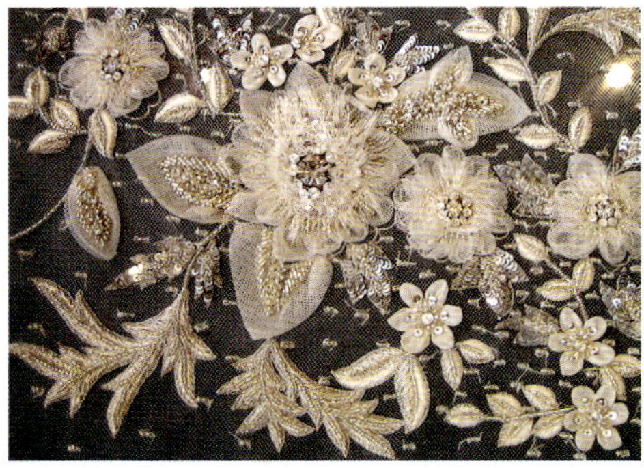

CLOCKWISE:
Drafting patterns for bias placement (JC)
Beading layout (JC)
Approval sample from India (SP)
Sketch come to life (JC)
Developmental beading swatch (SP)

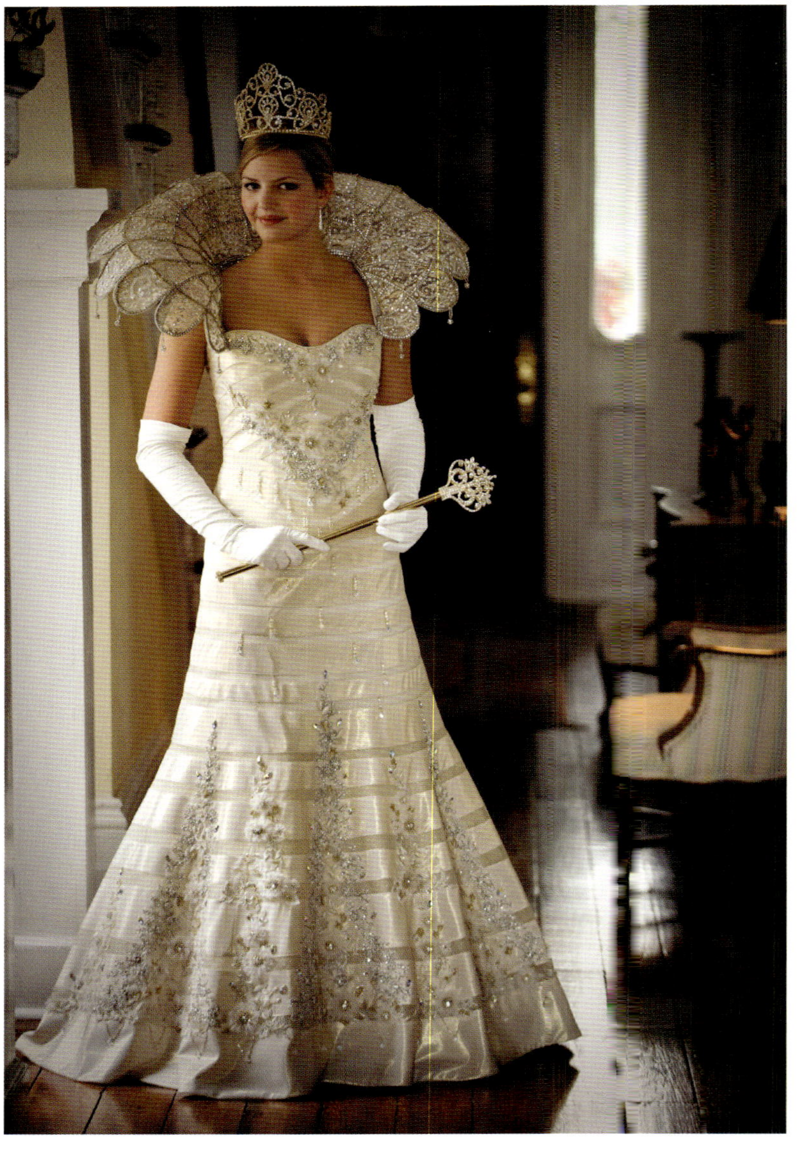

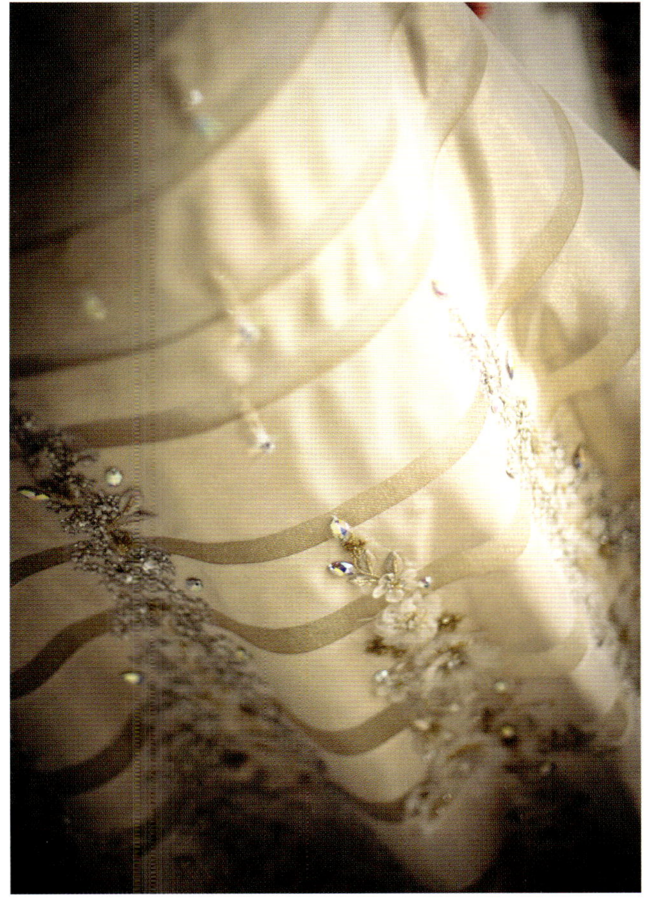

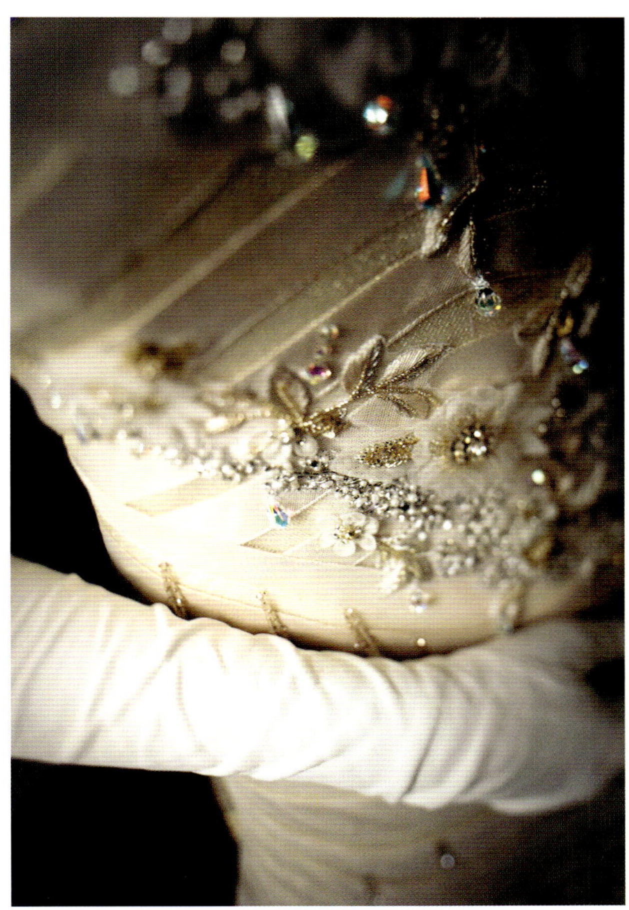

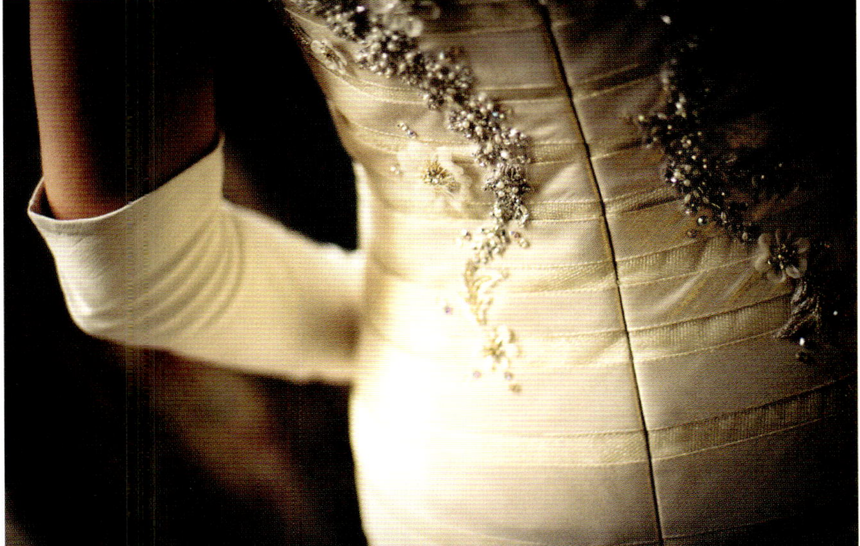

Skirt banding (JC)
Bias sculpted midriff (JC)
Back detailing (JC)

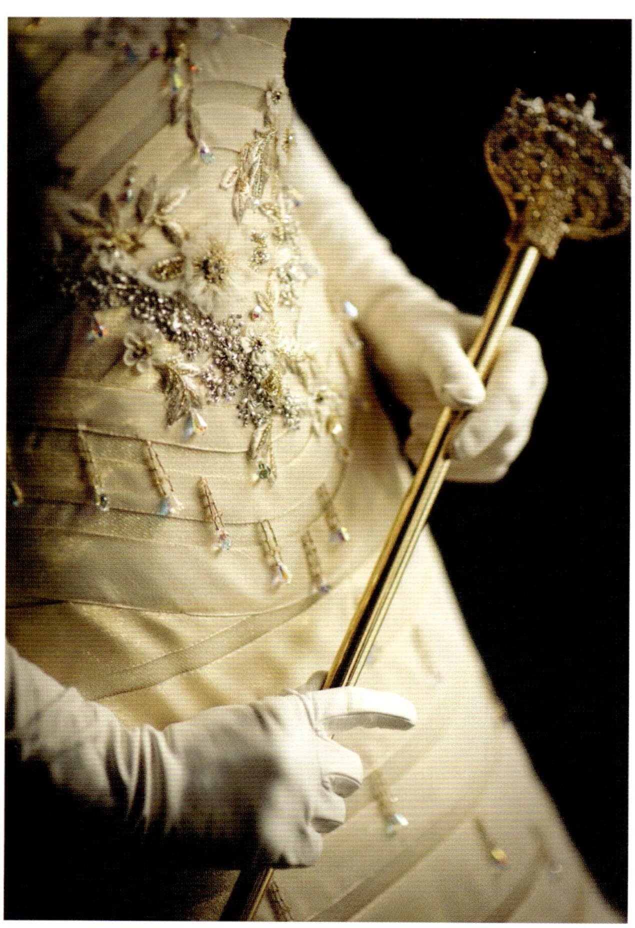

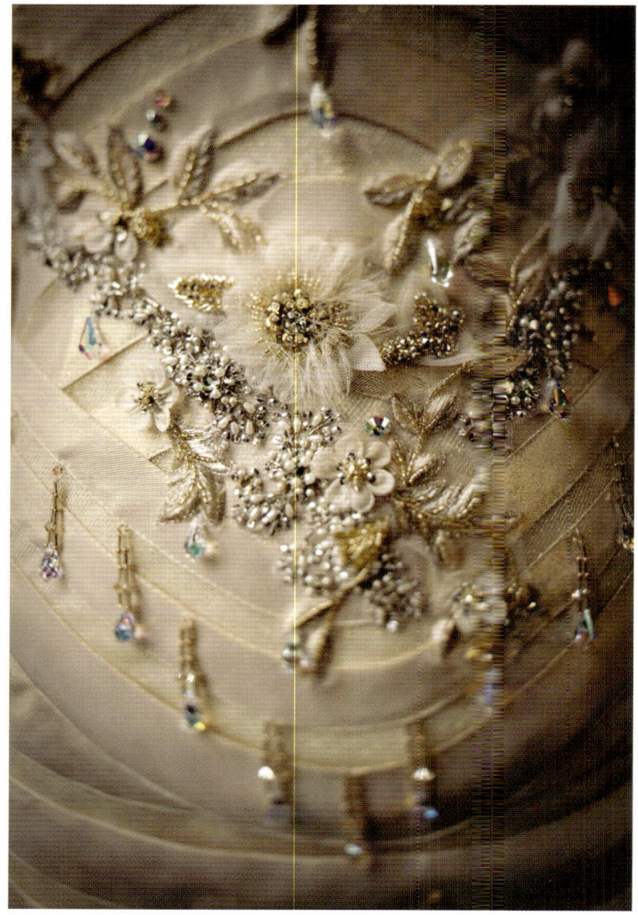

Waist defined with bias, beading, and crystal drops (JC)
Arcs appliquéd with embroidery (JC)

OPPOSITE PAGE:
Light through tulle highlighting bandwork (JC)

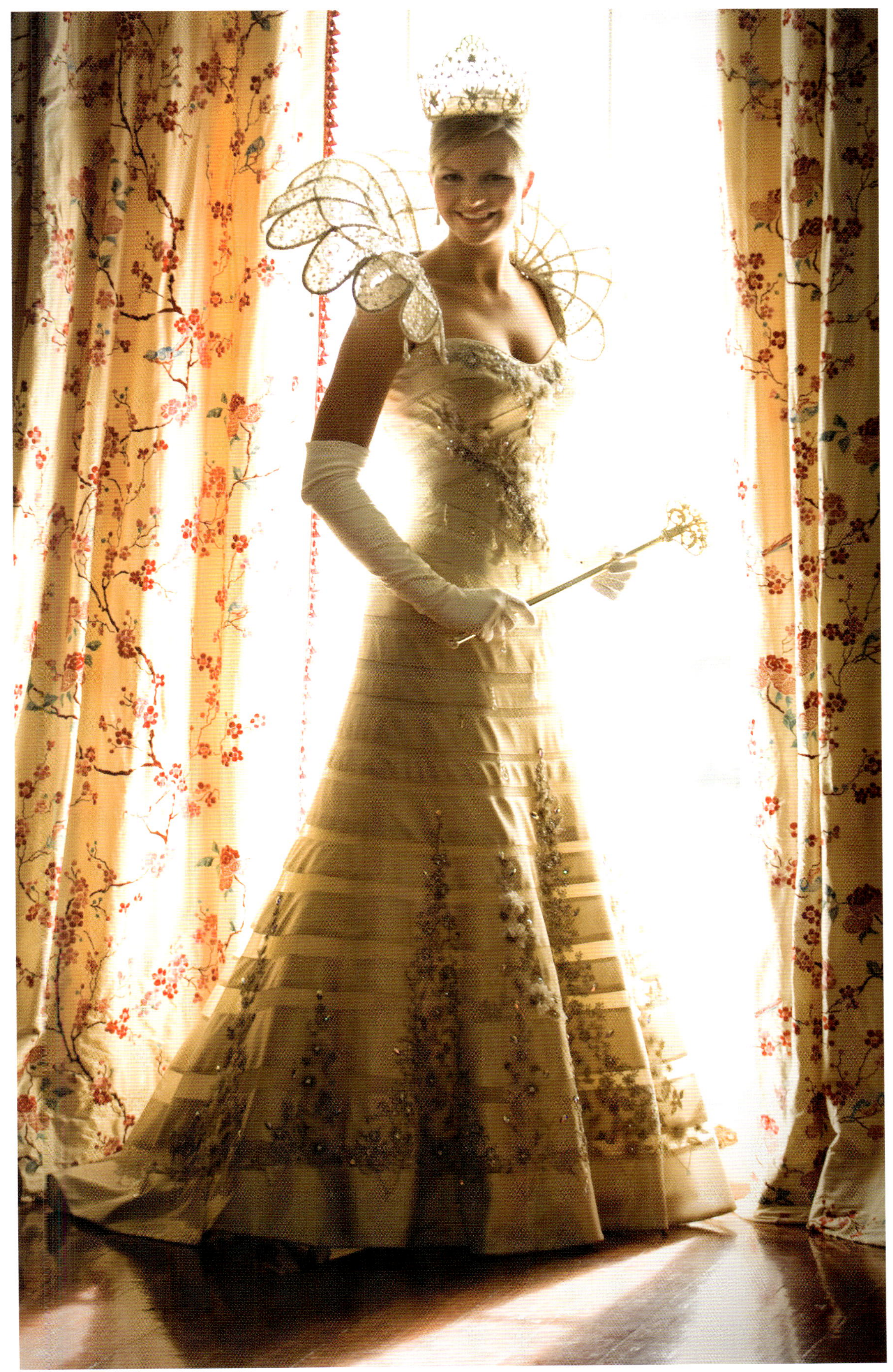

EMILY, ATHENIANS QUEEN

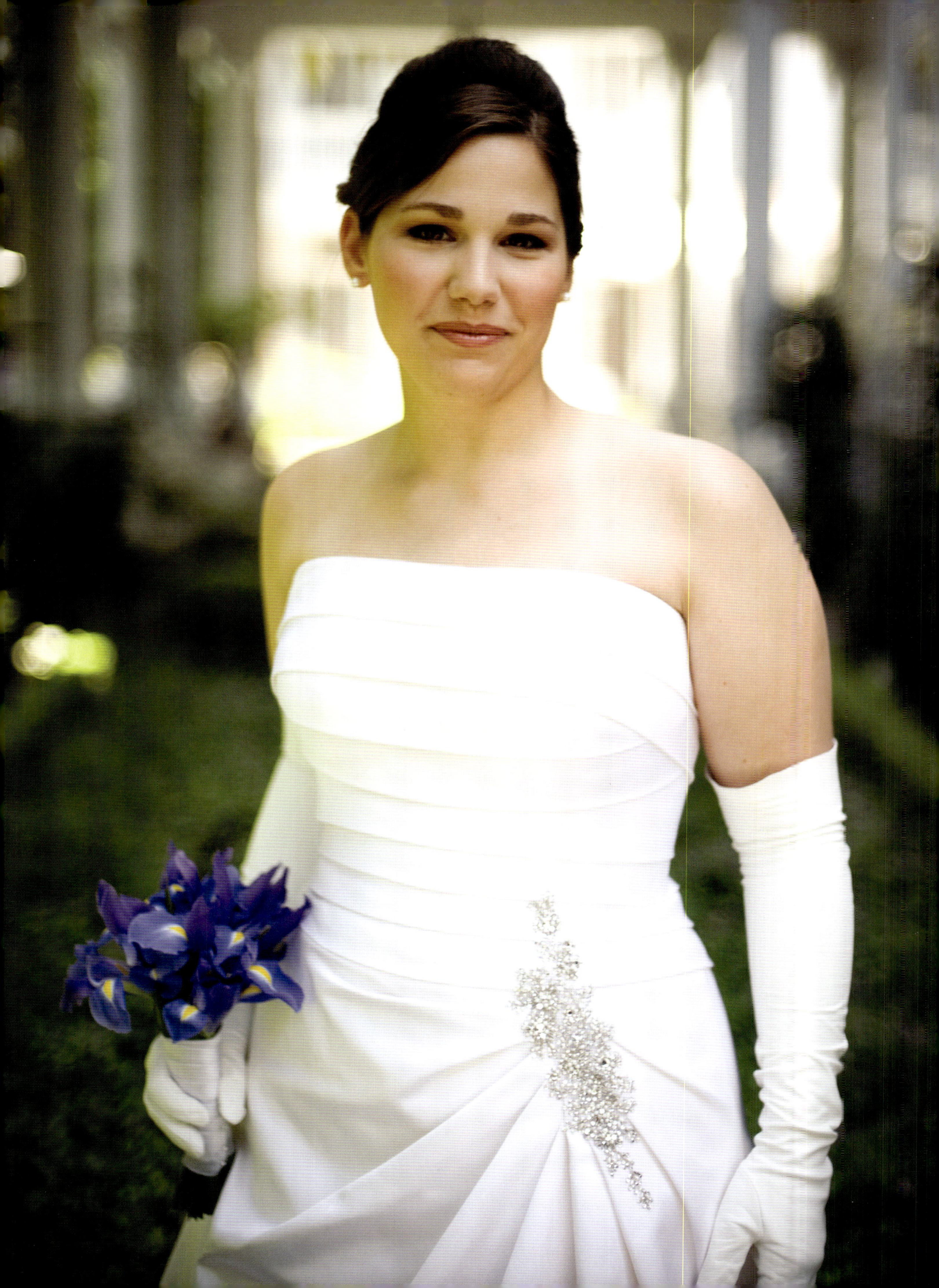

Jackye, Achaeans Maid

During her debut season, a New Orleans debutante may need an extensive wardrobe of white gowns. She may field a myriad of invitations, yielding a full calendar of presentations and royal reigns. It is not unusual for a client to turn to me for two or more gowns for one debutante season, as Jackye did.

Following her reign as Queen of Olympians, Jackye was presented as a maid in the Krewe of Achaeans. This krewe dates back to 1947 and presents a traditional Mardi Gras court of maids, queen, and king. The maids wear white ball gowns similar to that of the debutante. Full skirts are necessary for the appropriate look on the ballroom floor and allow for the traditional deep curtsey.

Jackye's preference was for a draped bodice and full A-line skirt. Jackye's personality was captured in a clean, tailored gown. The strapless hourglass silhouette flattered her shape. A rich double-face satin lent the formality necessary for the occasion.

The concept was initially sketched and then further developed through muslin draping. We developed the foundation and the gown silhouette through drafting with flat pattern methods. The foundation was meticulously drafted to Jackye's measurements. The constructed foundation and gown base served as a perfectly shaped and proportioned blank canvas on which to drape. We manipulated and sculpted large blocks of muslin in various ways until the right three-dimensional shape emerged from what was a one-dimensional block of muslin. Linear, geometric folds of muslin eventually sculpted to the bodice in horizontal rhythm. The draping continues into the skirt in a radiating pattern as deep folds repeat to the floor. The vertical folds of the skirt muslin were draped to elongate the grand ball skirt. The bodice draping wraps around the torso without the need for side seams, falling to a V below the back waist. The muslin of the skirt back was draped in an inverted V pattern of folds extending into the train.

The gown was finished with buttons and beading. Square satin-covered buttons turned on the diagonal create a diamond effect down the center back of the bodice. The beading combines rhinestones, lochrosens, metallic coils, and pearls. The silver beading mimicking encrusted jewels adorns the hip and back train.

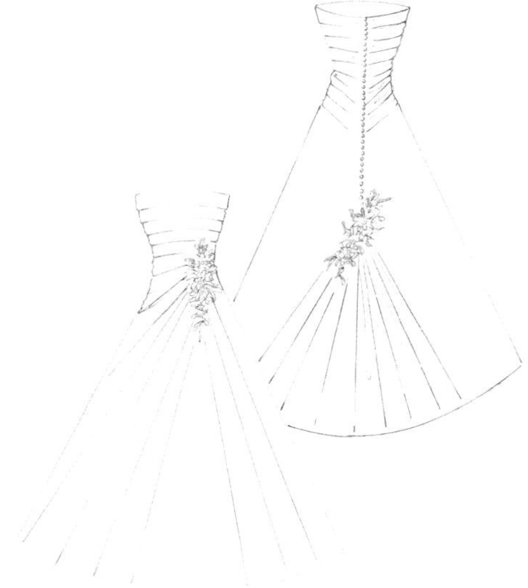

Front and back sketches of Jackye's gown

OPPOSITE PAGE:
Maid's portrait (JC)

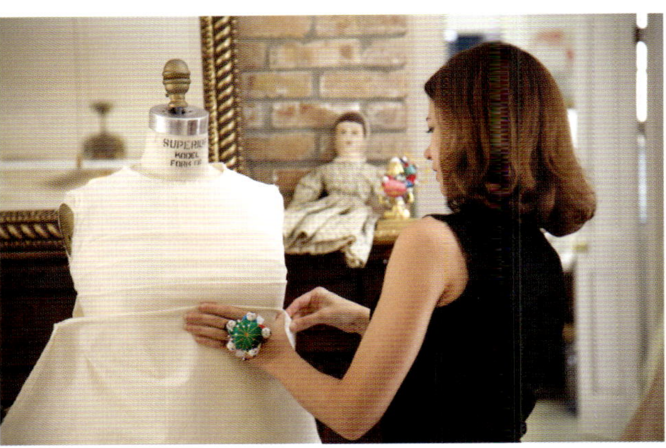

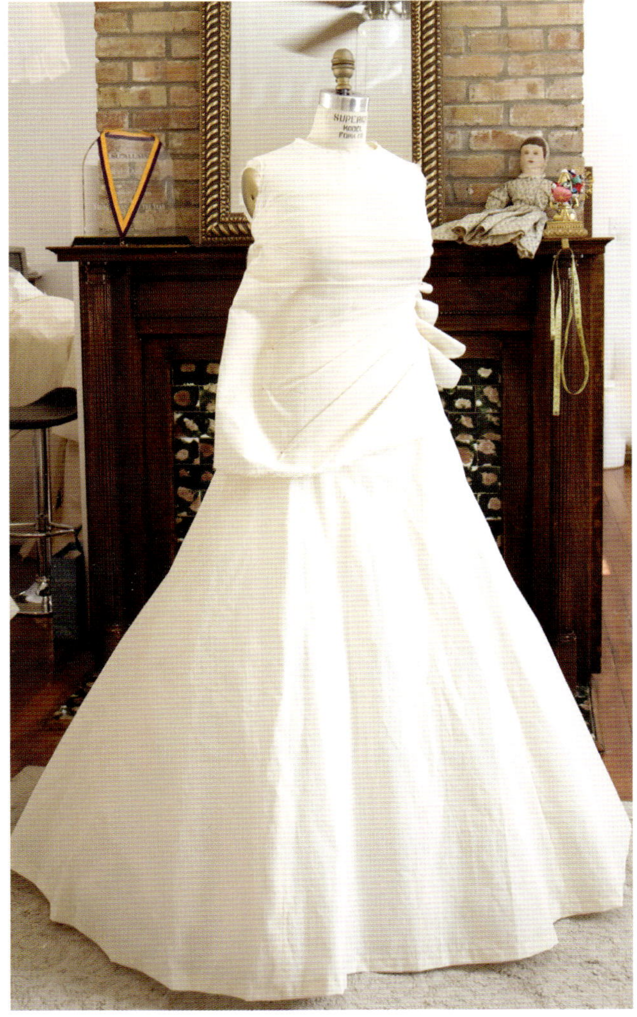

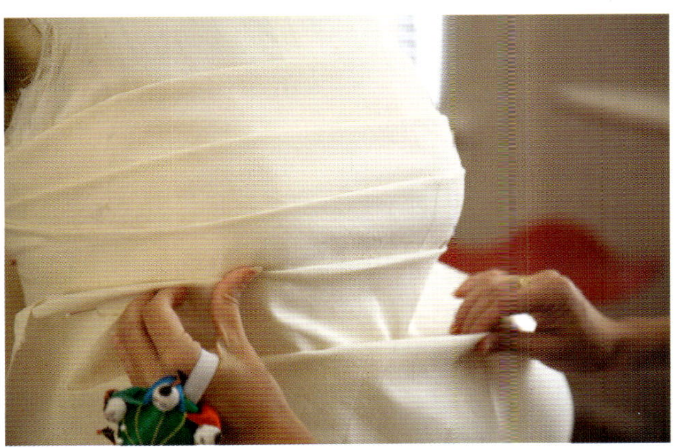

ABOVE:
Draping a muslin block (BB)

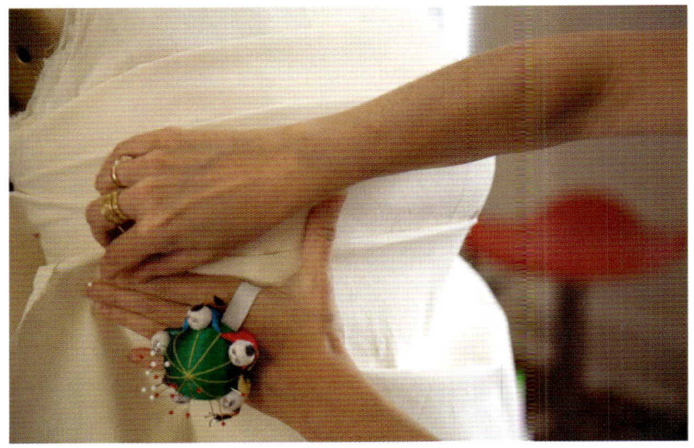

RIGHT:
Draping to shape the bust (BB)

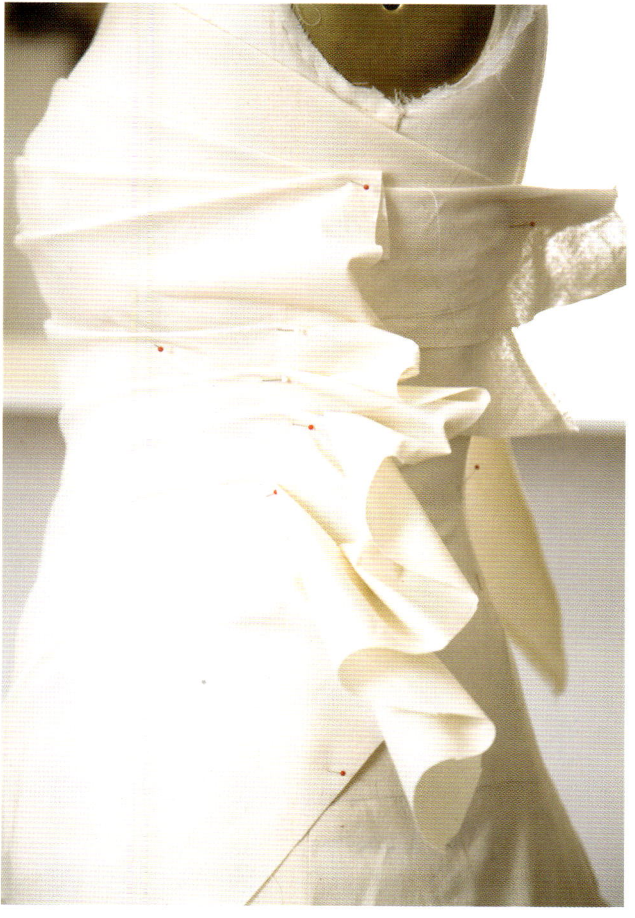

CLOCKWISE:
Sculpting design detail on the mannequin (BB)
Radiating hip detail blending into horizontal bodice draping in muslin (SP)
Skirt back muslin mock-up (SP)

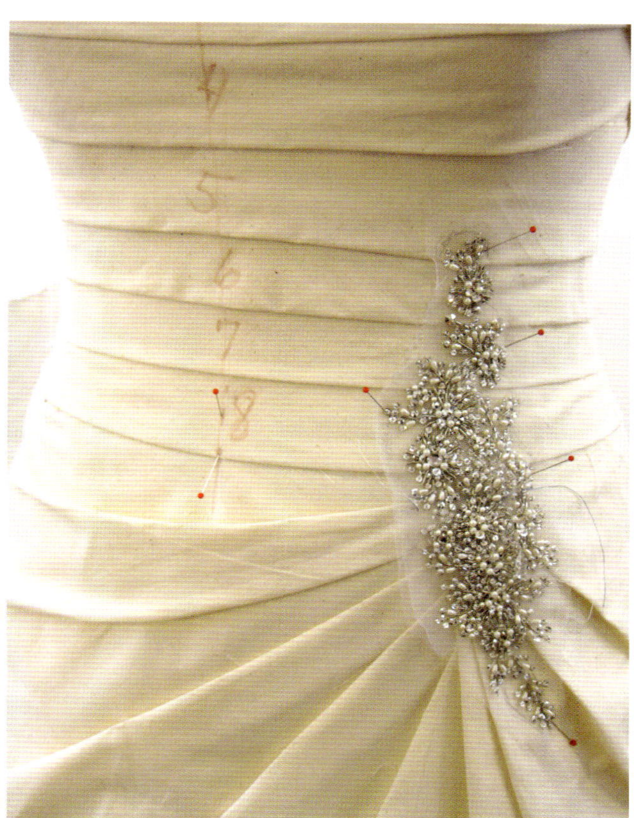

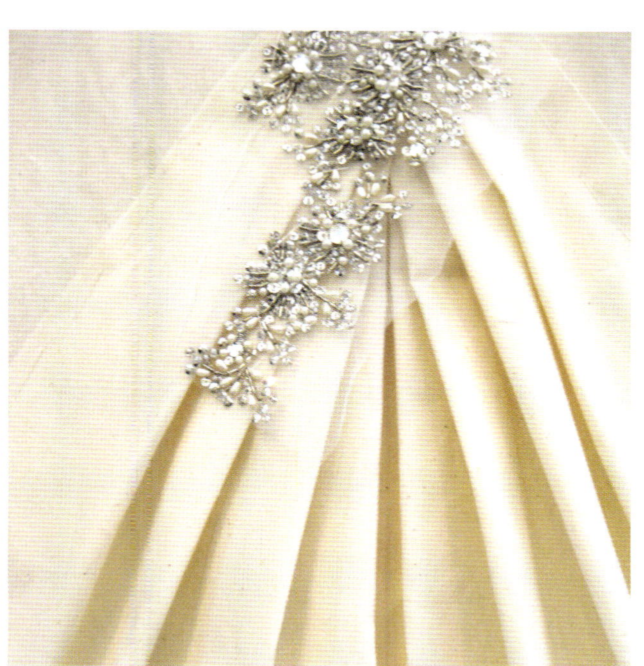

Muslin draping finishing in a back V (SP)

Draping the actual satin around the bodice with side seams eliminated (SP)

Diagonal buttons (JC)

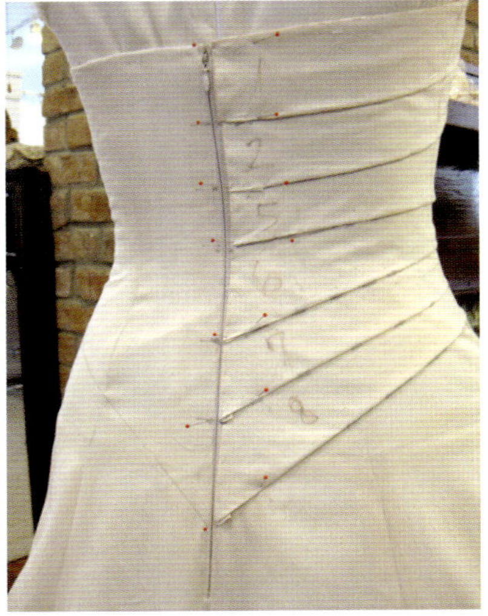

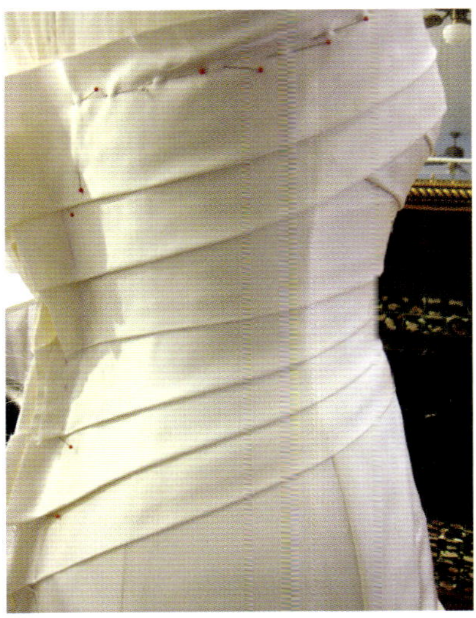

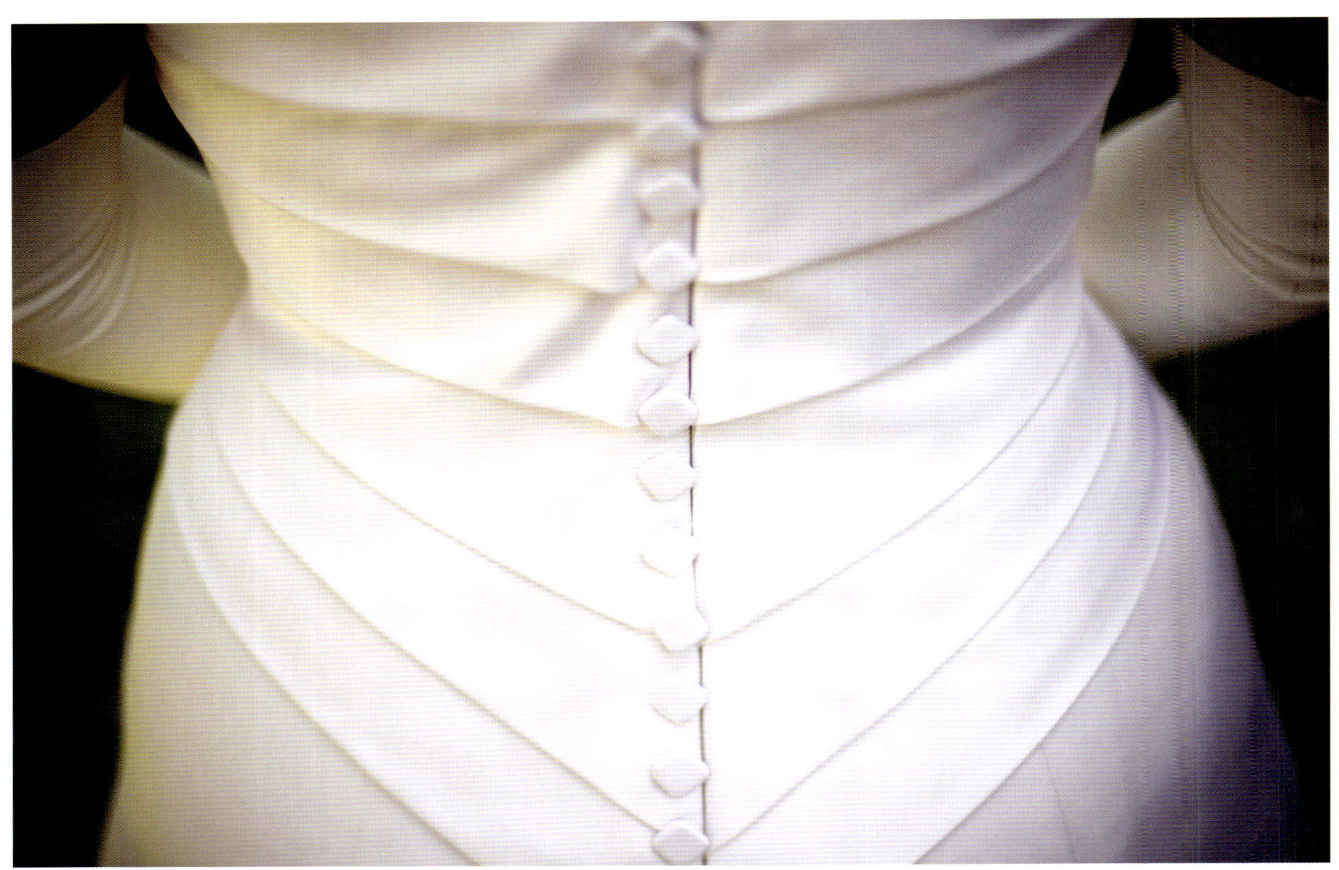

OPPOSITE PAGE:
Finished hip detailing (_C)

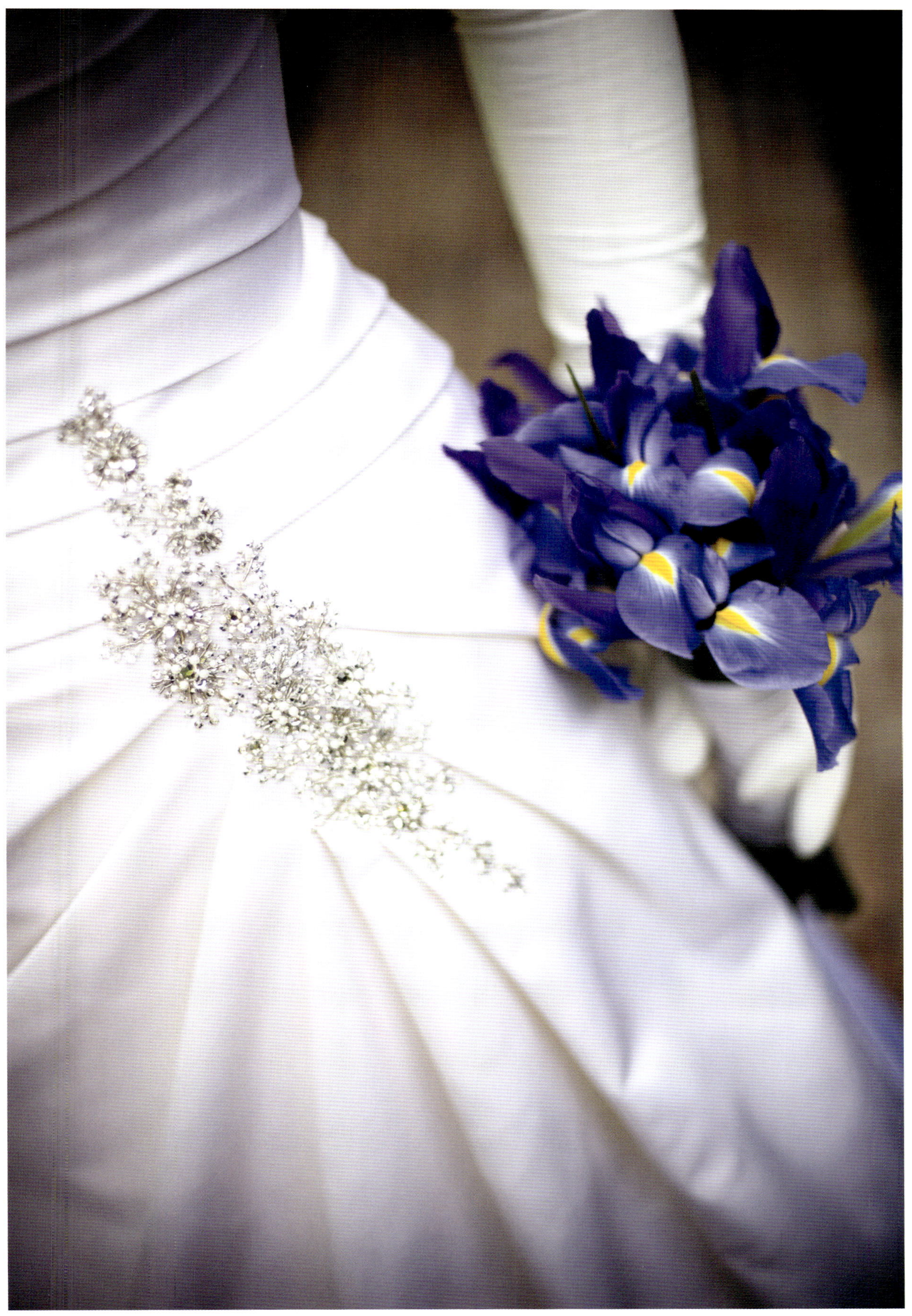

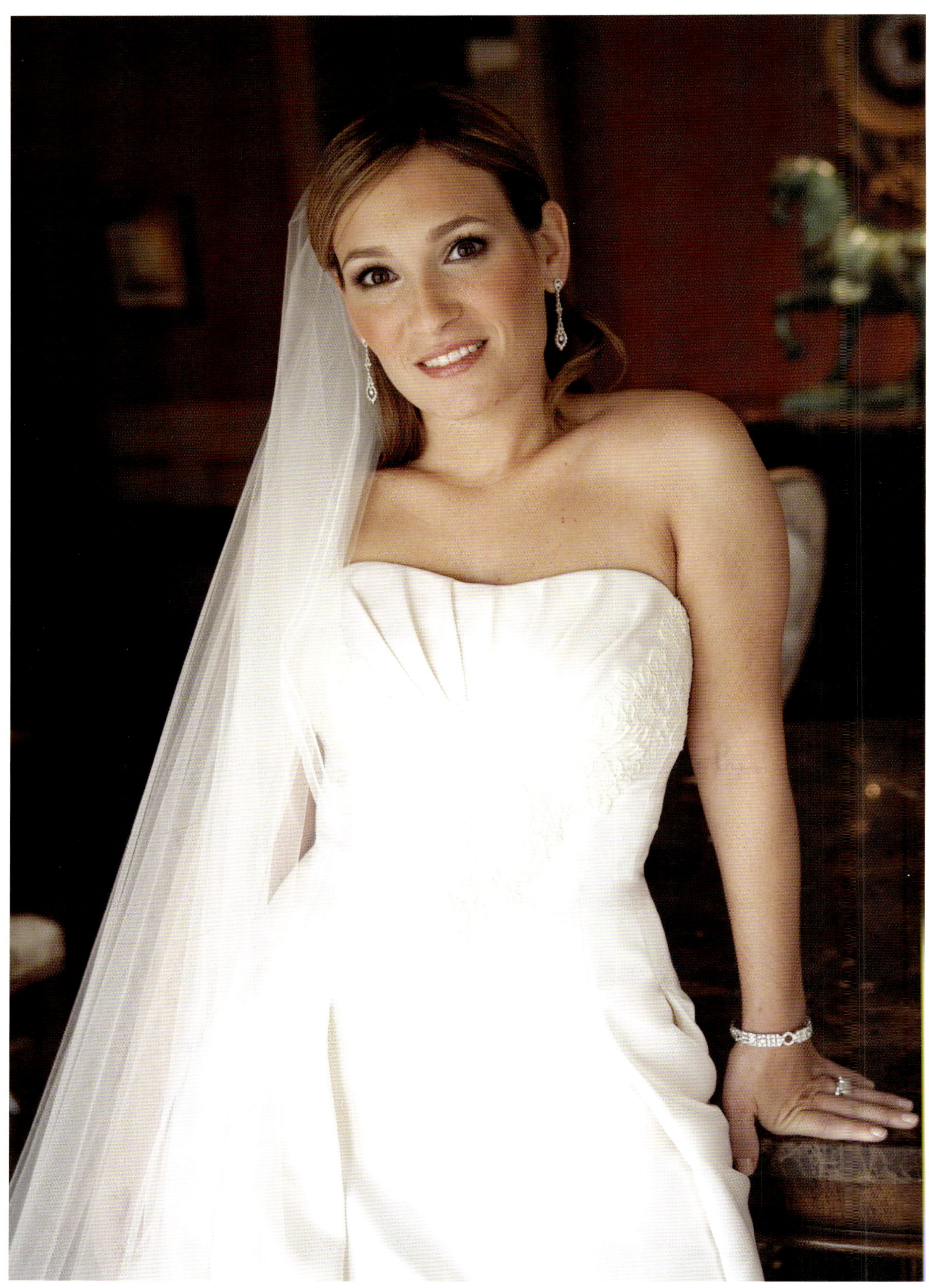

Lauren, Bride

Laurens wedding was a formal white-tie affair. The ambiance of the Grand Ballroom of the Ritz-Carlton and the formality of the traditional Temple Sinai ceremony called for a silhouette of classic opulence. Ivory double-faced satin with a hint of blush provided both the richness and luxuriousness appropriate for the evening October wedding. Ivory re-embroidered Alençon lace added a subtle variance in tonality when layered over the satin. The fabric choices and Lauren's preference for a strapless ball gown guided us in designing a fashionable, yet timeless, opulent silhouette.

Pleats draped in the strapless neckline bring attention to the face and décolletage before blending into the midriff's lace appliqué. Satin pleated banding defines the top of the back bodice. Lace extends from the pleated bands and trails down the center back bodice, elongating the torso. Satin-covered buttons line the entire length of the center back. Five seams shape each side of the bodice before releasing into deep pleats. The fullness from the pleats continues into a generous ball skirt with sweeping train. The deep front inverted pleats frame the center front panel, adorned with appliquéd lace. The hem of the front panel is finished with a continuous row of knife pleating extending beyond the lace. The remainder of the hem is bordered with lace. Shaped knife pleats from the front are repeated, extending beyond the lace at the center back sweep.

The satin pleated trim was created by drafting blocks. The length of the block was calculated by multiplying the front panel width by three. Pleats create three-to-one fullness. The width of the block was calculated by multiplying the desired length of the front pleats by two. Seam allowance was also added. The block was folded in half lengthwise and pressed. The fold of each pleat was marked and pressed into place across the width. The same proportions were applied to create the back hem pleat detailing.

We mended two pieces of lace together to create a beautiful finish to the cathedral-length veil of ivory illusion. A spray of appliquéd lace floats along the center back of the veil. In the appliquéd spray is a hook that allows the veil to be bustled. Organza ribbon extends the length of the veil and delicately frames the face.

"I wanted to feel like a princess, and Suzanne Perron did it for me. She is amazing," Lauren said.

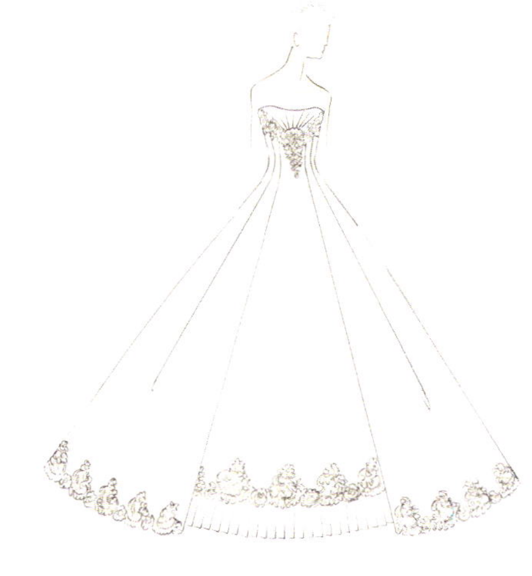

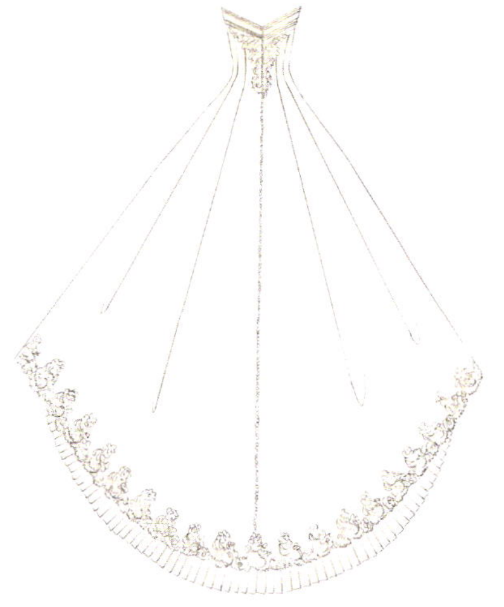

Front and back sketches of Lauren's gown

OPPOSITE PAGE:
Veil completes classic look (BB)

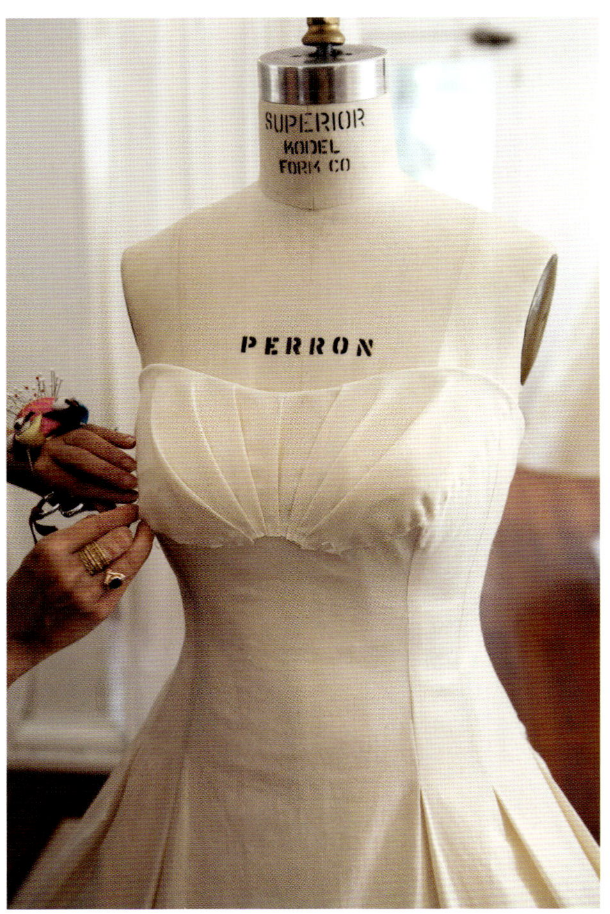

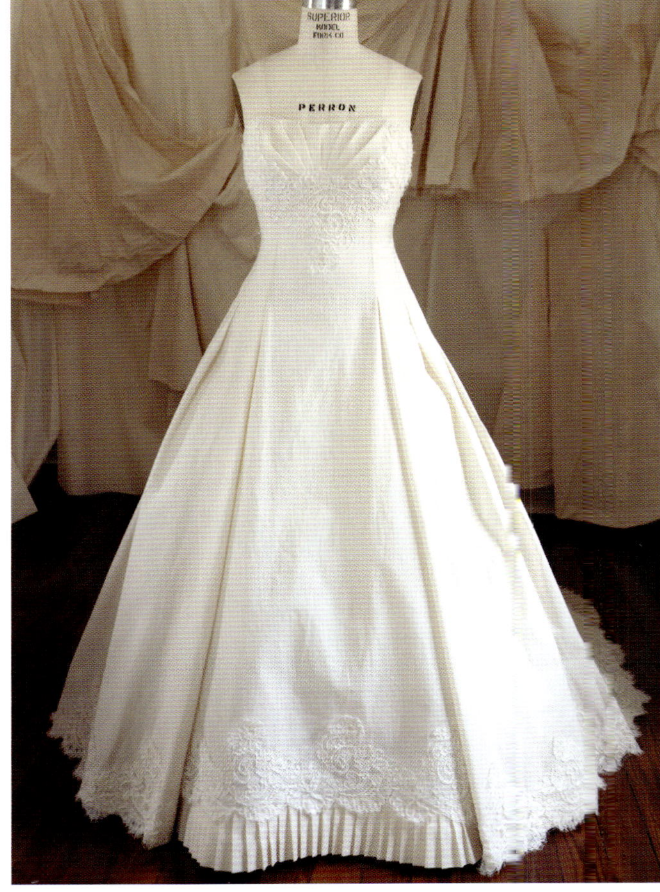

Muslin draping of bodice pleating (BB)
Muslin prototype (BB)
Muslin hem pleating with lace detail (SP)

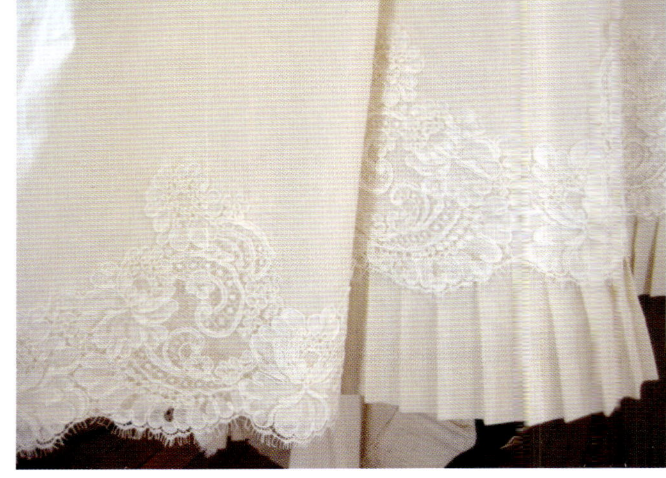

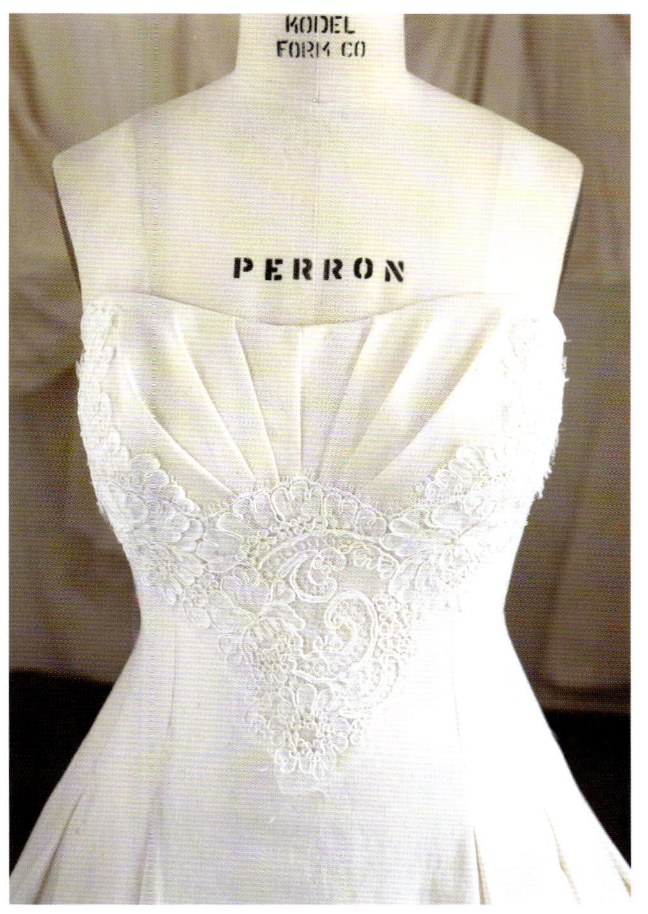

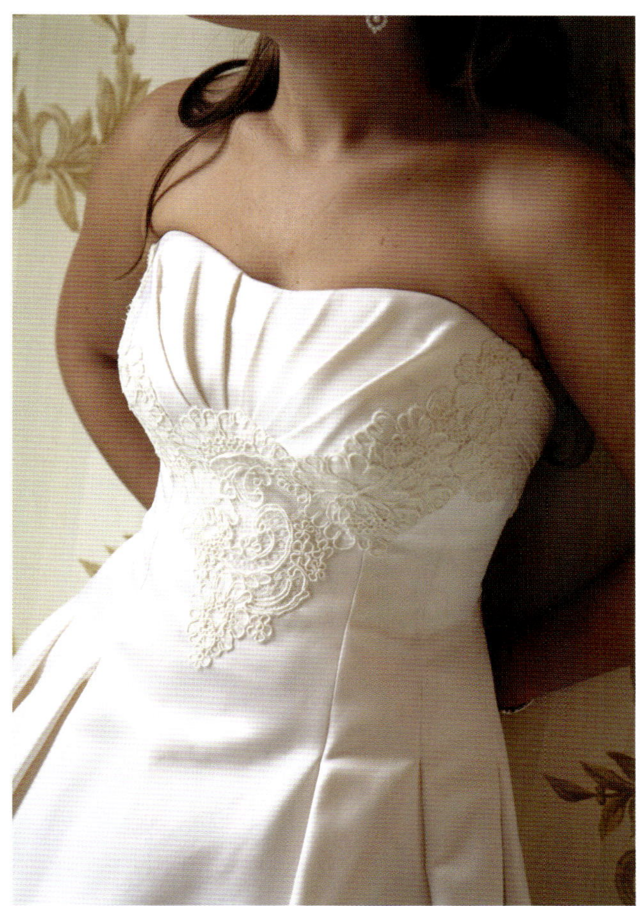

Bodice muslin draping (BB)
Finished satin bodice draping (BB)

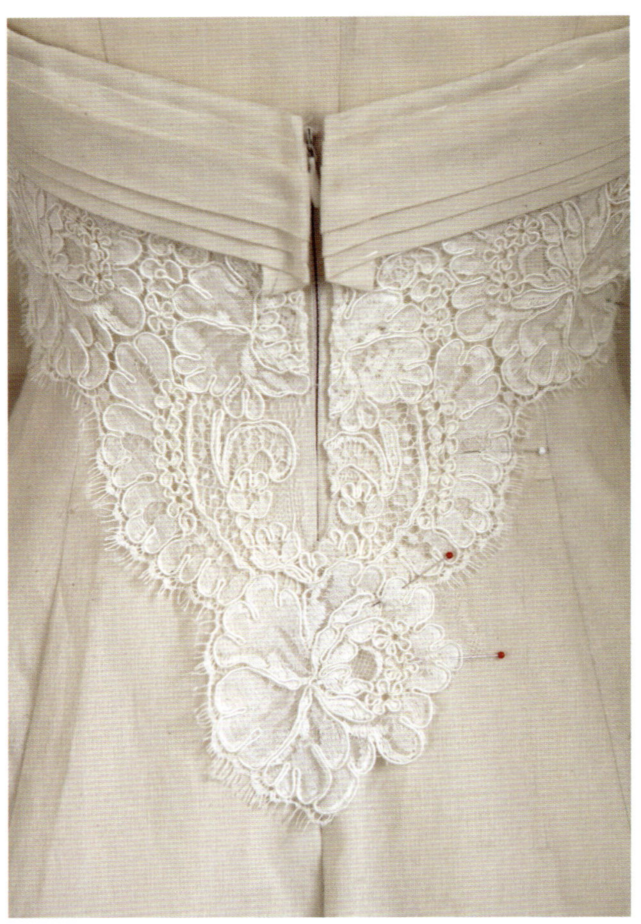

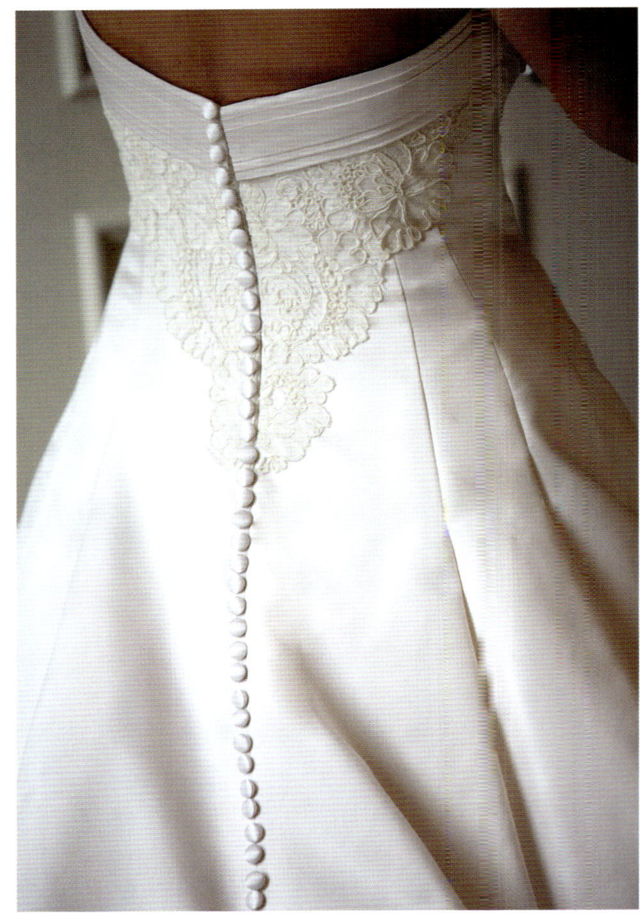

Back bodice muslin draping (SP)
Back bodice finished in satin (BB)

OPPOSITE PAGE:
Full-length gown portrait (BB)

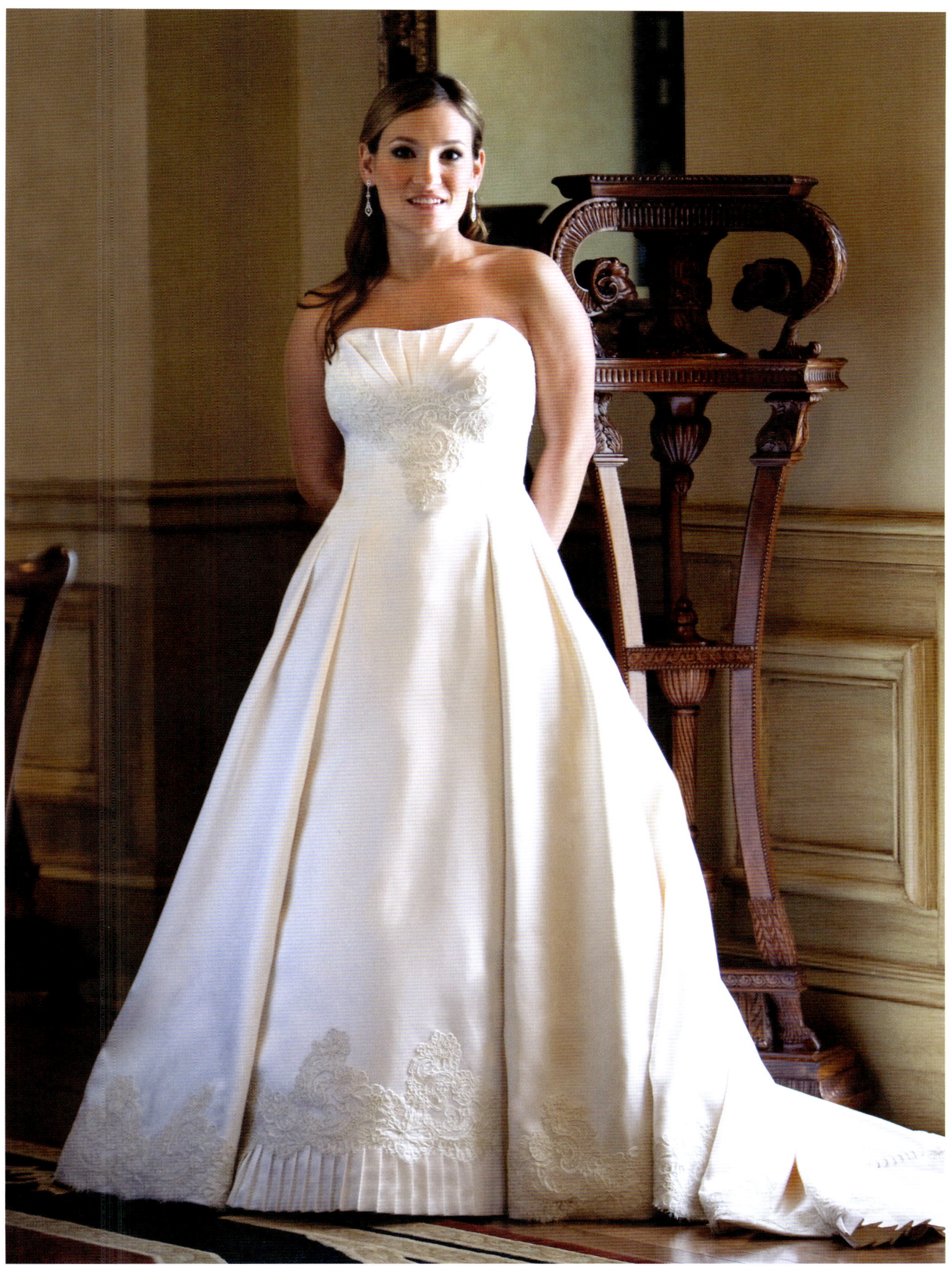

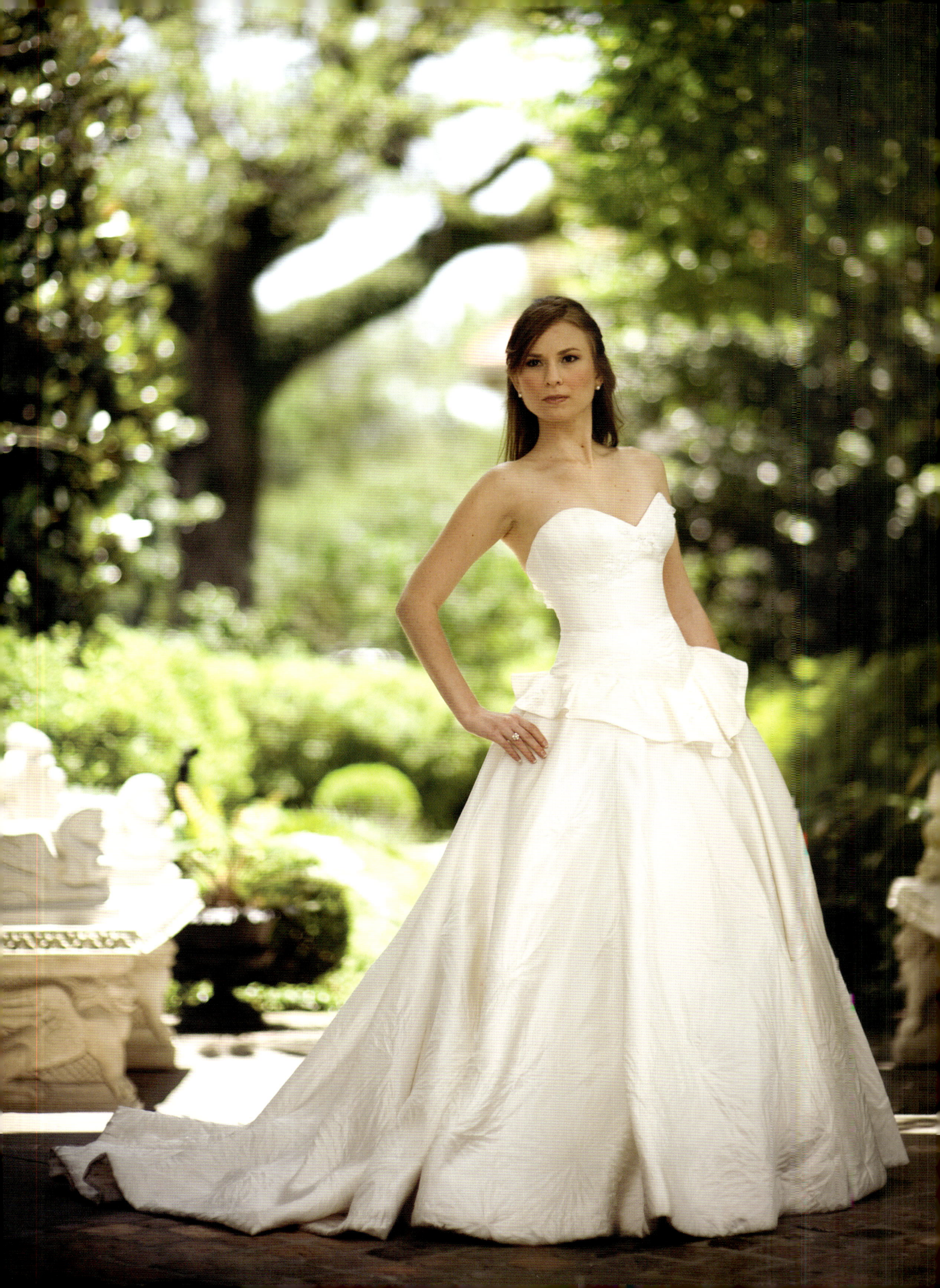

Sarah, Rex Maid

Sarah's Rex gown was my first opportunity to make an opulent debutante gown for the ultimate of Mardi Gras events, the Rex Ball. The meeting of the Rex and Comus courts is the culmination of the Mardi Gras season. This ambitious project was inspired by a photograph of a gown found by the client in a back issue of *Vogue* magazine. Inspiration can come from a variety of sources in art, history, and the fashion community. Designers are inspired by the work of the great masters of the past as well as the genius of the current industry leaders. I do not care to and will not copy other designers' work, but I often do find inspiration in the work of other designers. In this instance, we were inspired by the voluminous skirt, shaped peplum, and textured fabric.

The first step was to develop the muslin silhouette. The second step was to develop the textured fabric. The final step was to develop the proper finishings. The ball gown silhouette featured a strapless sweetheart neckline. A fitted bodice was draped to sculpt to the inner foundation. The ball gown shape of the skirt was supported with a full crinoline, the highest ruffle starting at the basque waist. We used three half-circle pattern pieces to create the skirt volume. The half-circle–shaped patterns allowed for tremendous volume in the hem with less volume in the hips. The flounce of the peplum was achieved through draping over the assembled muslin garment.

We experimented with two texturing techniques on satin-faced organza. This is a tightly woven, semi-opaque, plain-weave fabric with a shiny, pearl-like finish. Because of the fabric's innate characteristics and sheen, creasing can be permanent. The same characteristic that makes this fabric problematic for a client who wants to appear pristine after riding in the limo in her gown also makes this fabric ideal for texturing. One technique we experimented with produced an all-over random crinkling. The other technique was a more labor-intensive, orderly circular texturing with density toward the hem. The circular pattern was our preference. The shapes of the three skirt patterns, seven bodice pieces, and three peplum pieces were thread marked on blocks of the satin-faced organza. The circles were then marked within the pattern pieces with an air erase marker. We took care to match circles in seams and to gradate from dense, larger circles at the hem to smaller, less dense placement blending into untextured organza. The circles were stitched with long running stitches. The threads were pulled tight, twisted around the gathered centers, and tied. The blocks were rinsed and spun dry in my sister's washing machine.

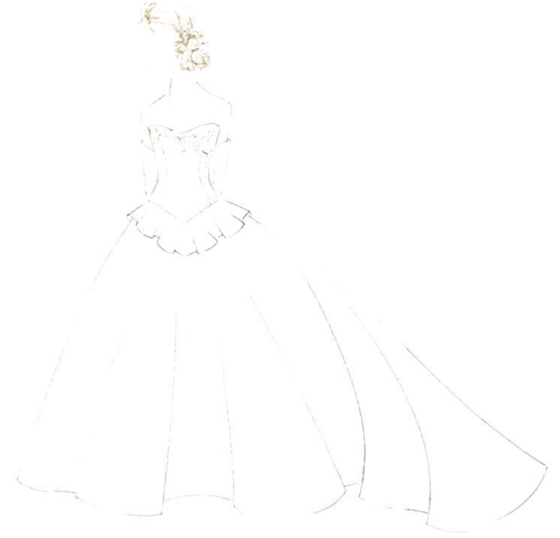

Sketch of Sarah's gown

OPPOSITE PAGE:
Design assistant Kelly modeling voluminous textured silhouette (JC)

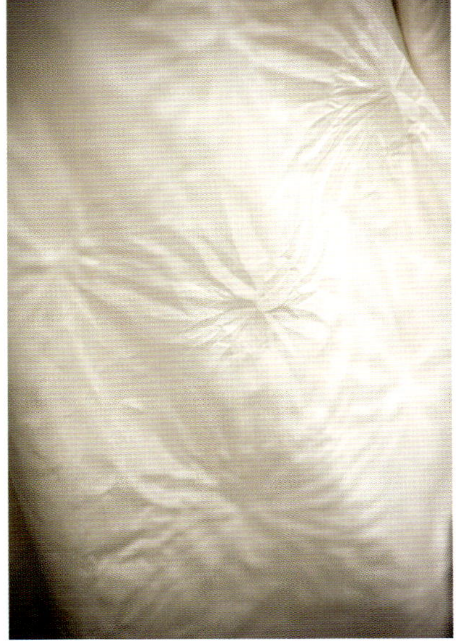

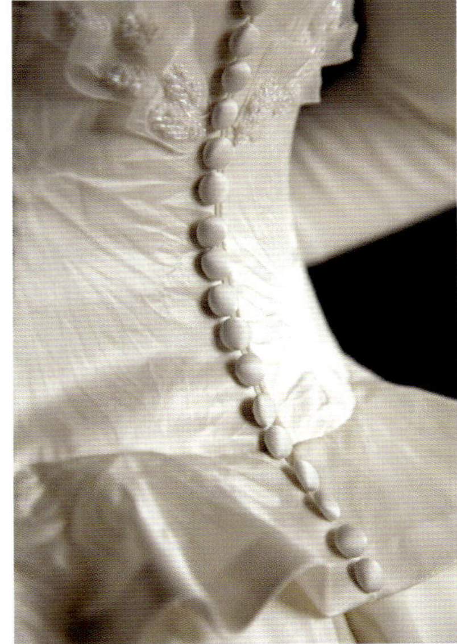

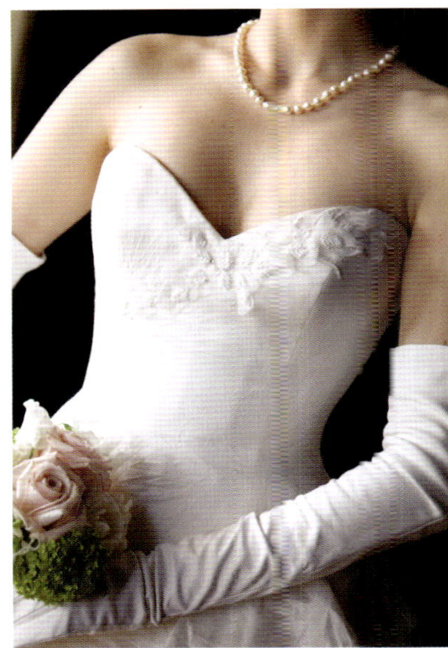

CLOCKWISE:

Fabric textured in a radiating starburst pattern (JC)

Back button detailing (BB)

Fitted bodice sculpted to shaped inner canvas foundation (BB)

Peplum accentuates hourglass shape (BB)

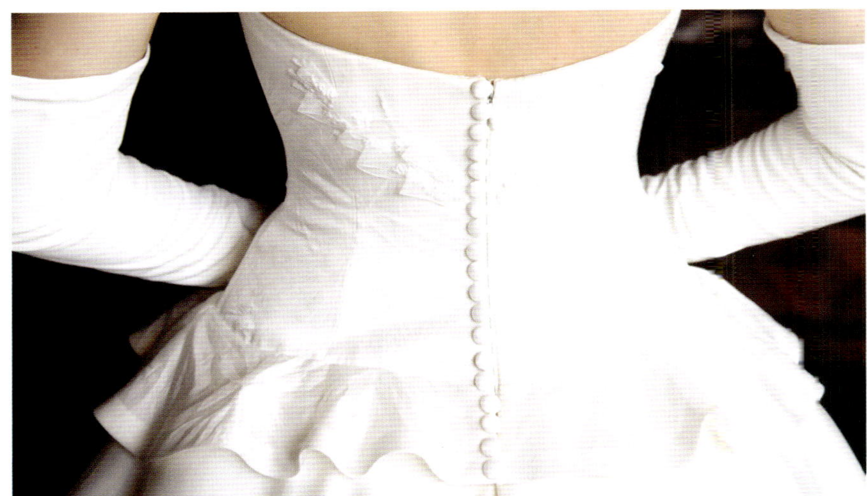

We used additional steam and pressure from the iron to permanently crease the fabric. The gathered blocks of fabric were allowed to sit and dry for weeks before we unfurled them. When the threads were released, radiating creases were exposed. The final task in preparing the fabric was to press the crinkled fabric as flat as possible. We went through gallons of water in our gravity-feed steam iron before the fabric was flat enough to cut. Once the blocks were pressed as flat as possible, the fabric was cut to match the actual pattern pieces.

We applied special finishes to create a very specific look. The skirt pieces were stiffened by layering satin and heavy crinoline behind the textured organza. The layering yielded a crisp, rustling effect. The structure of the skirt was continued in the reinforcement of the fold of the hem. The lofty, soft-rolled shape was kept puffy and rounded with quilt batting framed to the hem and facing seam. We hemmed the peplum with a bias band carefully hand stitched in place to create a hint of body and definition. Buttons line the center back bodice while sprays of beading adorn the bodice and hem for the finishing touch of glimmer.

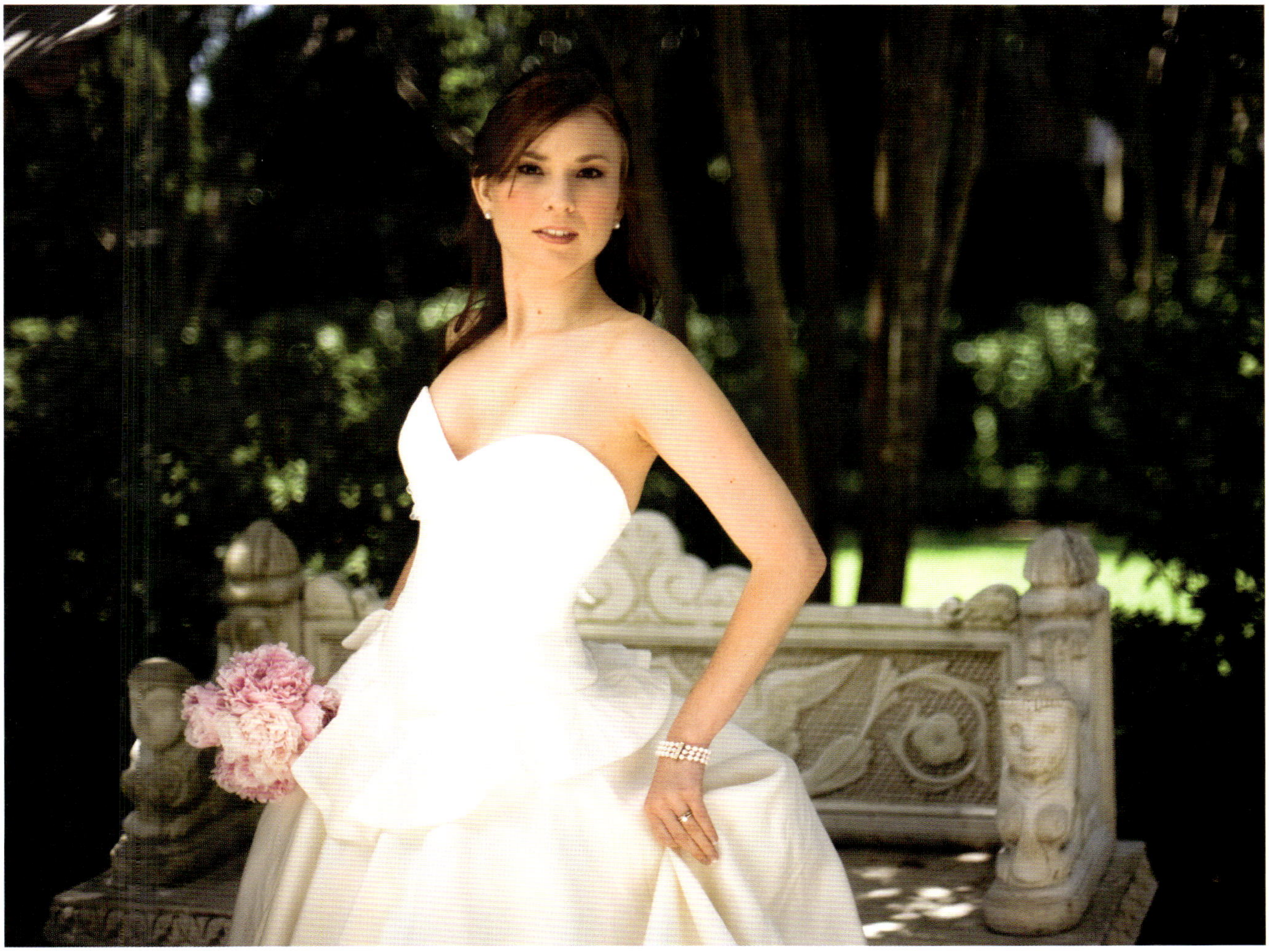

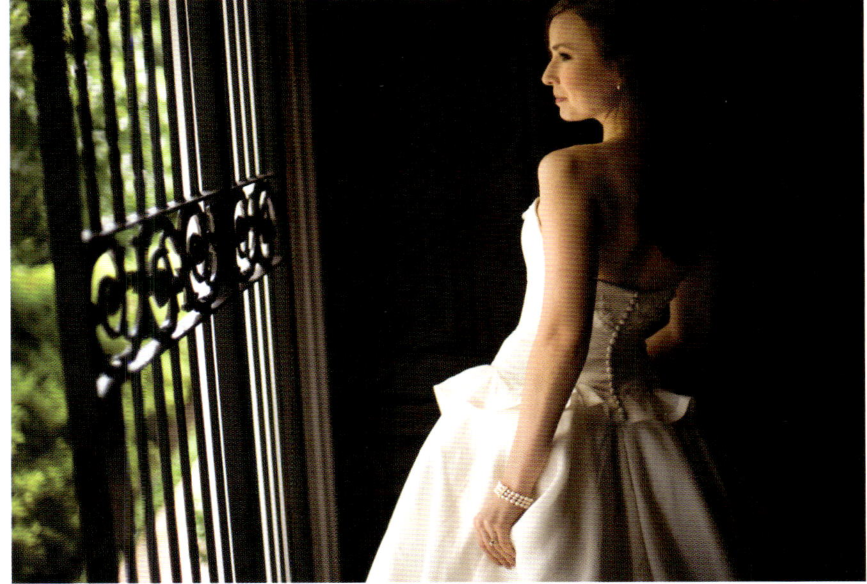

The gown with peplum fluttering around the basque dropped-waist seam (JC)

Dramatic gown profile (JC)

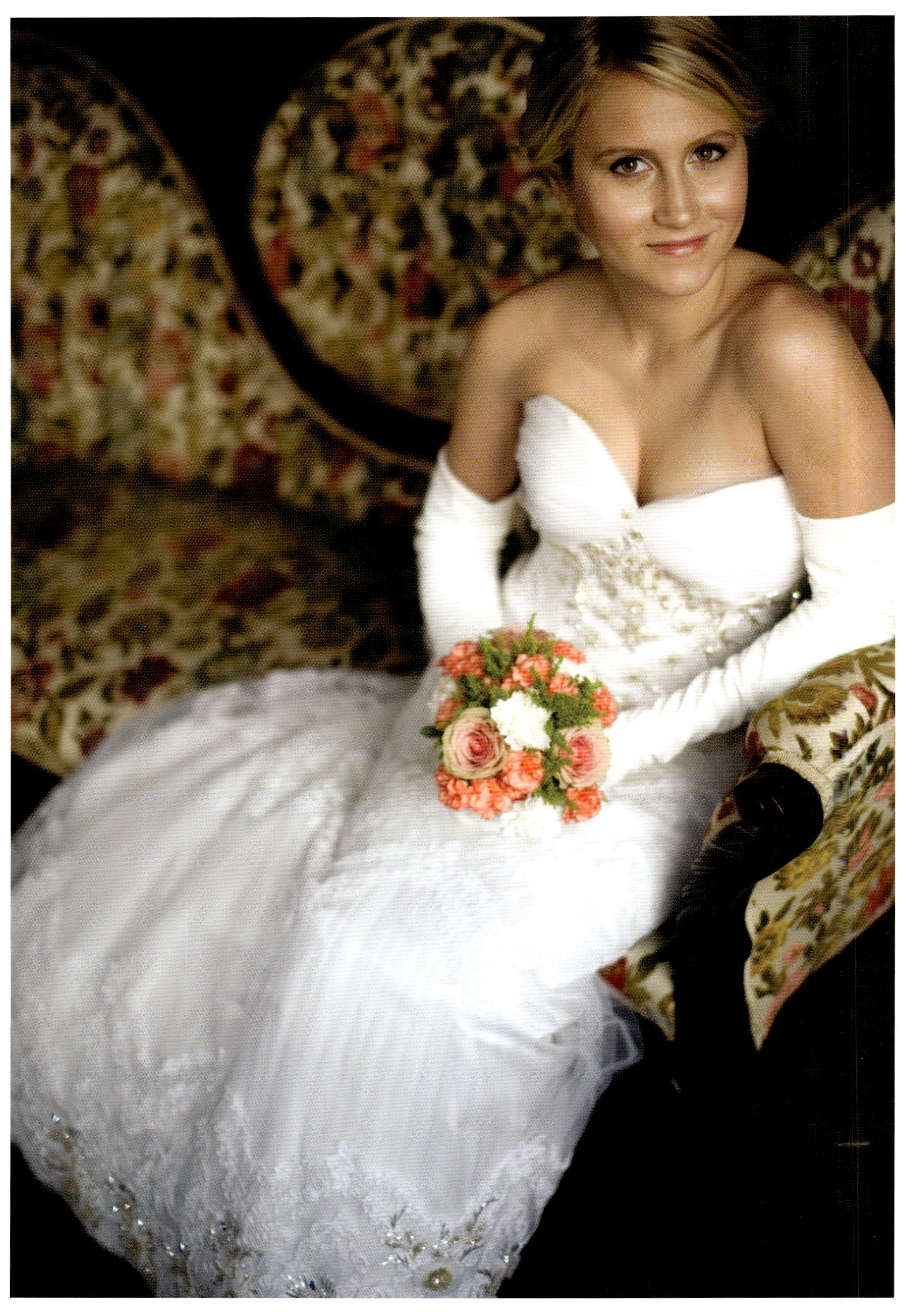

Francesca, Harlequins Queen

Francesca reigned as Queen of Harlequins. As the Harlequins organization traditionally recognizes young women prior to their debutante year, the gown should be less beaded and more youthful than most other queens' gowns. The gown needed to be regal and ball worthy while having the appropriate appearance for a younger sub-deb. Our goal was to create visual interest through fabric manipulation and lace placement without heavy all-over beading.

Francesca's preference was for a sweetheart neckline and soft trumpet shape. She left the majority of design decisions to me. I prepared sketches with fabric, lace, and beading swatches to communicate the concept I had in mind. Once she and her family were enthusiastically receptive to the concept, we began the long hours of work.

The most unique feature of the gown is the lace floating between bands of pleated tulle. Painstaking pattern work preceded the first cut or stitch. Engineering tulle and lace requires careful planning. Having the perfectly fitting muslin as a design tool was invaluable. We placed and adjusted lace on the muslin to achieve the most pleasing proportions. We then marked the lace placement on the muslin before transferring those lines to the paper pattern. These markings were crucial guides in layering the hand-pleated tulle on the princess panels. The tulle was hand pleated and pinned into place following the paper pattern guidelines. Once all of the pinned, pleated tulle was stitched in place, princess seams were stitched. The directional folds of the tulle camouflage the princess seaming. The center back seam was left open to allow for easier handling. The lace was then applied in continuous bands around the gown, yielding seams virtually invisible.

The lines of the scalloped lace border create the illusion of a basque waist seam. Gathered tulle wrapping the bust line is secured in place with center front beading. Additional scalloped border edges the gown hem and train. Gold and silver beading combine for subtle light reflection along the bodice and hem. The floral embroidery is enhanced with foliagelike sprays of bugle beads and Swarovski bicones. The gold picks up the hues of the Harlequins mantle, and the silver enhances the crystal hues of the collar.

For Francesca's reign as Queen of Harlequins, she wore this gown with all the dressings of crown, scepter, collar, and mantle. We photographed her in the historic setting of Latrobe's on Royal Street in the French Quarter, focusing on her beauty and the gown without the additional royal accoutrements.

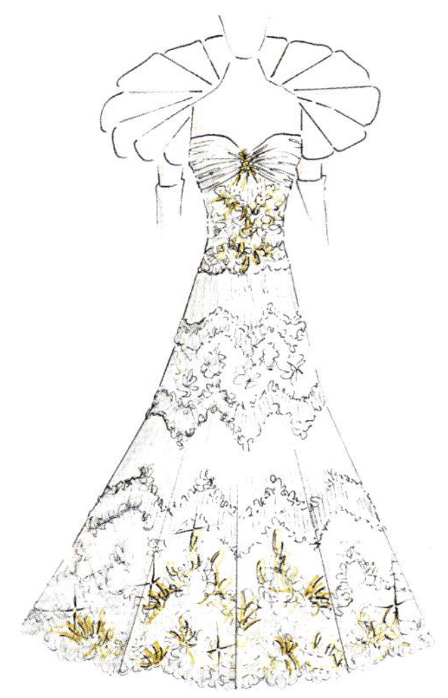

Sketch of Francesca's gown

OPPOSITE PAGE:
Gathered tulle adorning bodice and skirt (JC)

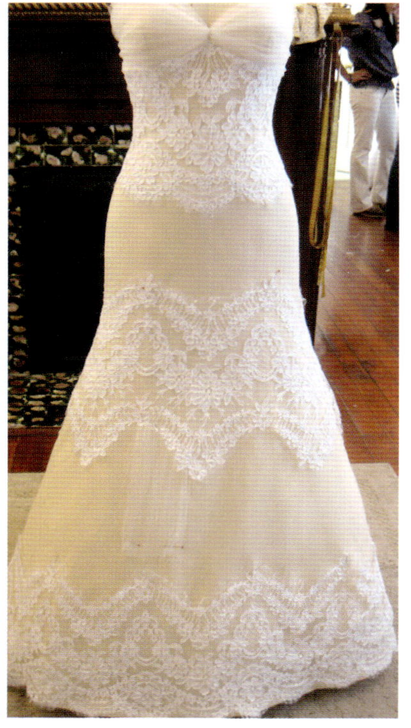

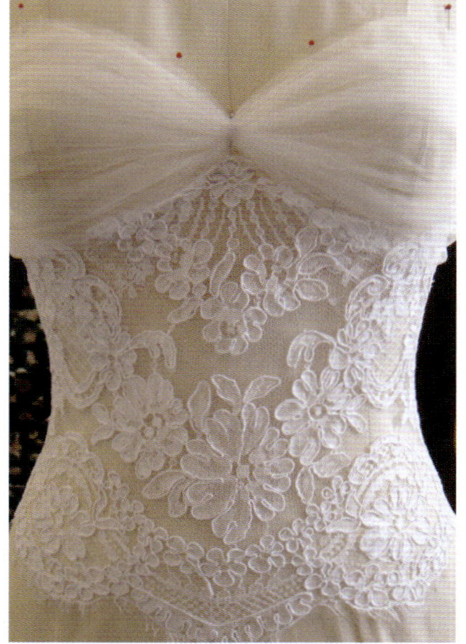

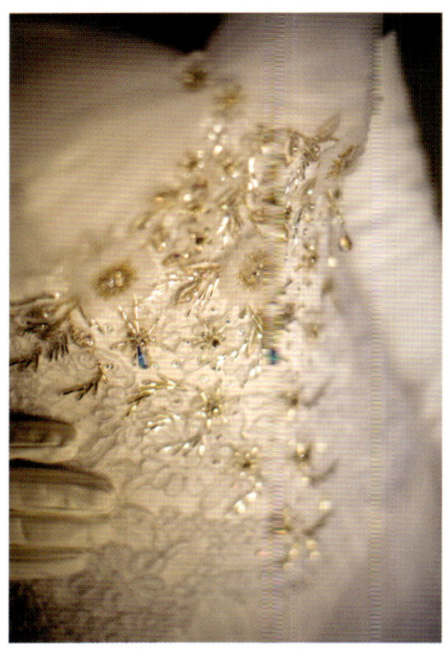

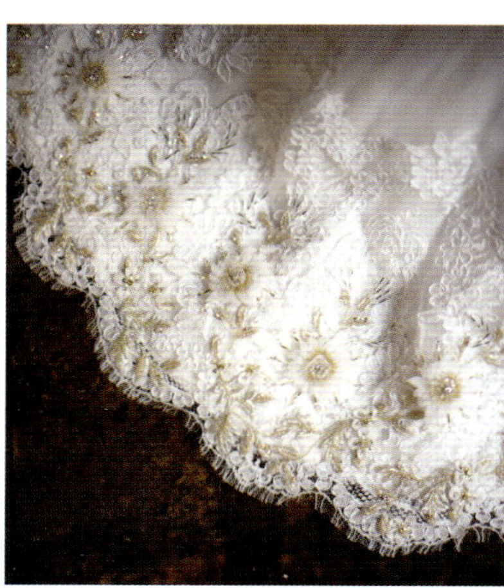

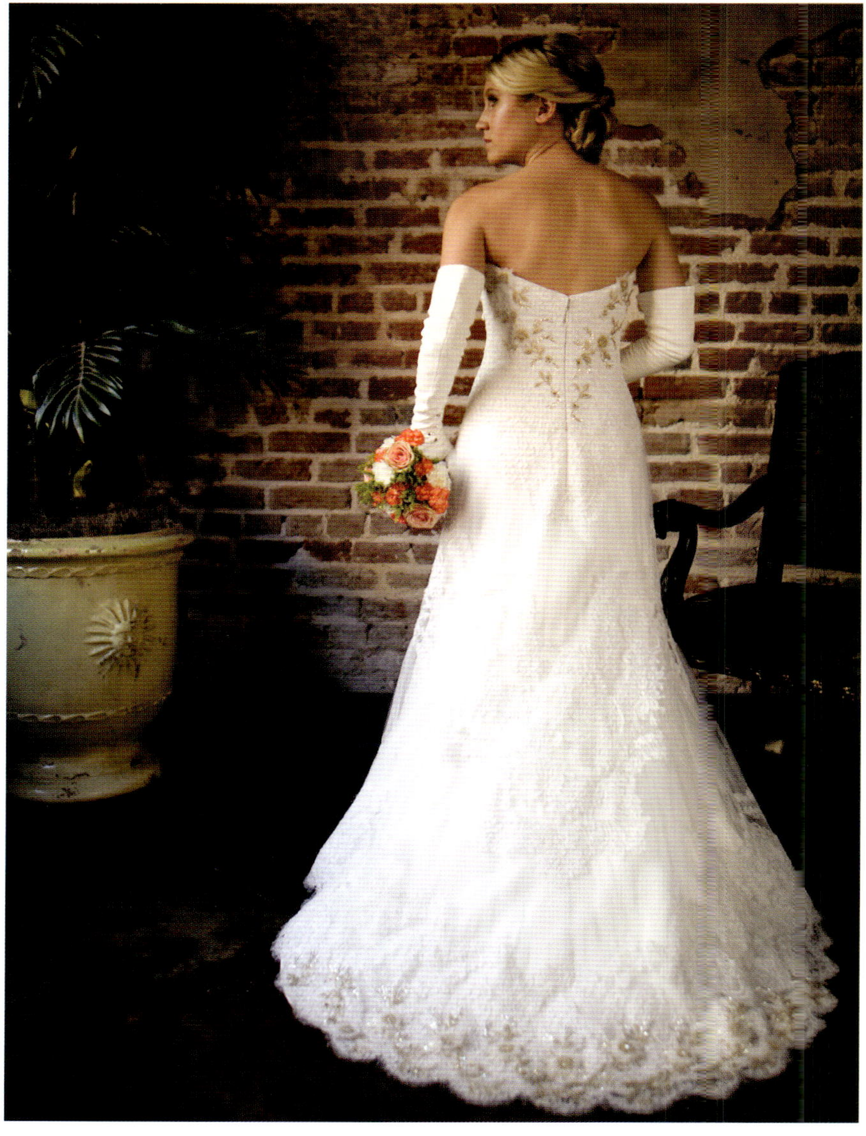

CLOCKWISE:
Lace and tulle placement worked out on muslin prototype (SP)

Lace and tulle draped to muslin (SP)

Gold and silver beading adorning the bodice (JC)

The gown's back and sweeping train adorned with lace, tulle, and beading (JC)

Beading adorning the scalloped lace of the back hem (JC)

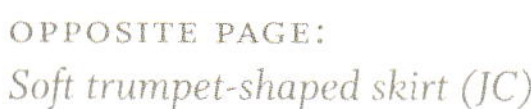

OPPOSITE PAGE:
Soft trumpet-shaped skirt (JC)

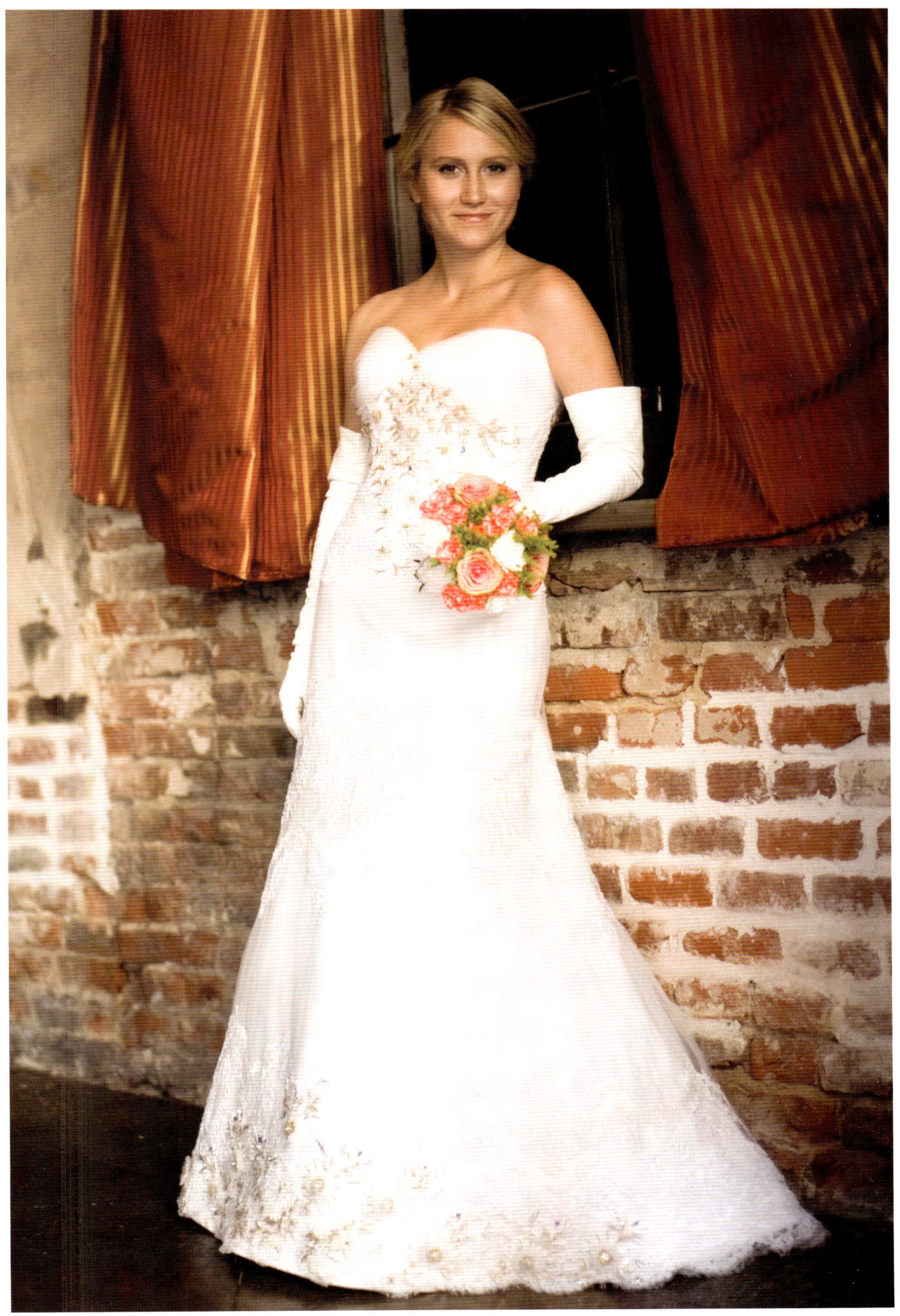

FRANCESCA, HARLEQUINS QUEEN

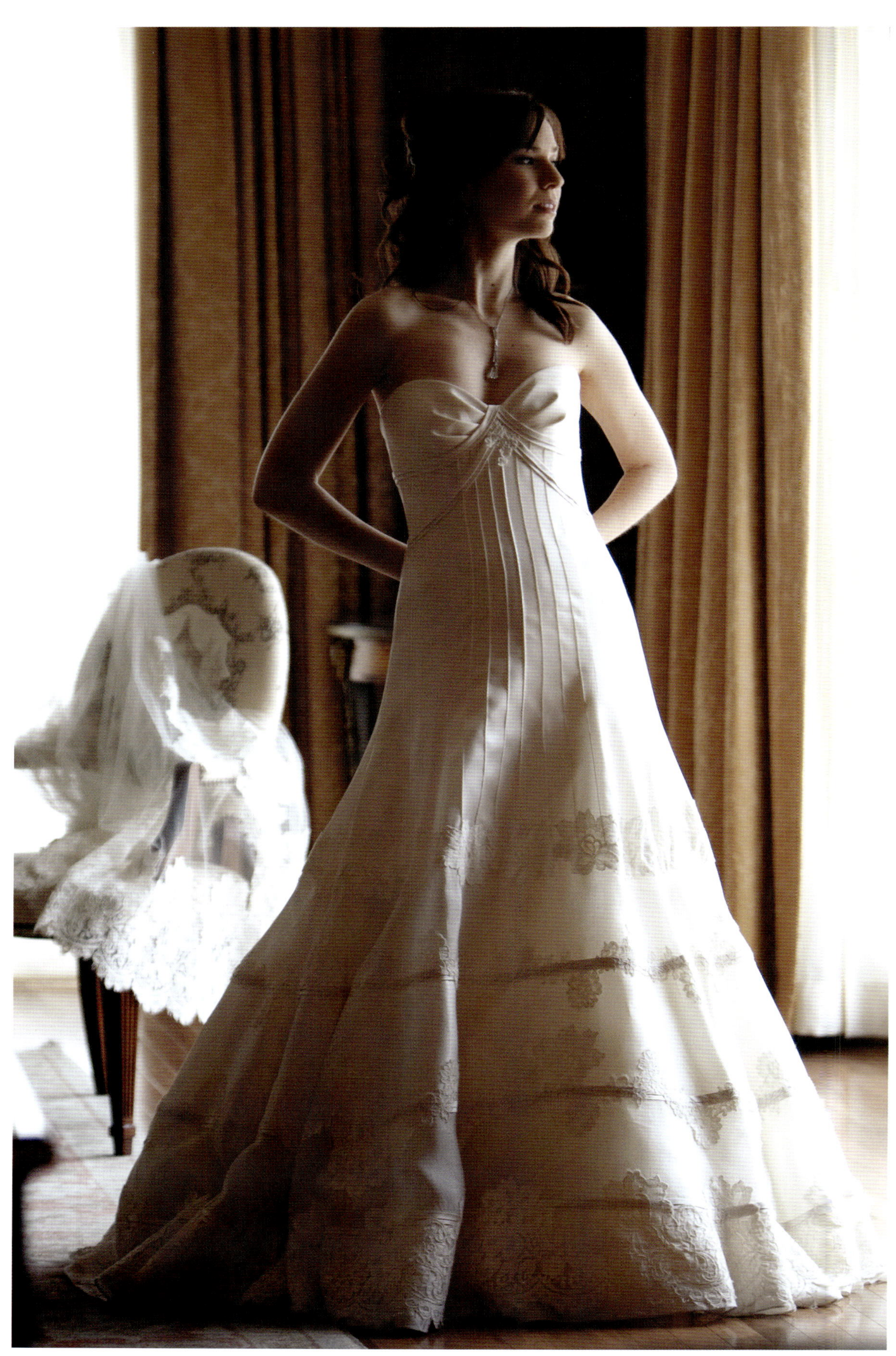

Jenny, Bride

A Garden District church and a French Quarter reception provided the perfect setting for my first wedding gown in New Orleans. Jenny was the ideal New Orleans client to start with. We had met years ago when she was the local sales director for Vera Wang bridal gowns. The post-Katrina timing should have been problematic, but it actually helped connect us. She was engaged, extremely knowledgeable about gowns, and an integral part of getting my business going.

Jenny chose a sketch from a collection of spec drawings I had done. When I thought of the perfect gown for Jenny, this sketch was the first to come to mind. She went directly to the same sketch, too. The layers of satin-faced organza, tissue organza, and lace created a light, airy silhouette perfectly appropriate for her June wedding. The silhouette featured a curved, dropped-waist seam and an empire band trimmed in bias satin. The skirt shape would skim the hips before billowing into a voluminous hem.

As I began to bring the sketch to life on the mannequin, the amount and type of detailing in the bodice of the original sketch seemed to shorten and cramp the torso. Working with Jenny's proportions, I began making adjustments to elongate the torso. The straight empire seam became two inverted V's. Dozens of pin tucks were stitched vertically to elongate the torso. The crispness of satin-faced organza pin tucks created a structured effect beautifully juxtaposed to the softness of the lace. The dropped-waist basque seam was completely eliminated in favor of the new vertical detailing. A longer, more ethereal silhouette emerged as I manipulated the design details.

The voluminous skirt is encircled with textural details. The vertical seams of the satin-faced organza are intersected by horizontal bands of lace, tissue organza, and satin. The sheer insets of tissue organza allow light to pass within the layers of the skirt. The double folds of bias-silk satin accentuate the change in fabrication. A wide border lace was cut into bands for appliqué. The widest section with scalloped edging lines the gown's hem. A section of lace in the shape of continuous vines borders the middle seams. The largest of the flowers from the lace pattern were cut and overlapped along the highest of the horizontal seams. To ensure the airiness of the skirt and to create the loft necessary to see the fabric variances and lace detail, dozens of tulle circles were cut and layered between the lining and the outer detailed layer.

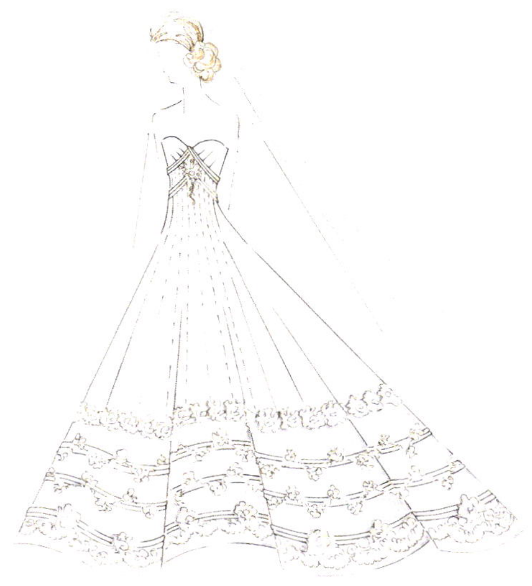

Sketch of Jenny's gown

OPPOSITE PAGE:
Design assistant Kelly modeling banded, appliquéd skirt with translucent layers (BB)

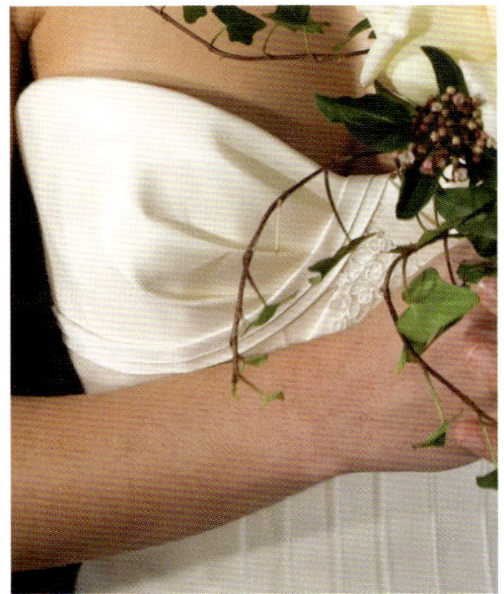

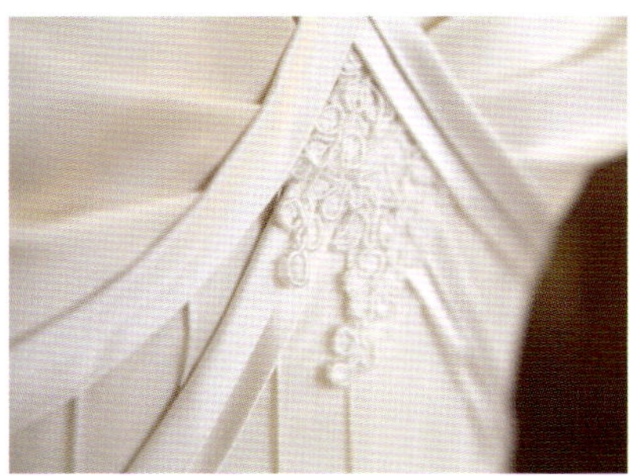

CLOCKWISE:
Bodice shaped with soft pleats (SB)

A-line silhouette with a modified sculpted shape (BB)

Bodice detailing of pleats, pintucks, and folded bias satin bands (BB)

OPPOSITE PAGE:
Bands of lace, tissue organza, and bias satin circling the skirt and hem (BB)

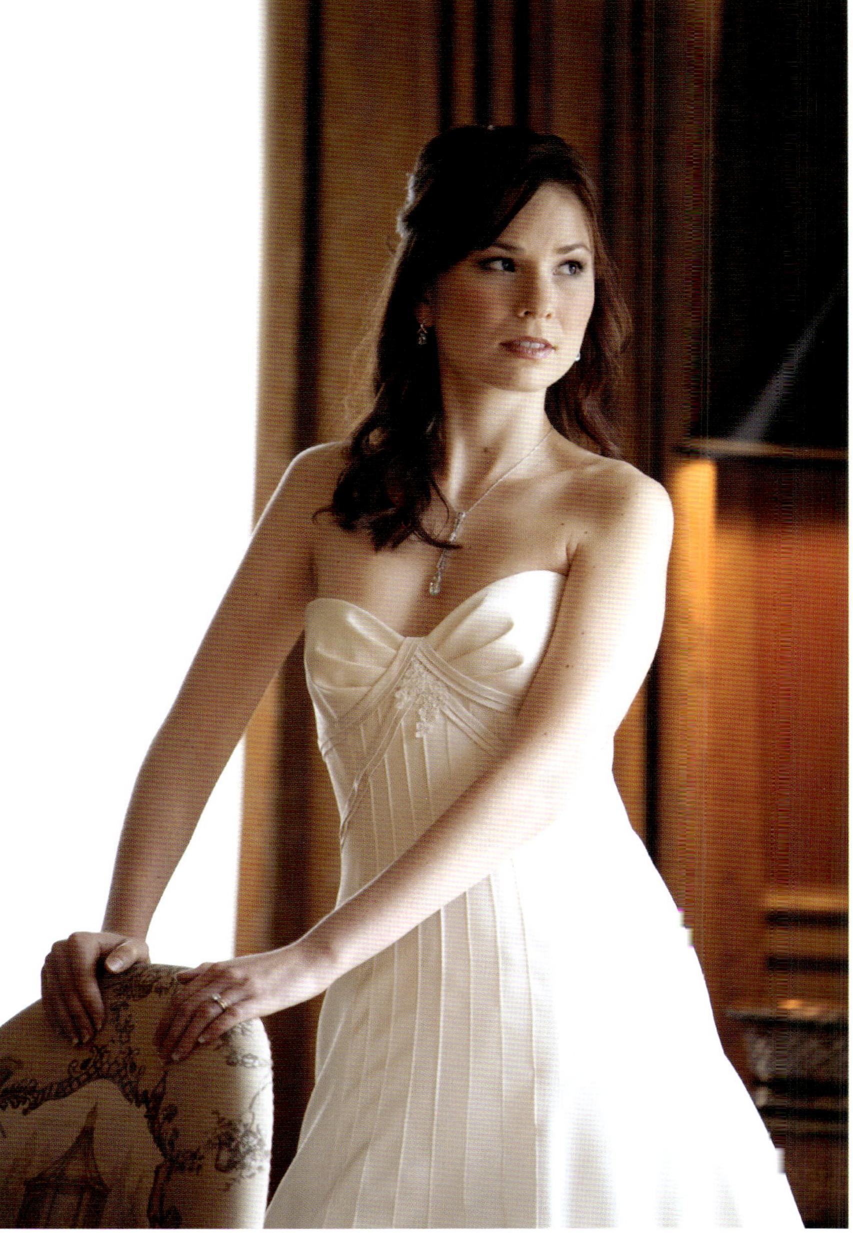

Other details added to the luxury of the gown. The bust was shaped with deep folds of organza. We used lace appliqués to adorn the center front bodice where the satin bands miter. Fabric-covered buttons dot the center back of the gown. A long veil of tulle illusion with lace border and center medallion completes the look. The veil's border lace delicately frames the sweeping lace hem of the gown.

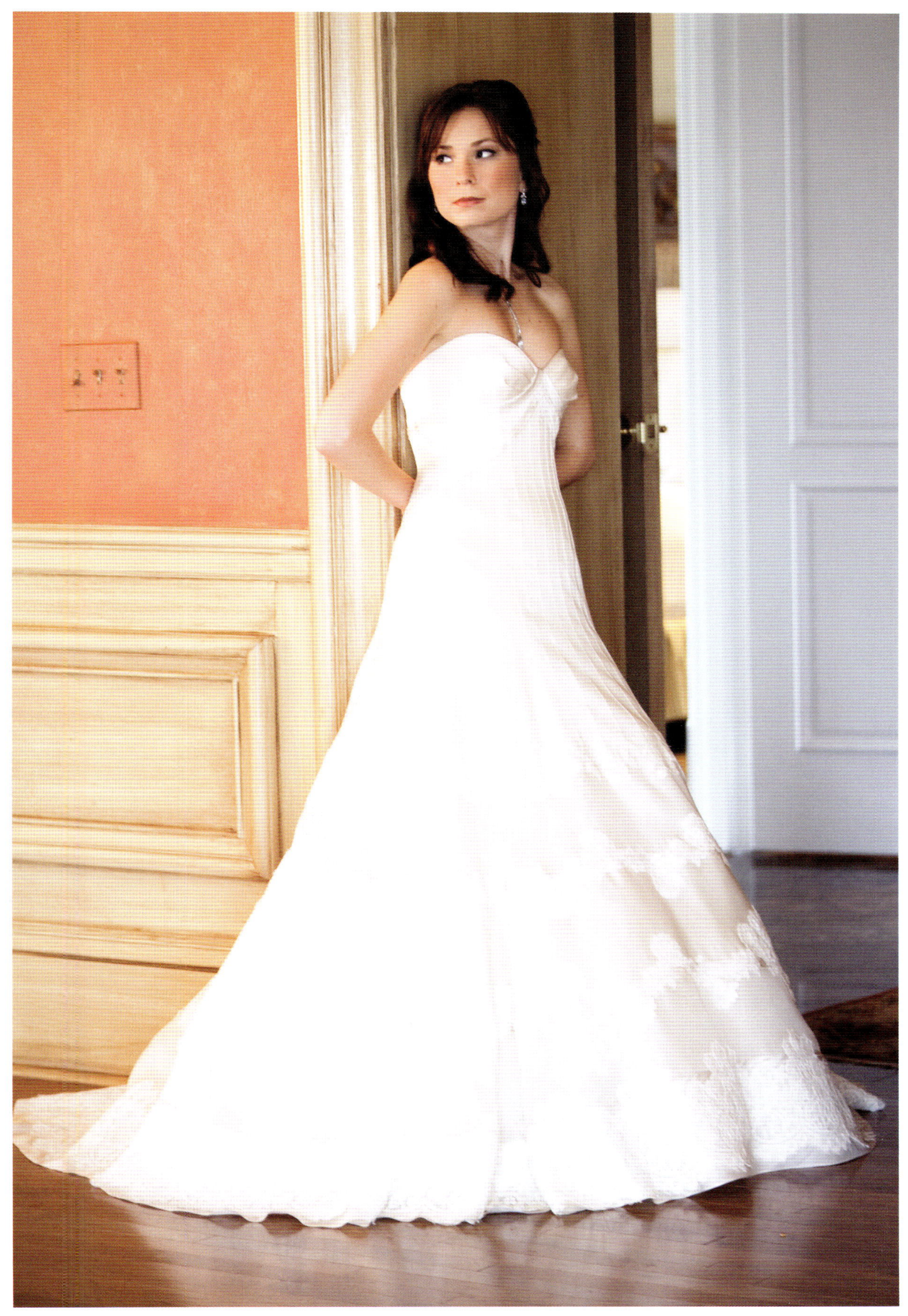

Floral lace appliqués blending pintucks with first tissue organza tier (BB)

Hem finished with a wide scalloped lace (BB)

OPPOSITE PAGE:
Pintucks elongating the torso (BB)

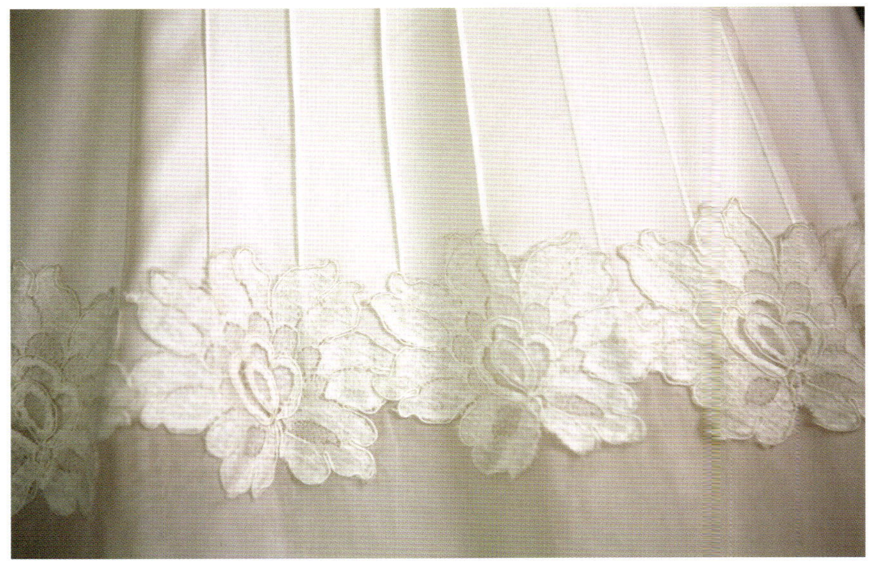

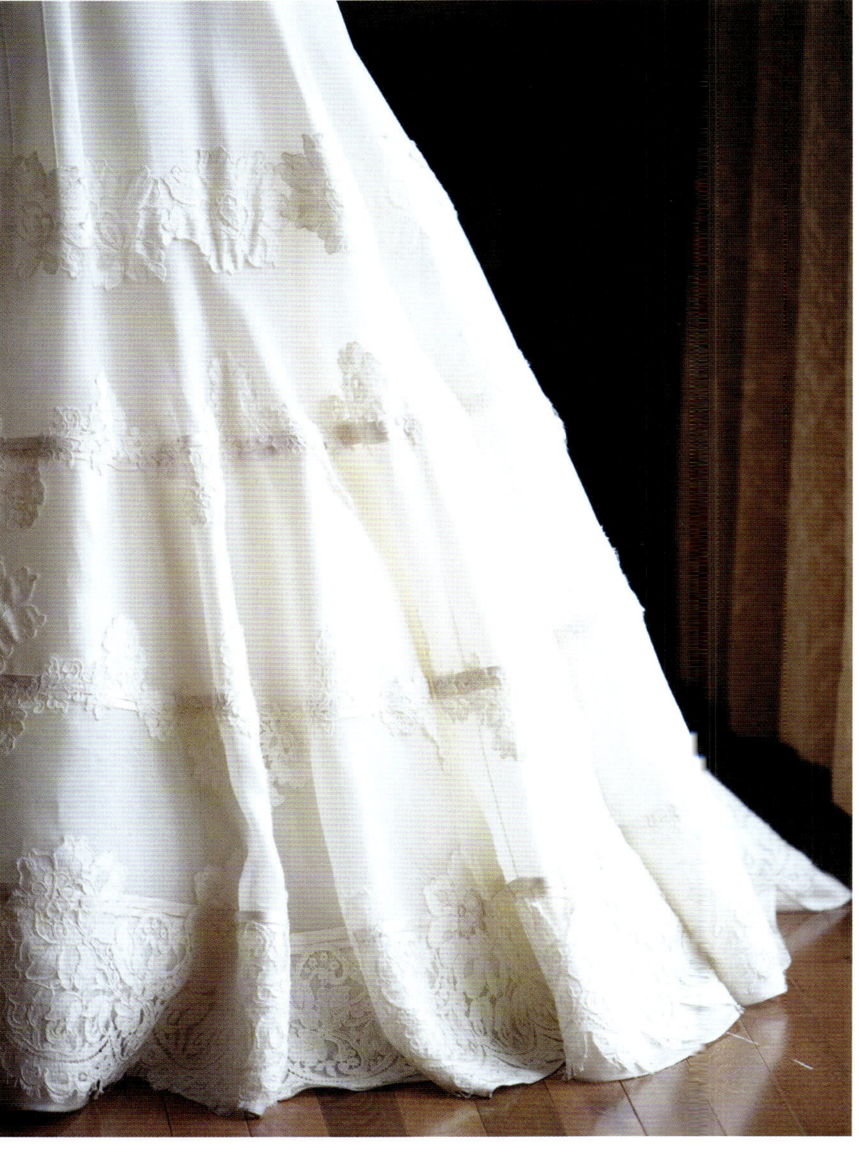

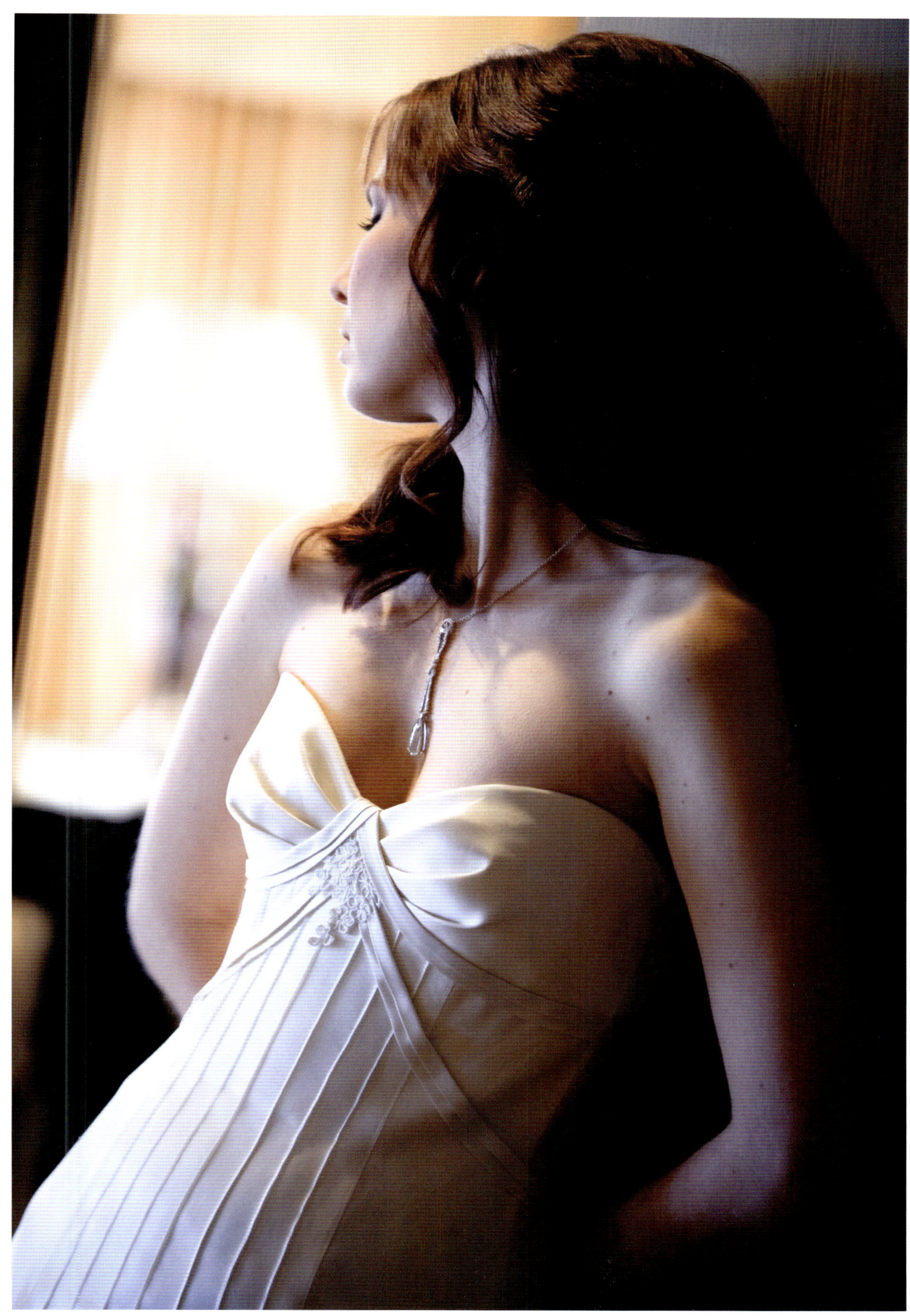

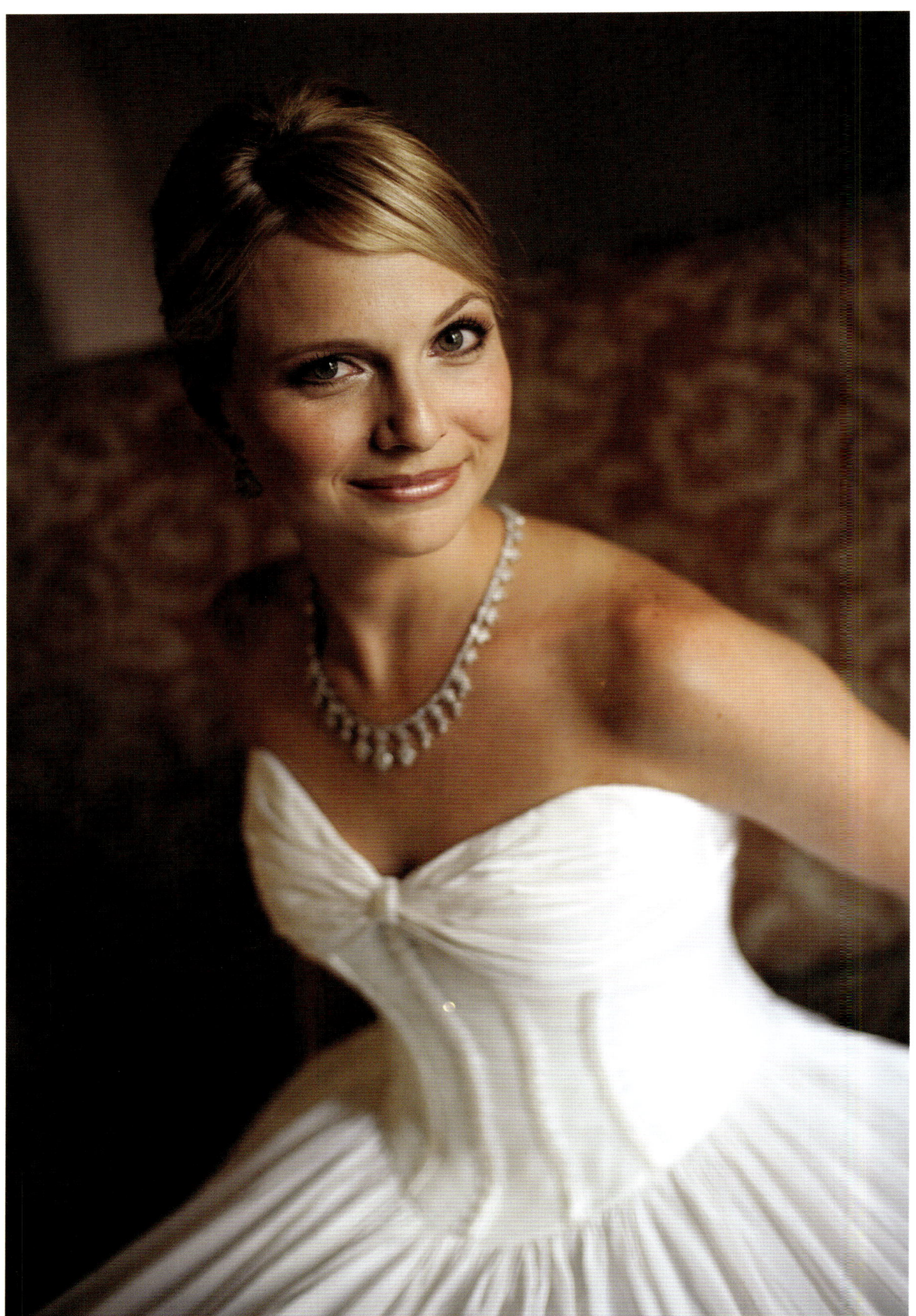

Kelly, Rex Maid

Kelly and her mother came to my shop when planning her wardrobe of gowns for her debutante season. We discussed several gown options, with the gown for the Rex Ball being of utmost importance.

Kelly chose a design directly from my sketchbook for her Rex gown. The design details were originally rendered on a subtle trumpet silhouette. We changed the trumpet skirt to a full ball gown skirt, keeping all other details true to the sketch. The sweetheart neckline, corseted bodice with cinched waist, and voluminous ball skirt were perfectly suited to create a stunning effect on Kelly's petite frame. Embellishing the traditional ball gown silhouette with numerous tulle, crystal, and satin details set it apart from the sea of white gowns on display during the season.

Satin bands accentuate dramatically curved hourglass bodice seams. The panels between the bodice seams were covered with a layer of tulle gathered perpendicular to the seams. Taffeta shirring wraps around the bust and over side seams from the center-front beaded band to the back princess seam. Stopping the shirring short of center back allowed for the back princess seams to extend the full length of the back bodice, creating a more elongated back bodice detailing.

We further embellished the satin band trim with bridal looping and Swarovski crystal aurora borealis bicones. We concealed the base of the bridal looping under the satin bands. The amount of looping exposed varies for different effects. On the front bodice, the loops hug the satin banding with a crystal between each loop. Along the princess seams, more of the looping is exposed and secured into triangular shapes with hand-sewn crystals. In the four bands of the skirt, nearly 2,000 hand-sewn crystal bicones secure arcs of the loop trim.

The skirt is a continuous length of taffeta of nearly five yards. We cut and marked two flat insets of tulle the same length as the taffeta to create a supportive base for the gathered detailing. We cut the blocks of tulle with enough length to accommodate a shirring ratio of six to one. The shirring blocks totaled 30 yards per band. These blocks were gathered to predetermined measurements and framed to the underlying support blocks. The flat under layers provided support and control points for the shirred layers. The insets required 120 yards of shirring—the length of a football field goalpost to goalpost. The tulle gathered insets around the entire circumference of the voluminous taffeta skirt allowed for light to pass through the skirt, creating a glowing, floating effect. The hours invested in the fine detailing were well worth it when Kelly elicited a gasp from the audience as she stepped into the spotlight on the night of her event.

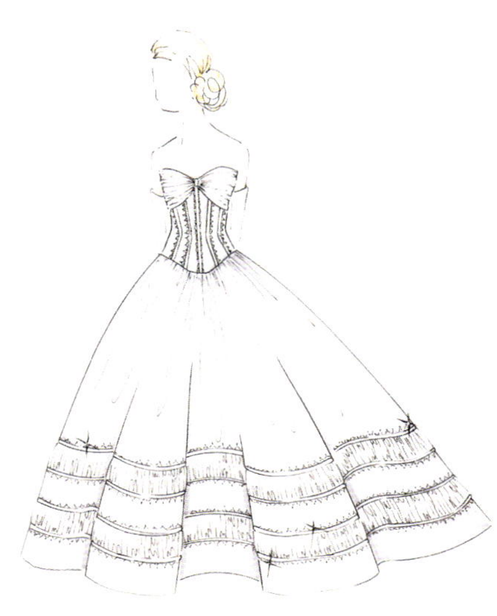

Sketch of Kelly's gown

OPPOSITE PAGE:
Client Ainsley modeling gown featuring gathered silk taffeta bodice and full ball gown skirt (JC)

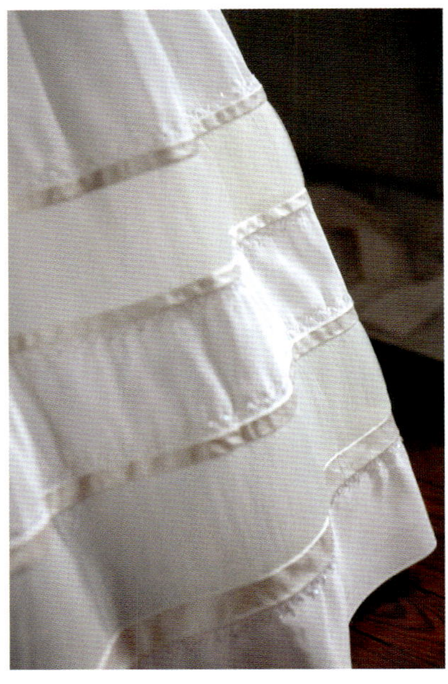

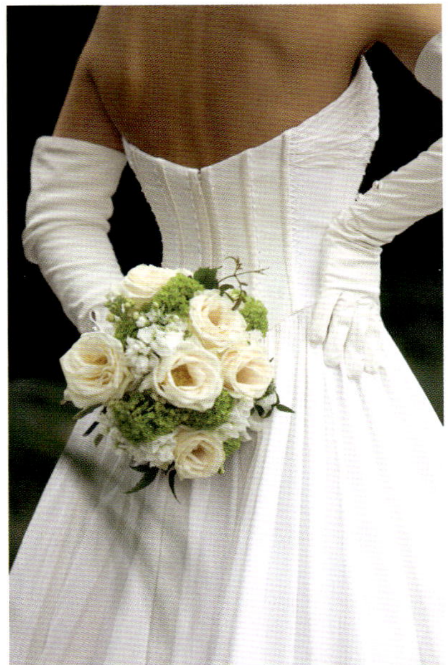

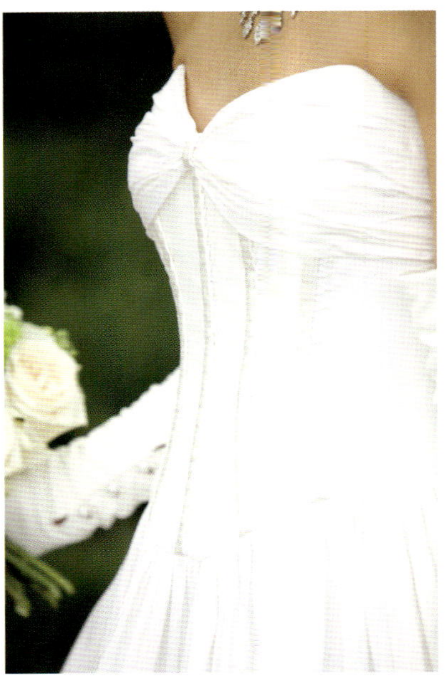

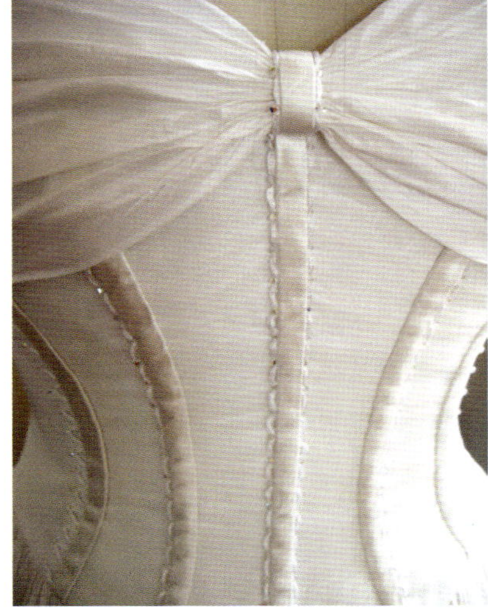

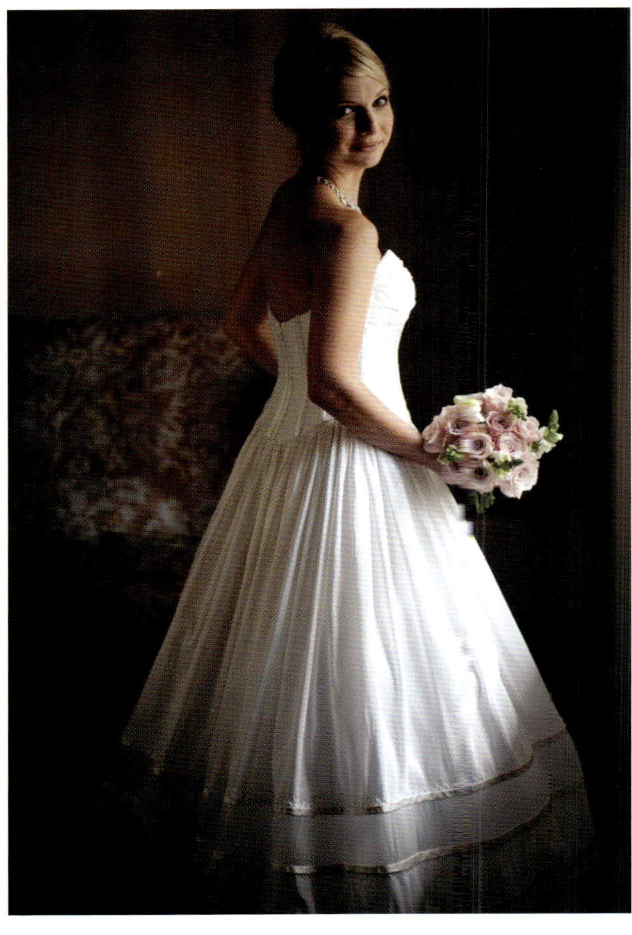

CLOCKWISE:

Skirt insets of gathered tulle defined by satin banding (JC)

Satin bands defining back bodice seam and framing center back closure (BB)

Tulle gathered horizontally between bodice vertical seams (BB)

Airy silhouette created by gathered tulle and taffeta (JC)

Satin banded seams adorned with crystals and cording (BB)

OPPOSITE PAGE:

Tulle insets allowing ligh· ·o travel through the skirt (JC)

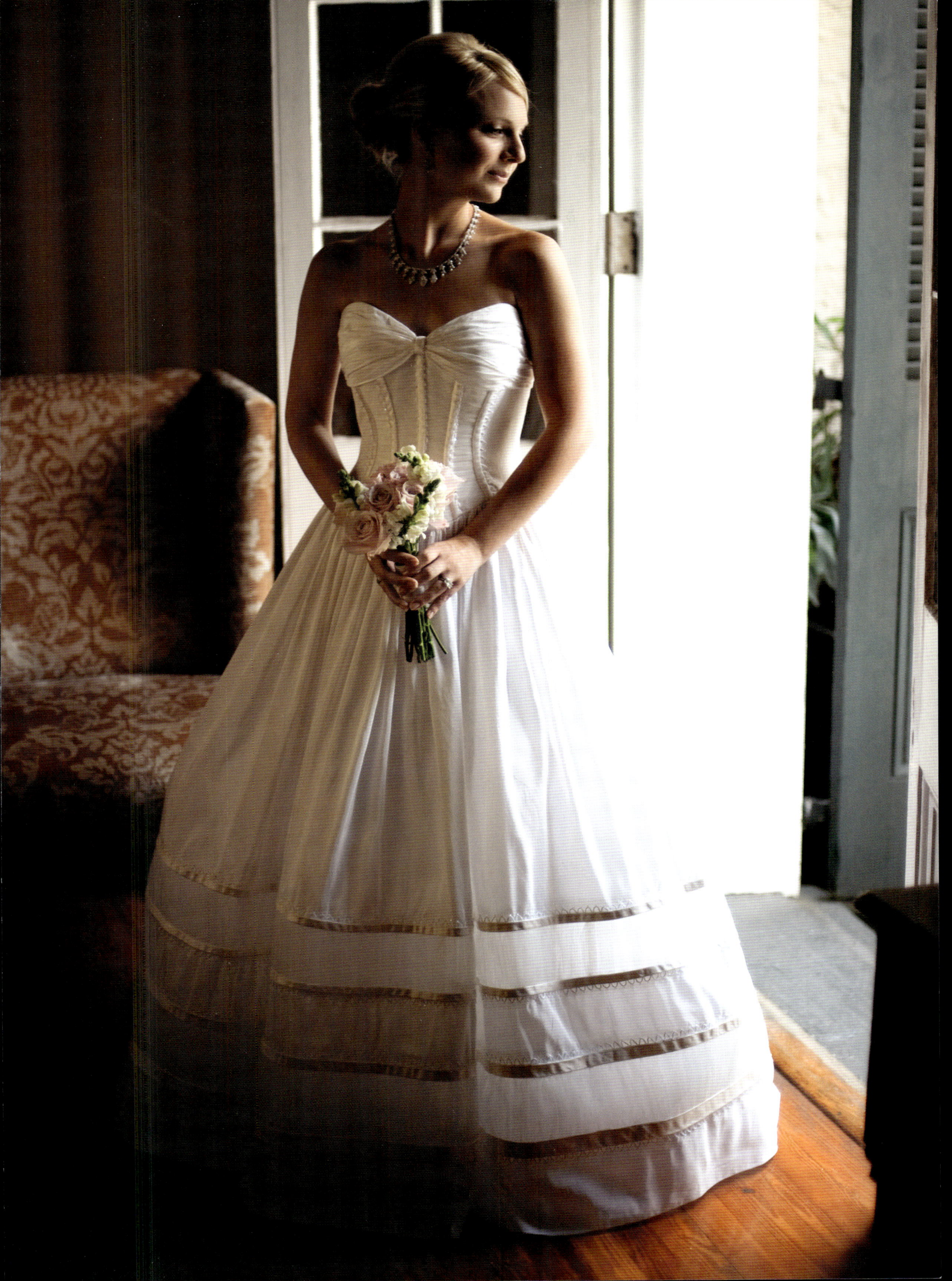

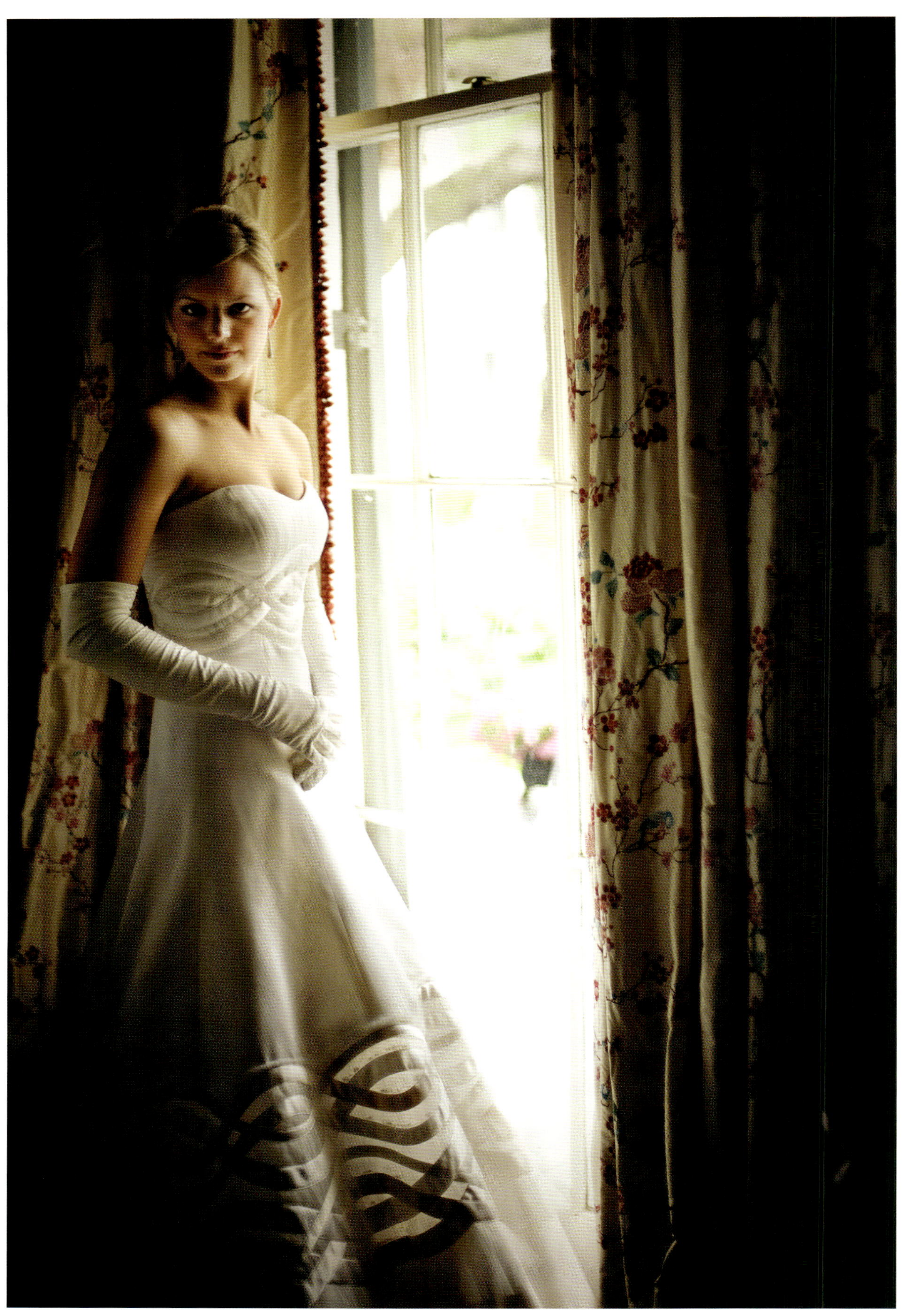

Emily, Rex Maid

With the Rex Ball being the culmination of the Mardi Gras season, I strive to make each Rex gown a one-of-a-kind standout with unique design techniques and finishes. It can be a challenge to push the boundaries of creativity within the confines of a traditional all-white ball gown. Emily came to me in my third season of designing gowns for the Rex Ball, and I set out to make her a gown that would live up to and even exceed the standard set in previous years.

Emily and I originally talked about creating a full ball gown silhouette. I had sketched a gown with a full ball skirt and pleated detailing I thought only someone with Emily's height could pull off. I played with a full crinoline shape and blocks of fabric on a mannequin adjusted to her height and shape. As I stepped back to get perspective on the proportions, I saw that the ball gown silhouette was just too much gown. With so much length below the waist, the full skirt became overwhelming in volume. I knew I needed a different direction for Emily's gown.

Emily was open to my design ideas and trusted me with creating the perfect gown for her. When I decided to abandon the traditional ball gown shape, I settled on a strapless, princess-seamed silhouette that was fitted through the hips before flaring into elegant fullness at the hem. A graceful trumpet shape with most of the skirt fullness at the hem was far better suited to Emily's tall, athletic frame than the princess look of my original ball gown concept.

The juxtaposition of athletic with ethereal was my inspiration for developing the design detailing. Awareness of the theatrical lighting and the use of spotlights during the event presentation on the ballroom floor further shaped my creative thinking. Using the skirt of clean double-faced satin as a palette, I envisioned an inset of intertwining satin bands floating on gathered layers of sheer tulle. The loft and effervescence created as light traveled through the tulle inset would be further amplified by the light reflection of thousands of Swarovski crystals floating in pockets between the tulle layers.

The design detailing of floating skirt bands was continued in the bodice. The repeat of the bias banding detail in the bodice is twofold. One, the monochromatic blend of various shades of white and ivory in the banding adds dimension. Second, the bands control the artfully draped tulle extending from strapless neckline to the waist.

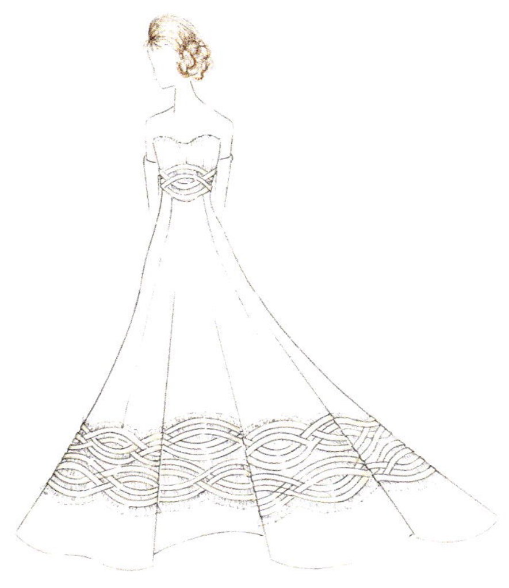

Sketch of Emily's gown

OPPOSITE PAGE:
Pattern of skirt detailing accentuated with light (JC)

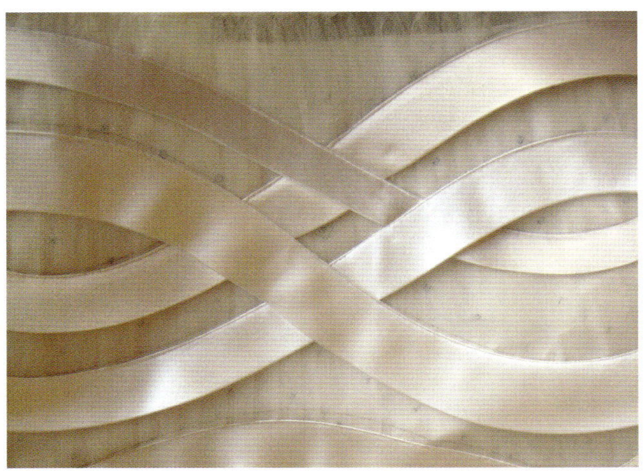

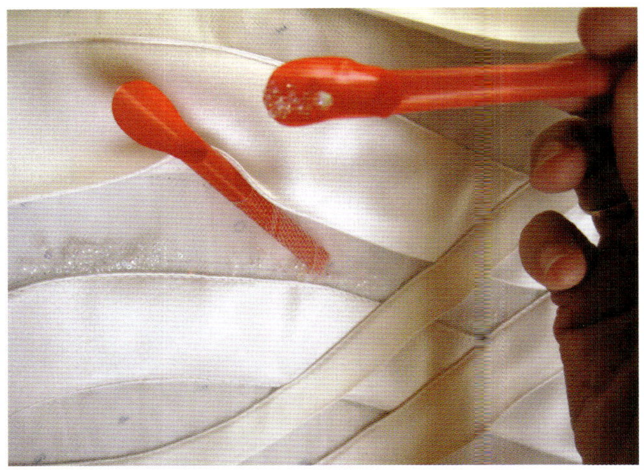

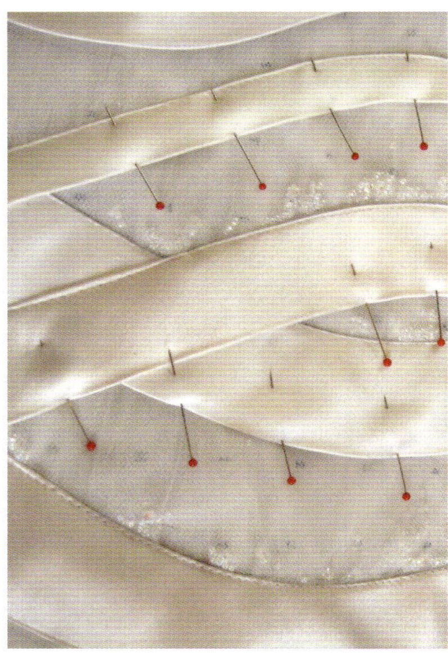

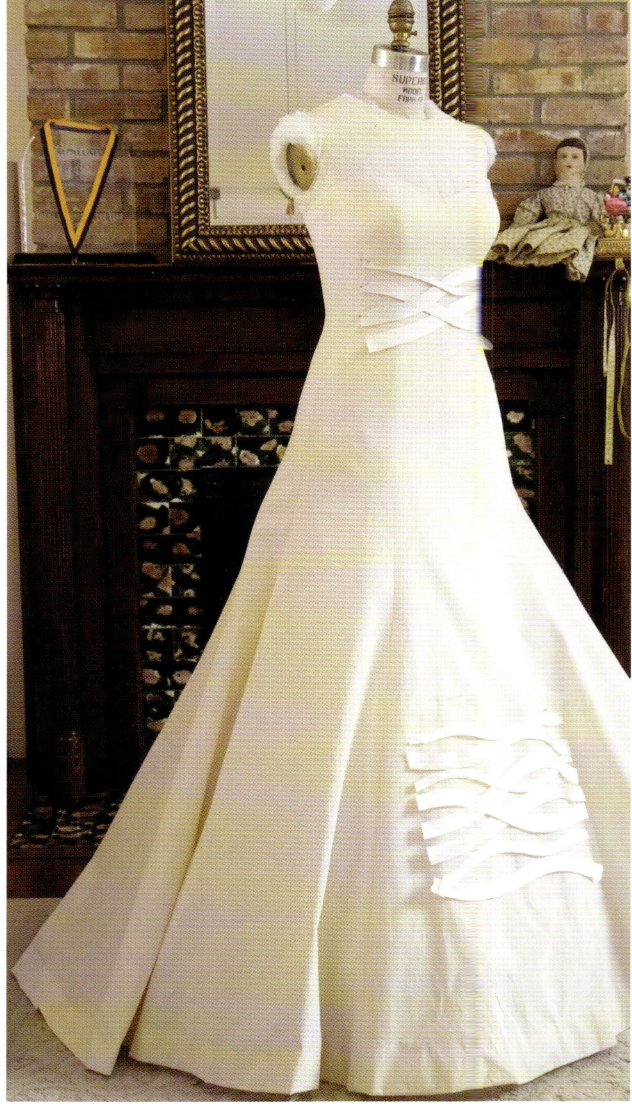

CLOCKWISE:
Development of bias banded and tulle inset (SP)

Placing crystals in pockets of tulle between bands (SP)

Muslin prototype with band placement for proportion (BB)

Bands pinned in place for edge stitching (SP)

OPPOSITE PAGE:
Graceful A-line silhouette with hem fullness (JC)

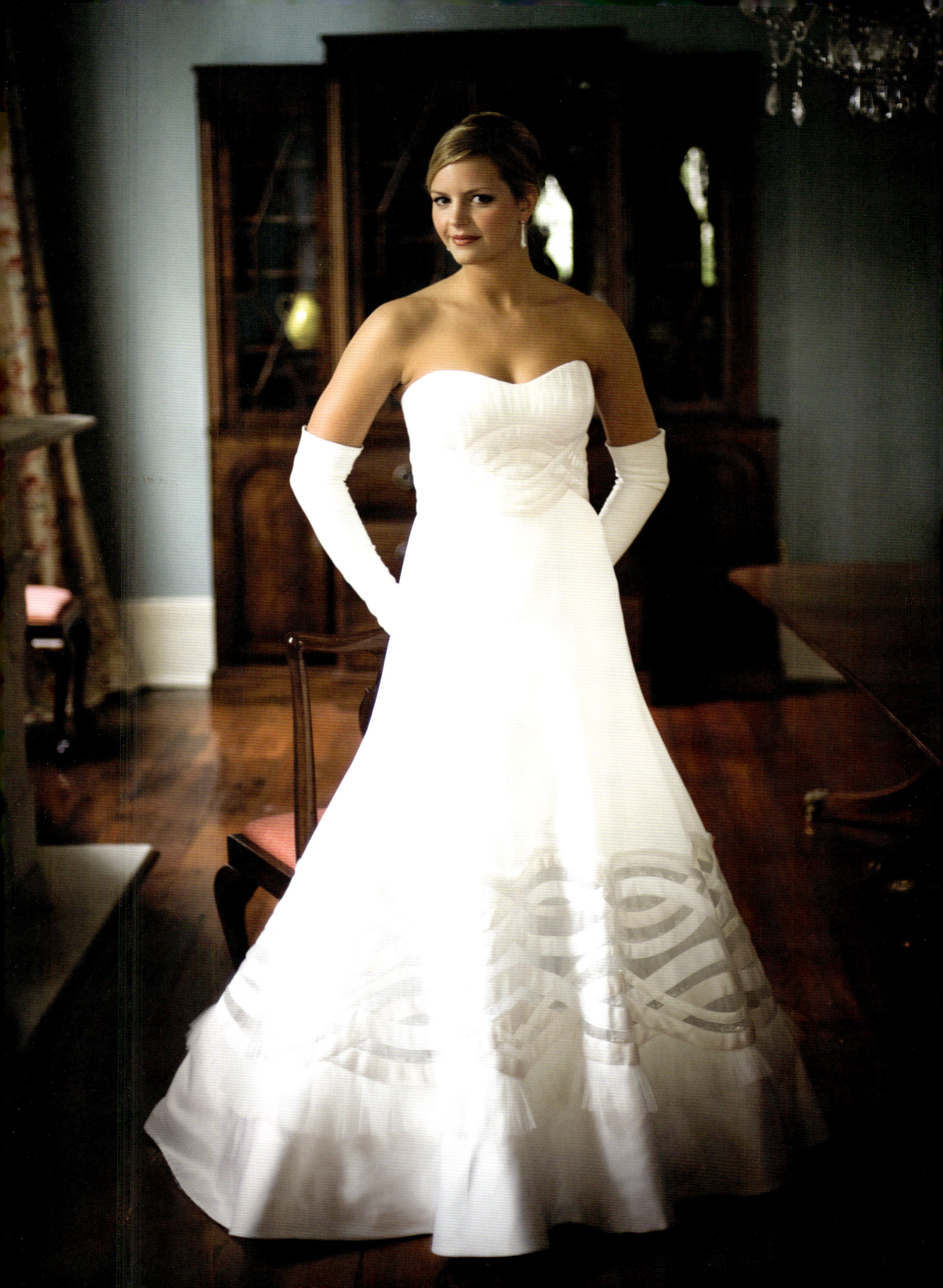

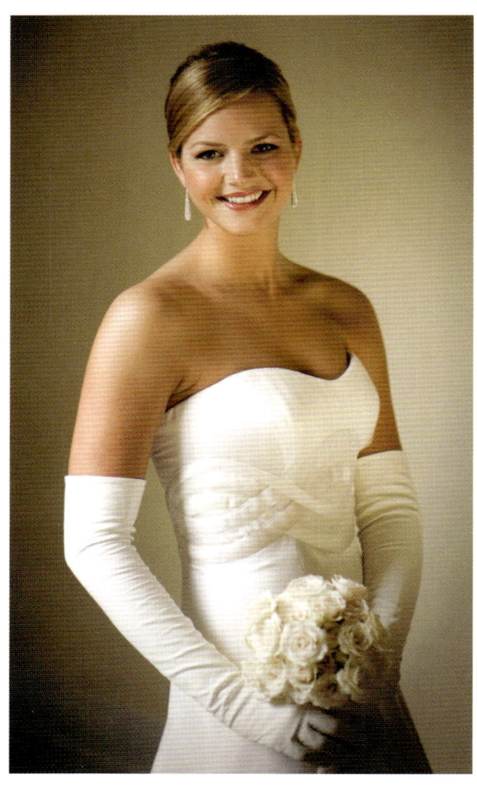

Gathered tulle draping from bodice banding to sweetheart neckline (JC)

Sweetheart neckline mimicing the arcs of the skirt detailing (JC)

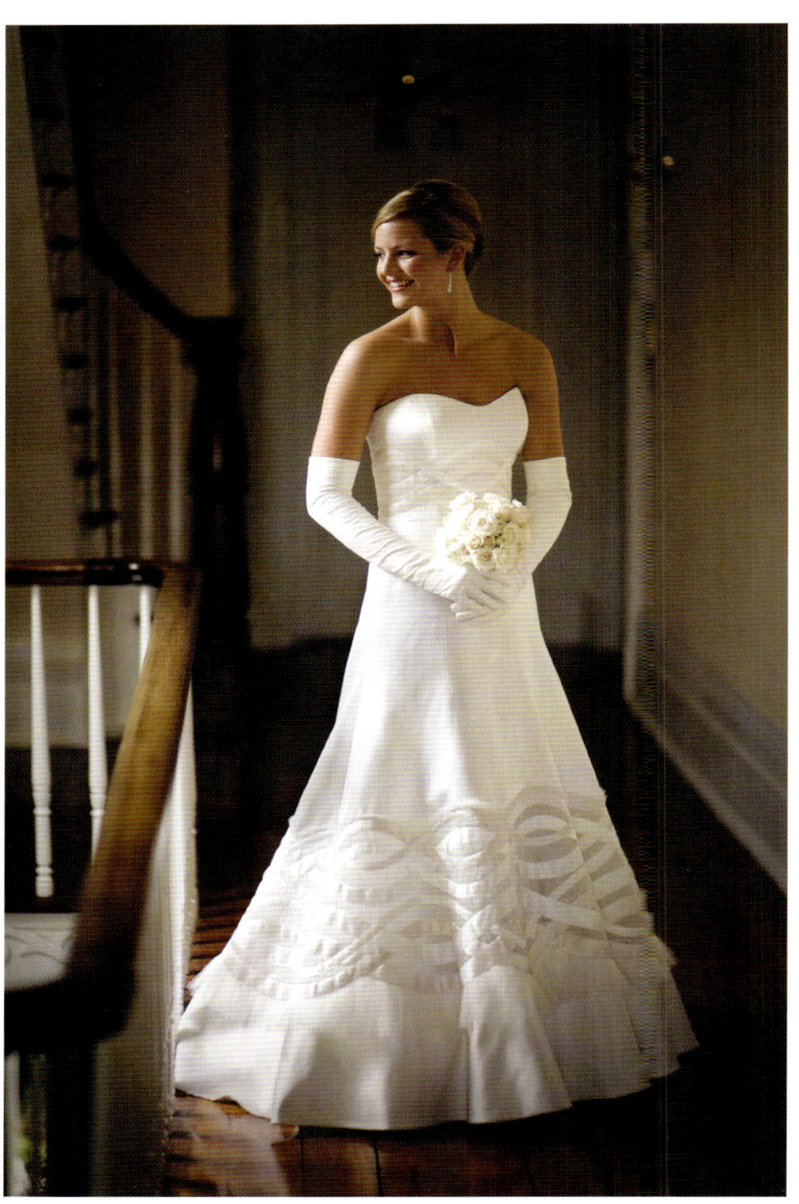

OPPOSITE PAGE:
Slight train and volume adding drama to skirt back (JC)

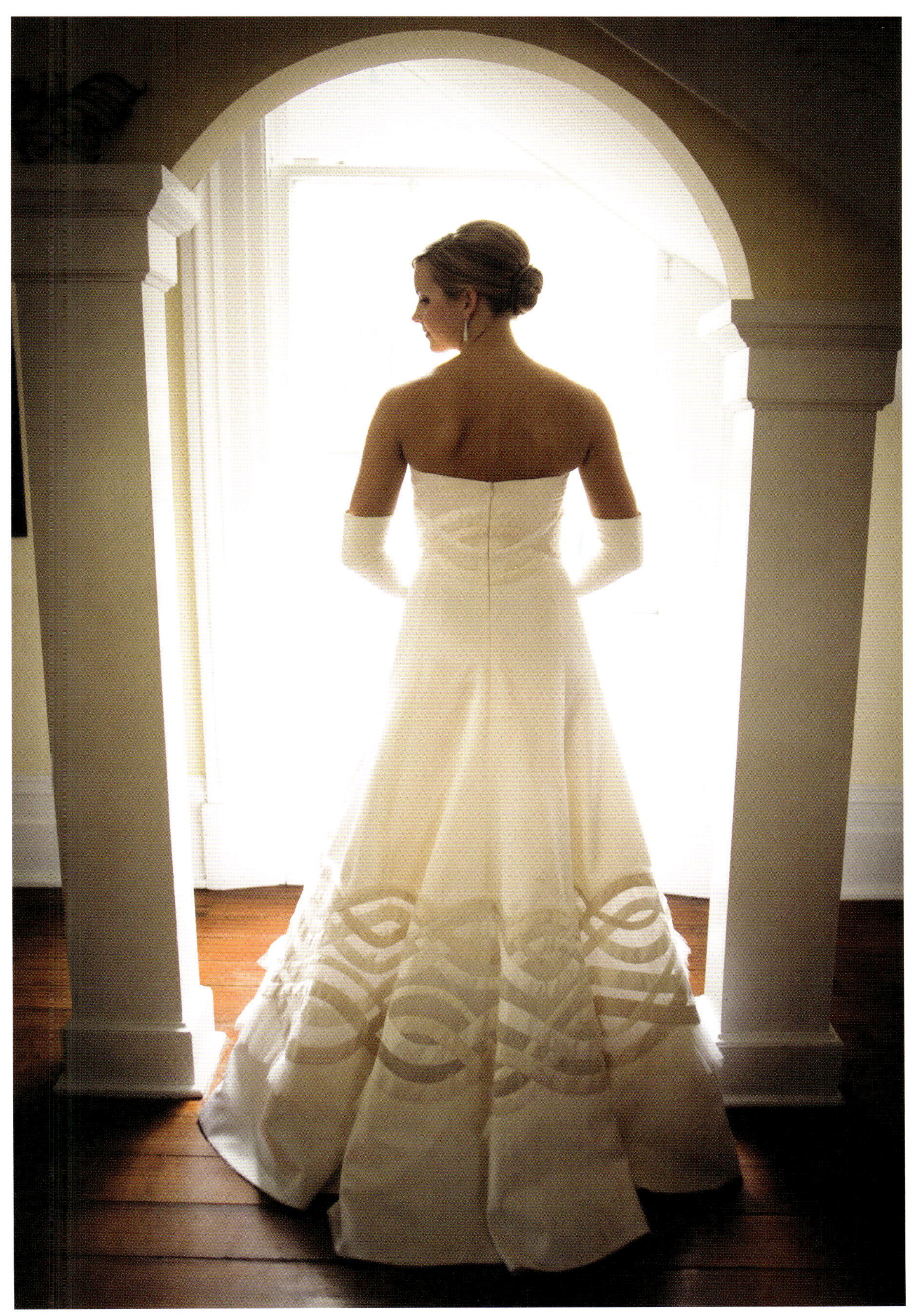

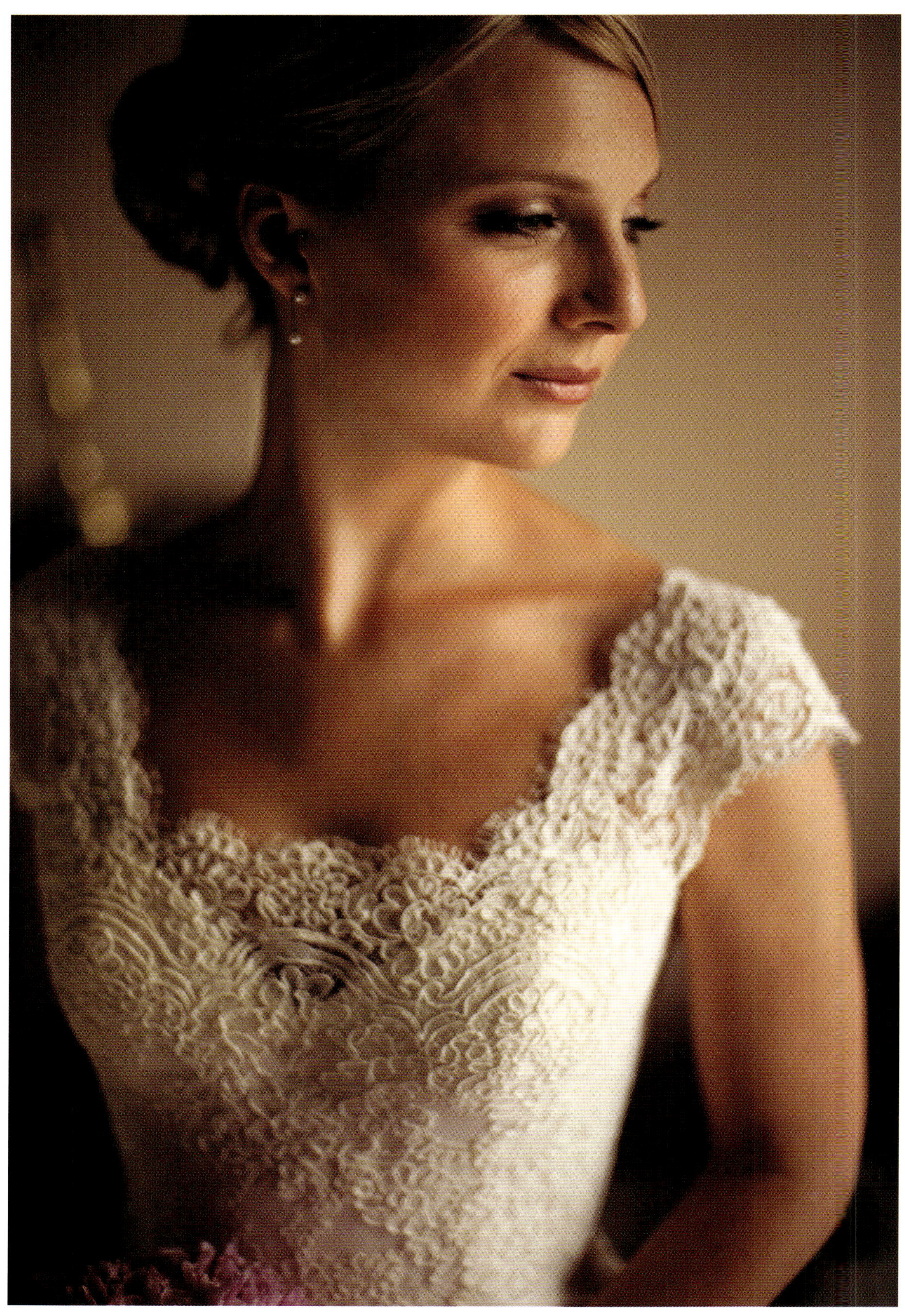

Ainsley, Bride

Ainsley had been shopping for wedding dresses for some time before she heard about our custom creations. She had an idea of what she wanted in a wedding gown and was not finding it in the bridal stores. Her shopping trips were ending in constant frustration. With her petite frame, she found trying on sample gowns many sizes too large and several inches too long exhausting. Not only did the sample gowns have too much length at the hem, but there was also too much length in the bodice, torso, and shoulders.

All that gown shopping had helped Ainsley form a pretty clear idea of the design elements she preferred in a gown. She wanted a modified trumpet skirt with hem volume and a long train. The desired shape would graze the hips and gracefully flare without evoking the look of a mermaid. Lace appliqué would adorn the bodice, neckline, and skirt. Bodice detailing of a V neckline, cap sleeves, and open low back were incorporated into the design. I sketched two options for her. One was all-over lace, and the alternative had lace appliquéd along the bodice and hem of a tissue organza over layer. We shared a preference for the tissue organza variation with lace accents.

The first muslin fitting was a great success. Happy tears are a perk in the bridal industry. They are a sign that I have done my job well. When Ainsley saw her gown muslin hanging in the dressing room, she and her mom both teared up. Both were relieved to see a gown combining all of her desired design elements and proportioned to her frame. Slight fit adjustments were pinned to achieve perfection of fit and proportion. We designed and draped a petite sleeve cap of border lace on Ainsley during the fitting. The sleeve cap was the perfect finishing touch to an already flattering silhouette complementary to the bride's personality and style.

Ainsley had decided to wear her mother's tulle veil with blusher for her wedding day. We paired the veil with the gown during the muslin fitting. We were able to shape the gown's sweeping train to correspond to the shape of the beautifully preserved heirloom tulle veil. The diaphanous layers of tulle elegantly framed the silhouette of the gown.

The silhouette, fabrication, and detailing were perfectly suited for the fall 2008 formal Catholic wedding. The gown's train layered with cathedral veil picturesquely trailed the aisle of the church. The lace-adorned gown captured the southern style evident in the reception venue of the Baton Rouge Country Club.

Before Ainsley and I began working on her wedding dress, she had narrowed her selection to two gowns if she had to purchase one at a traditional bridal re-

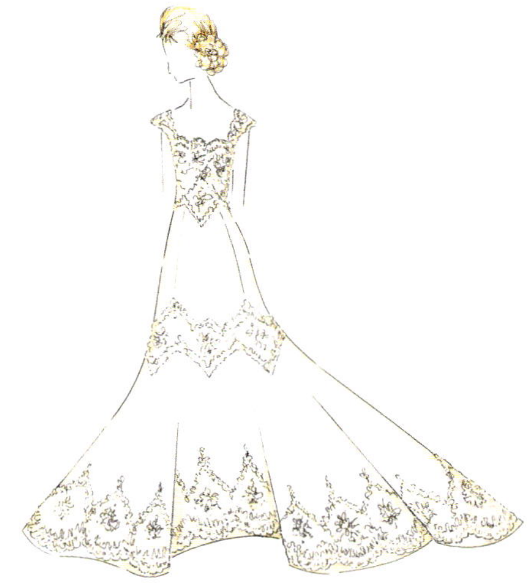

Front sketch of Ainsley's gown

OPPOSITE PAGE:
Cap sleeves designed by draping are flawlessly mended into bodice (JC)

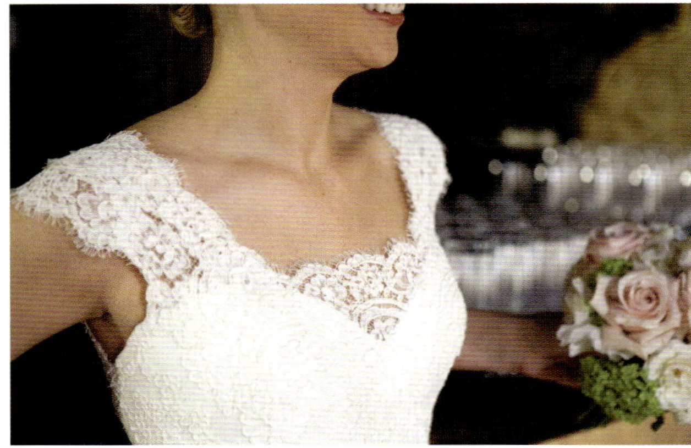

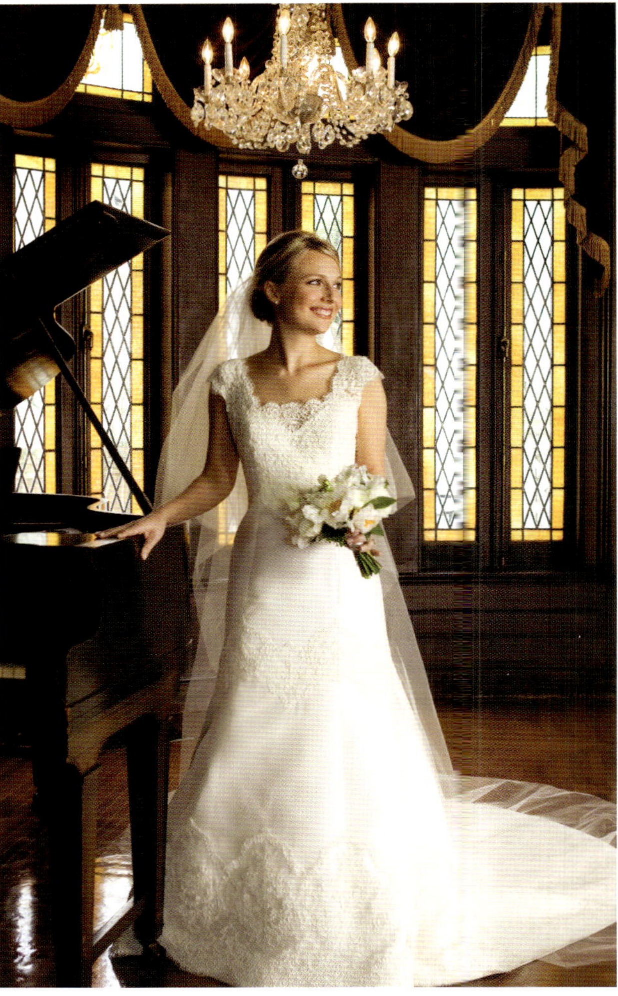

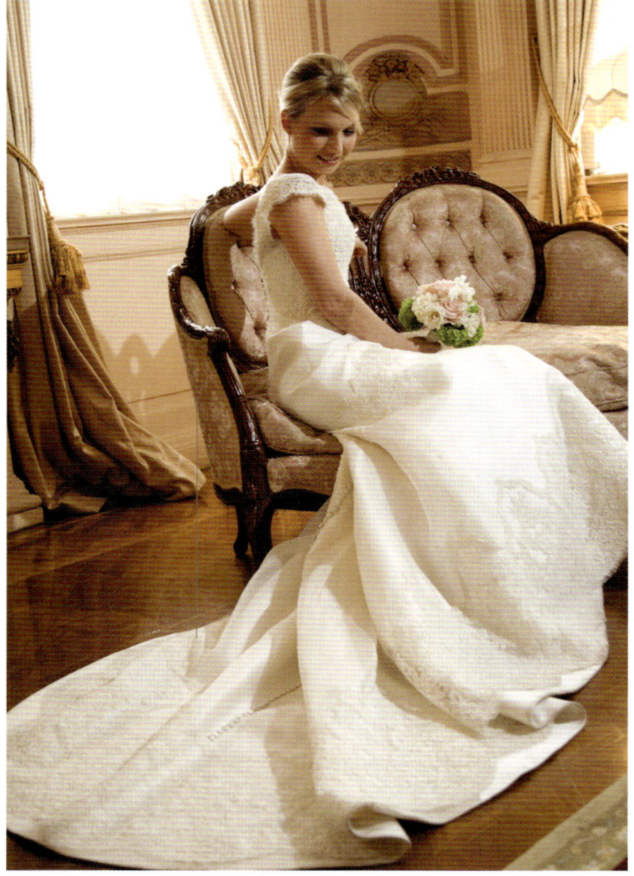

tailer. The weekend before her final gown fitting, she and her fiancé attended a wedding. The doors at the back of the church opened, and the bride was standing in the gown Ainsley would have most likely purchased had she not worked with me. With so many of the same guests due to attend her own wedding, she was relieved her gown would be unique . . . and she did not have to explain to her fiancé why she was crying.

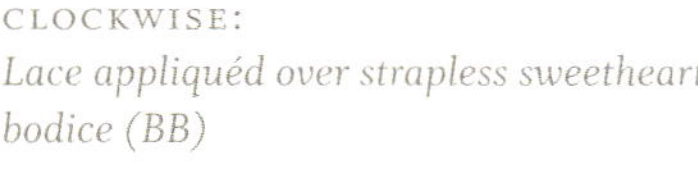

CLOCKWISE:
Lace appliquéd over strapless sweetheart bodice (BB)

Train shape designed to follow shape of heirloom veil (BB)

Voluminous skirt and train edged with scalloped lace (BB)

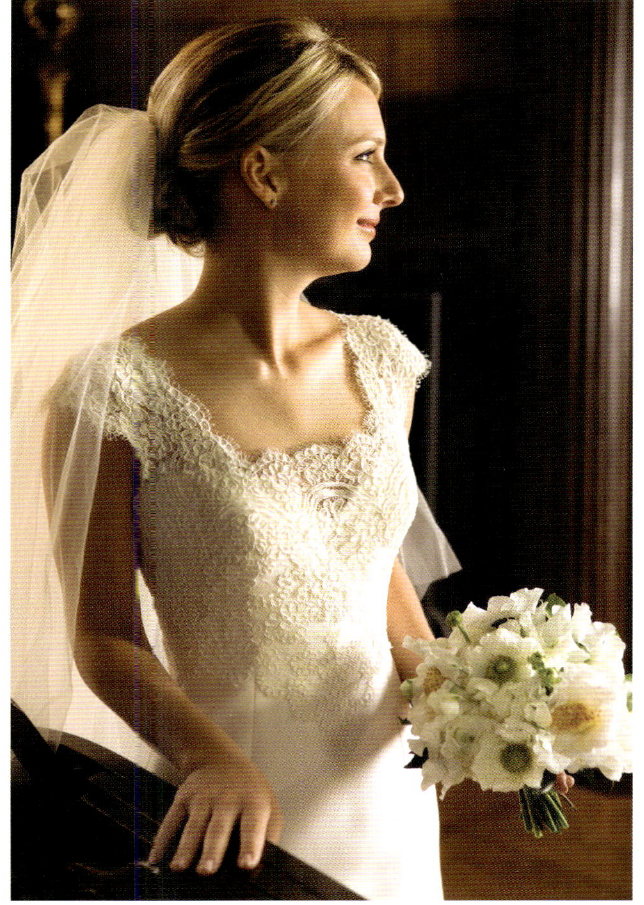

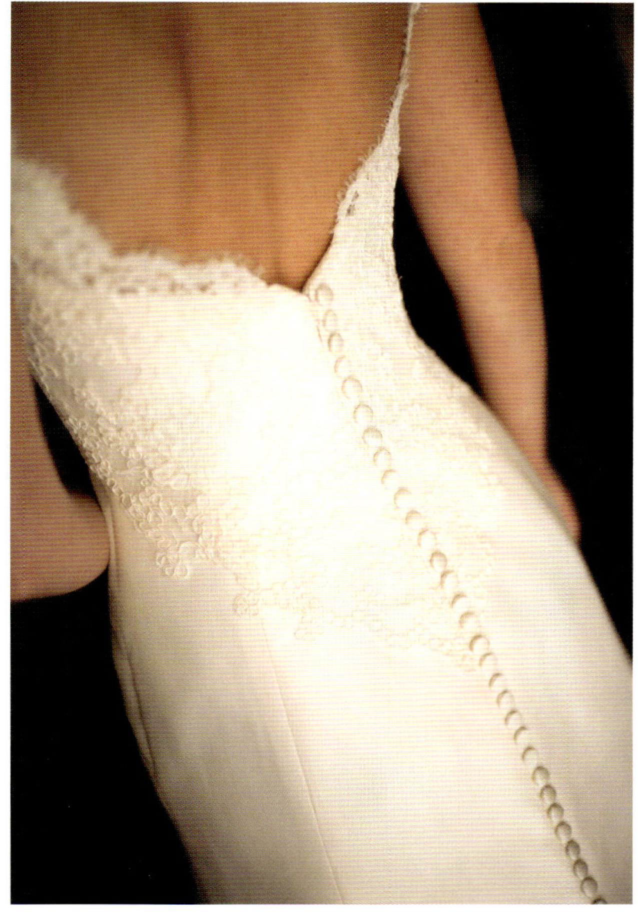

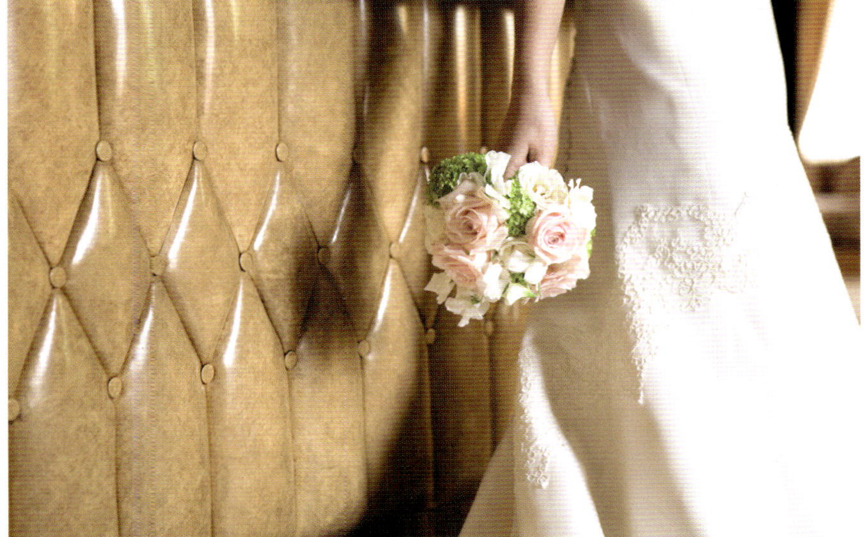

Lace appliqué continuing through the bodice (BB)

Covered buttons lining center back of the silhouette sculpted to the bride's petite frame (JC)

Angular shape of skirt appliqué (BB)

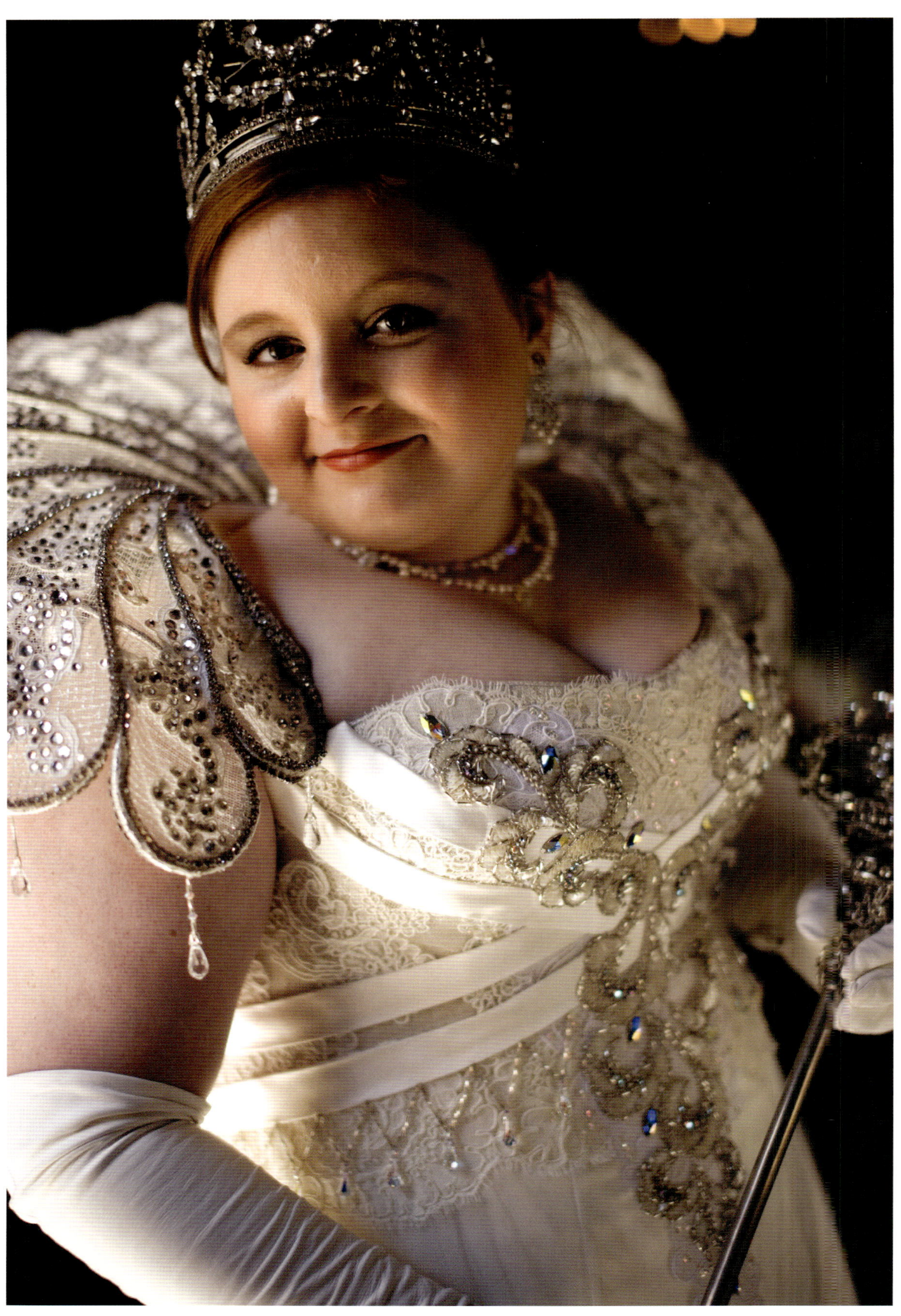

Eleanor, Olympians Queen

I am often asked how I develop a client base. There is no better way to attract future clientele than to create exceptional gowns for current clients. There is no more target-rich audience than a Mardi Gras ball or a wedding. When Eleanor began preparing for her reign as Queen of Olympians, she looked back at queens' gowns worn the previous year. Her two favorite queens' gowns were both Suzanne Perron gowns.

Most New Orleans debutante and Mardi Gras organizations recognize college-age women during their junior year. With many of these students attending school out of state, scheduling fittings can be challenging. Eleanor presented an even greater than usual challenge. Not only was she attending college out of state, but she would be out of the country for the fall semester, participating in a study-abroad program in Italy. Planning and scheduling were crucial in creating Eleanor's gown with limited fitting opportunities. She would be returning from Italy just one month prior to her reign. We were able to fit a foundation and muslin prior to her overseas departure. The final gown design and beading were finalized via email. When she returned from Italy, we had all fabrics, beading, and trim in house and ready to go. After a quick fit check of the muslin, we began work on the actual gown. In a three-week window we went from muslin to completed beaded masterpiece.

We enhanced the gown silhouette by incorporating elongated vertical seaming and angled empire bodice lines. We knew we wanted godets of beading embellishing the vertical gown panels. Working with layers of satin, tulle, beading, and lace allowed us to create depth in both color and texture. Ivory with gold and silver highlights presented the color palette most flattering to Eleanor's coloring and auburn hair. The antique silver of the collar was best complemented with a blend of metallic hues.

Plumelike embroidery was inspired by a photo of vintage beading. We developed the beading by drawing the plumes to scale with notations for style, type, and color of beading and threadwork. Color coding and a key designated the placement of rhinestones, bugle beads, and sequins. The dense, labor-intensive beading was developed in partnership with an embroidery resource in India. Once a sample from India was approved, we proceeded with creating the numerous specific beading patterns required for the design. We developed separate beading patterns for the front bodice appliqué, the two back bodice appliqués, and the nine skirt panels. Blocks of ivory embroidery tulle served as the base fabric for the beading.

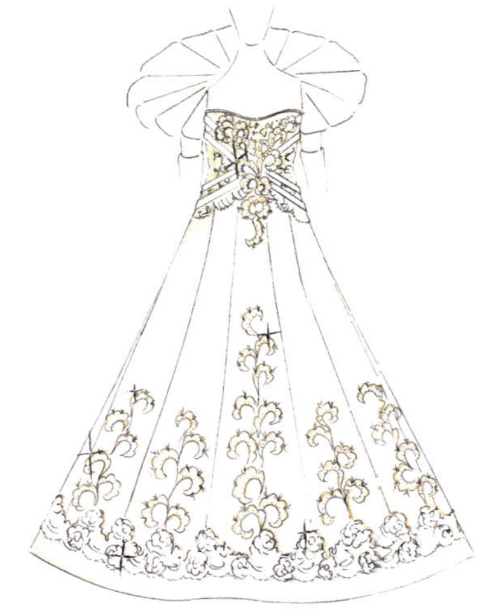

Sketch of Eleanor's gown

OPPOSITE PAGE:
Satin bands wrapping front bodice (JC)

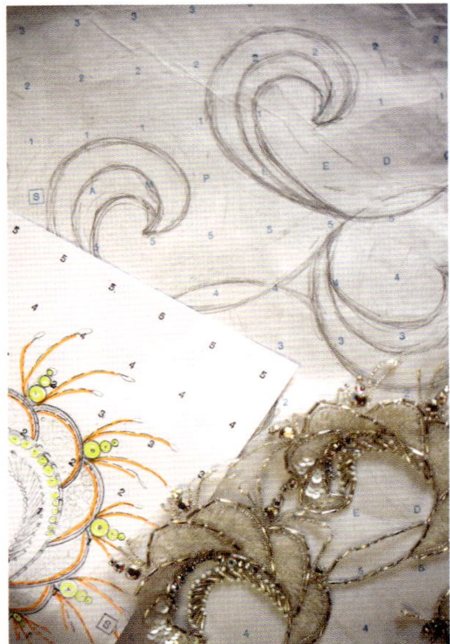

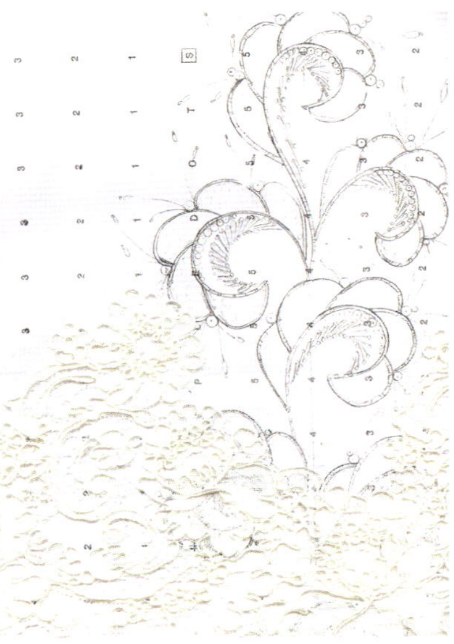

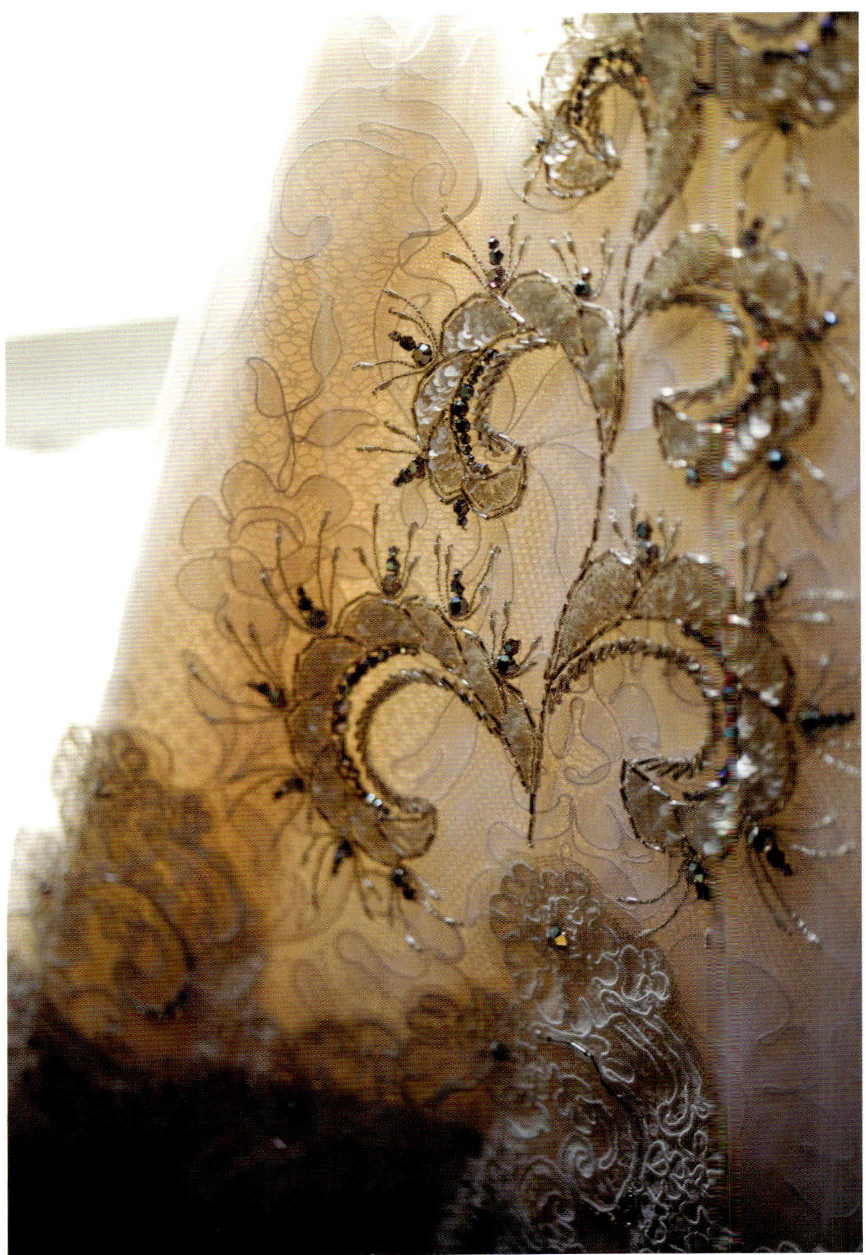

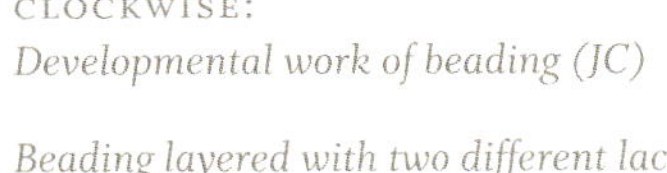

CLOCKWISE:
Developmental work of beading (JC)

Beading layered with two different lace patterns (JC)

Beading layout paired with lace (JC)

The gown evolved as the elements came together. When the beaded tulle panels of the gown were cut and assembled, the beaded plumes looked lost in the volume of the skirt. We added white triangles of lace appliqué to the ivory under layer, creating a frame behind each of the beaded plumes. The lace triangles were not part of the original design but were the element that really set the gown off.

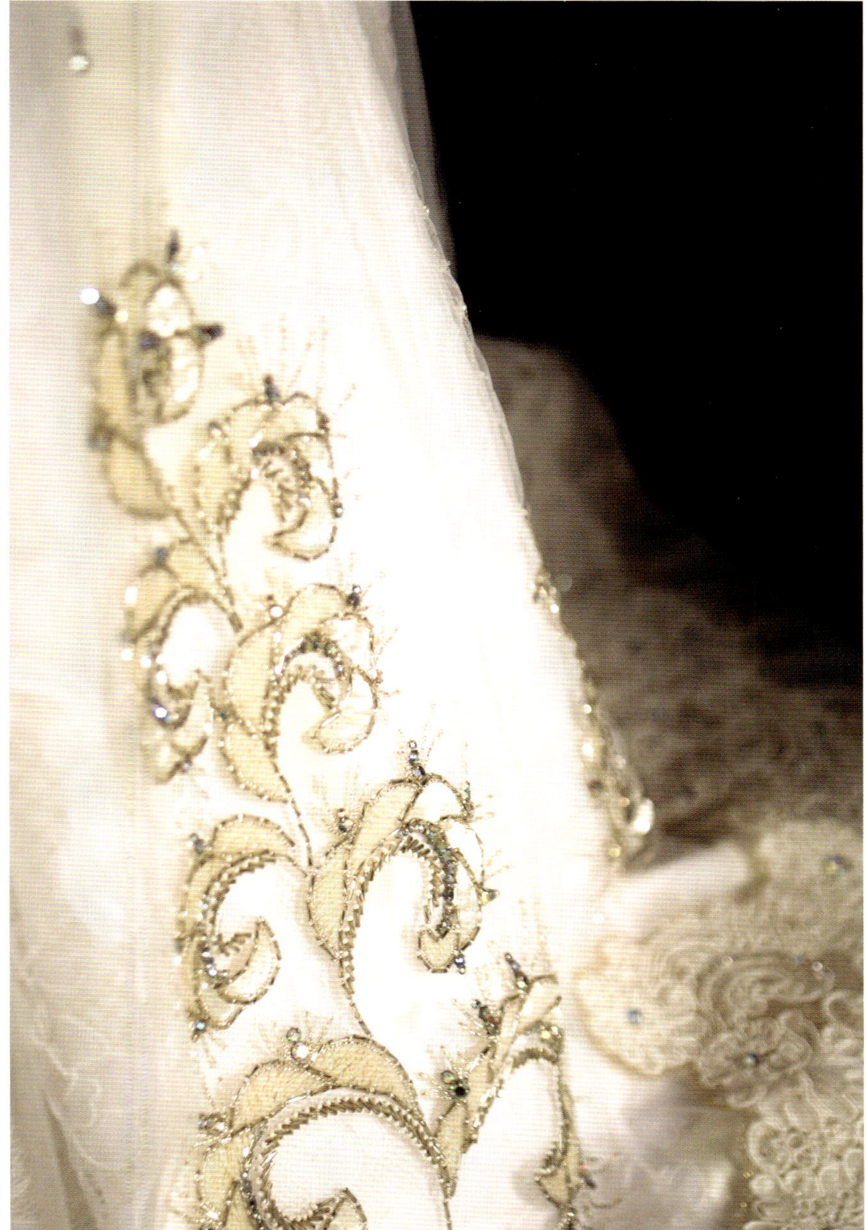

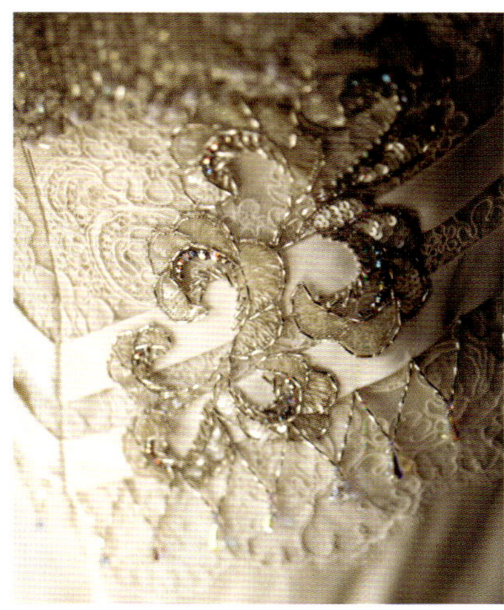

Hem of beaded tulle finished in scalloped lace (JC)

Back bodice featuring lace, beading, satin bands, and crystal drops (JC)

The lace empire bodice was finished with two silk-satin bands wrapping the front bodice before continuing to create back V detailing. White lace under the band and a beading appliqué over the band mimic the layering of the skirt. Bugle bead and crystal drops fall from the satin bands for additional light reflection. Hand-sewn Swarovski crystal navettes also accent the bodice embroidery.

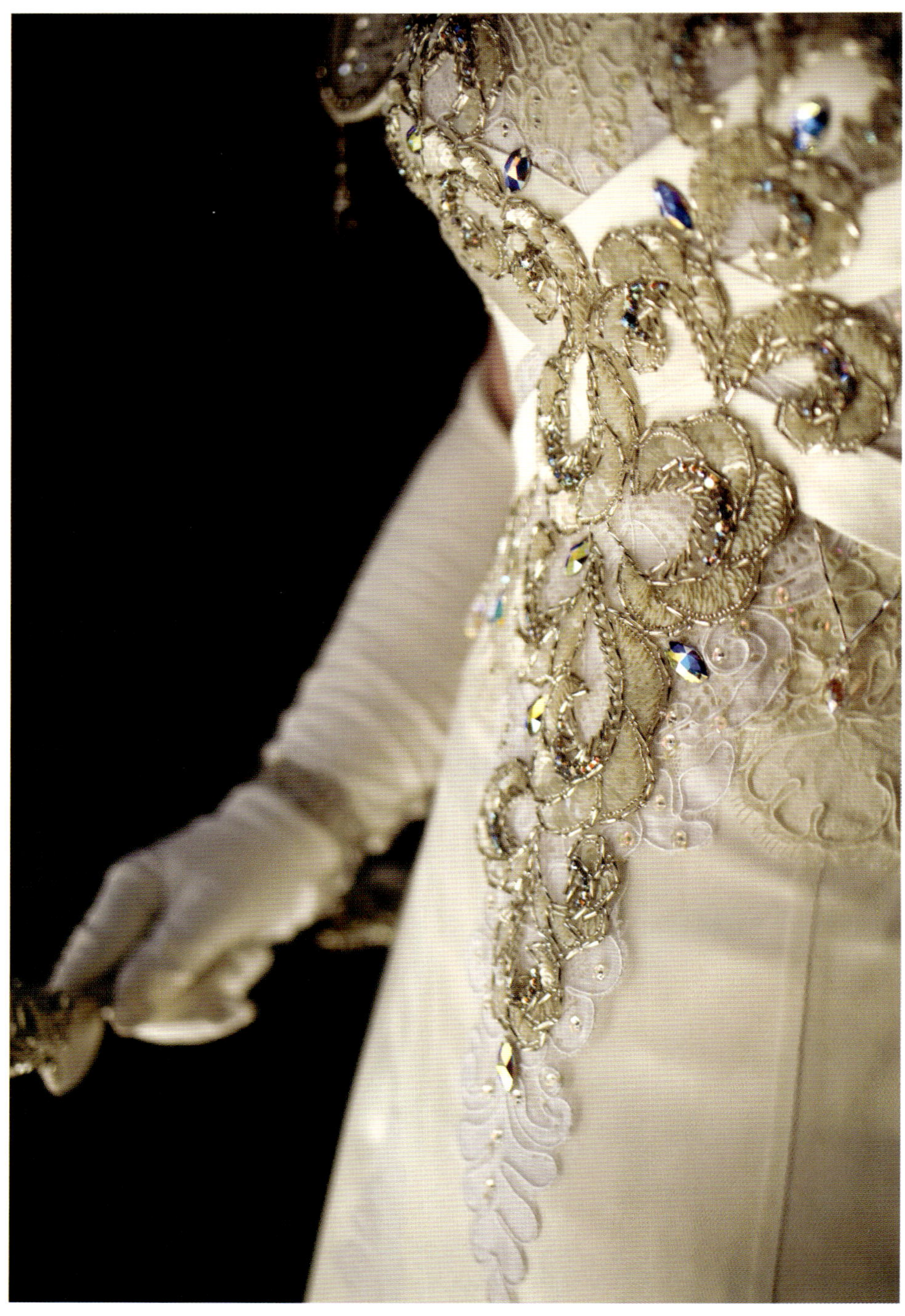

Front bodice beading detail with lace accents (JC)

OPPOSITE PAGE:
Formal queen's portrait (JC)

Acknowledgments

When working in fashion, you rarely operate independently. Others will inspire you, others will train you, and others will recognize your talent. Designers are most often either part of a team or the head of a team. A designer's concept will look only as good as the quality of sewing, draping, and patternmaking used to execute that concept. The quality of fashion photography is as dependent on the expertise of the model and the artistry of the photographer as it is on the quality of the garment. This book project is not unlike that. Countless individuals have played a part in shaping my design experiences and in shaping this book. I have had the privilege of teaming up with numerous talented artists and professionals in making this book a reality.

I would like to thank MaryKatherine Callaway, Margaret Lovecraft, and the LSU Press for initiating this project. I sincerely appreciate Margaret Lovecraft's perseverance and patience in the process while my body of work continued to grow and develop until the content for a book was more substantial. I thank book designer Michelle Neustrom for her creative input. I am also grateful to the LSU community as a whole, including the LSU Alumni Association, the LSU Foundation, the School of Human Ecology, and LSU Media Relations for their generous support of my endeavors.

Among my business goals was to hire and train local talent as well as offer quality fashion-design internships locally. I am grateful for the work of my assistants and numerous student interns. Kelly Pourciau was my first assistant. She is an LSU graduate who became a part of the business in the very beginning. Thank you, Kelly, for being a great designer, model, and friend. Kelly's help in training and supervising interns has been invaluable, and I praise God for perfectly weaving Christian community through my business by bringing Kelly to work with me. Kelly Casey is an LSU graduate who first interned with us and then joined us after graduation. Thank you, Kelly, for filling numerous roles from design assistant to model to photographer and Photoshop expert. Arnaz Bhujwalla graduated from the Fashion Institute of Technology before returning to her hometown of New Orleans. I thank her for becoming part of our staff and sharing her knowledge of jewelry and lingerie design.

I wish to thank all of my clients, who have entrusted me to be an integral part of their special day. In particular, I am grateful to clients who allowed me to photograph their gowns to share with you. I extend additional thanks to the clients who generously gave of their time to model their gowns in our photo shoots.

The city of New Orleans offers beautiful locations for photography. Many thanks to the homeowners who allowed us into their private residences and on their impeccably manicured grounds. Exquisite event spaces including the Elms Mansion and Latrobe's on Royal also served as backdrops for our photo shoots. The Van Benthuysen-Elms Mansion is a striking Italianate-style venue in New Orleans's Garden District, complete with period furnishings and lovely gardens and patios. Latrobe's on Royal is a historic gem in the heart of the French Quarter. The exposed brick, plaster walls, and cypress woodwork at Latrobe's added depth and texture to our photography.

I would like to thank Wellington & Co. for the use of precious jewelry and of their French Quarter building, a stunning example of a former New Orleans residence dating back to the eighteenth century.

Many talented artists have collaborated in each and every photo shoot. Katie Seghers Malone was responsible for the models' makeup. I appreciate Katie's subtle approach of using makeup to bring out the natural beauty of the client or model without being overdone. When a scheduling conflict kept Katie from our final shoot at Latrobe's, Marti Pourciau of the Face Place in Baton Rouge was an excellent choice to join our team. With a similar aesthetic of enhancing natural beauty, Marti's work blended in seamlessly. Anne Delacoix and A[illegible]is Gold provided the polished, elegant hair styles of the models and clients. I thank them for creating formal up-dos that complimented the youthfulness of the wearers while maintaining a sense of fashion.

My work comes to life on these pages thanks to many gifted photographers. I first and foremost thank Jason Cohen and his artistic vision that fills the majority of these pages. I am grateful to Brian Baiamonte for starting this project with me, and to the contributing photographers Susan Woodard, Skip Bolen, Jennie Westerman, and my mother, Caroline Perron. The initials of each photographer are indicated in the captions.

I owe special thanks to Yvonne Marquette Leake for her years of encouragement and mentorship as a teacher, co-worker, and contemporary. I appreciate her continually facilitating my relationships with talented LSU fashion design graduates and student interns.

My business success has been greatly impacted by the support of my family. I thank the Beary family for allowing me to make their guest house my home when I moved to New Orleans from New York City. I thank my immediate family for a lifetime of support of my desire to pursue fashion. I am grateful to my sister for letting me make her prom dress and for putting up with such an overachieving and overinvolved little sister. I thank my mother and grandmother for sharing their sewing knowledge and for providing an environment conducive to constant creativity. I greatly appreciate my father for every facet of his support—for every shelf, curtain rod, and hook installed in my shop; and for his aptitudes for building, problem solving, and attention to detail that obviously rubbed off on me.

I am forever grateful for the three amazing men in my life: my husband, William St. Paul, and our twin boys, David and Andrew, born in November of 2010. They are blessings more rich than I could ever have imagined. This journey I have made on my own is now much sweeter with them a part of it.

SUZANNE PERRON ST. PAUL